CONSTANT LAMBERT
his life, his music and his friends

Frontispiece: Lambert at the piano (1932).

CONSTANT LAMBERT

RICHARD SHEAD

with a Memoir
by
ANTHONY POWELL

SIMON PUBLICATIONS
LONDON

First published 1973

ISBN 0 903620 01 4

*Printed in Great Britain by
The Bowering Press, Plymouth*

for Ken Apolony
and to the memory of
Arthur Langford

"His greatness lay in his variety of purpose, in the way he squandered his gifts, in the way he would drop his own work to put his burning enthusiasm to the service of others."

Constant Lambert on Franz Liszt

CONTENTS

FOREWORD

Constant Lambert was born in 1905 and died in 1951, two days before his forty-sixth birthday. He was only twenty years old when Diaghilev presented his ballet *Romeo and Juliet*. Lambert was the first English composer to work for the Russian company. Three years later his setting of a poem by Sacheverell Sitwell, *The Rio Grande*, created a sensation. His musical output was not great (he published less than twenty works) but almost everything he wrote is at the very least accomplished and attractive, at best passionate and moving.

But Lambert was far more than simply one of a number of British composers not of the first rank whose music is suffering at present from an unjust neglect. He was also a fine conductor: for the ballet, in the concert hall, and – when he got the chance – in the opera house. As one of the three main architects of the Sadler's Wells (now the Royal) Ballet, he displayed enthusiasm, musical insight and a great capacity for sheer hard work (despite poor health), as well as a knowledge of the visual arts and of literature quite exceptional in a musician. "In Lambert lay our only hope of an English Diaghilev", wrote Ninette de Valois.

Through his work for the ballet, for the BBC and with the major British orchestras, Lambert exerted a powerful influence on British musical taste. In his book *Music Ho!* he deployed his wit and outstanding command of the English language to such effect that thousands who never saw him conduct nor heard his music were affected by his highly individual approach to the arts in general and music in particular. He played a major part in moulding the creative gifts of other artists now better known to the general public than Lambert himself: men like William Walton and Frederick Ashton.

From his youth to his death Lambert was a brilliant figure in the intellectual and social life of London. His circle of friends was wide and varied. It included, of course, fellow-musicians and ballet colleagues like Walton, Lord Berners, Darius Milhaud, Bernard van Dieren, Philip Heseltine, Louis Kentner, Alan Rawsthorne, Nijinska, Ashton and Margot Fonteyn. But Lambert also found that he had much in

9

common with writers like Anthony Powell and Peter Quennell, the Sitwells and Dylan Thomas, painters like Christopher Wood and Michael Ayrton, and journalists like Tom Driberg.

Lambert's intellectual and artistic gifts (Keynes called him "potentially the most brilliant person I have ever met") were not matched by an equal ability to handle the problems of his personal life. A prolonged childhood sickness left him in continual pain. He found it hard to build satisfactory emotional relationships with those he most loved. Like several others who came to maturity in the circle which revolved around Bernard van Dieren and Philip Heseltine, he drank to excess, and hard drinking, ill health, overwork and multiple disappointments drove him to a premature grave. But in his blackest moments he never lost a rare personal magnetism which struck everyone who knew him, a quality only half conveyed by words like "radiance" and "glamour". For parallels one must turn not to the world of music but perhaps to Johnson or Wilde, himself, like Lambert, a lover of the Café Royal. He was a complete man in an age of specialists.

ACKNOWLEDGEMENTS

Many people helped in the preparation of this book. I should like to thank Miss Margaret Dale; Dame Ninette de Valois; Miss Hilda Gaunt; Mrs Pamela May Gordon; Mrs Camilla Hole; Mrs Barbara King; Mrs Maurice Lambert; Dame Eva Turner; Mr Basil Ashmore; Mr Michael Ayrton; Mr William Chappell; Dr Ian Copley; Mr and Mrs Christian Darnton; the late Mr J. H. Davies, of the BBC Music Library; T. E. N. Driberg, M.P.; Mr Alan Frank, of the Oxford University Press; Mr Barrie Gavin; Mr Robert Irving; Dr Gordon Jacob; Mr Louis Kentner; Mr Walter Legge; Dr Patrick Lovett; Mr Richard McGrady; Monsieur Darius Milhaud; Mr Peter Quennell; Mr N. Plumley, of Christ's Hospital; Mr T. B. Radley; the late Mr Alan Rawsthorne; Mr Harold Rosenthal; Dr E. Rubbra; Mr Michael Somes; Mr R. Temple Savage; and Mr Raimund von Hofmannsthal.

Among the friends who have helped and encouraged me I should like to mention Miss Phyllis Blackburn, Mr Kenneth Apolony, Mr Hugh Davidson, Mr Martin Kinna, Mr Paul Reding and the late Mr Arthur Langford.

Especial thanks are due to Mrs Isabel Rawsthorne; to Dr Denis ApIvor and Mr Humphrey Searle, for allowing me to read and use their unpublished recollections of Lambert; to Mr Anthony Powell and Lady Violet Powell, for great encouragement and practical help; and to Mr Angus Morrison, for generously permitting me to use part of a chapter from his own projected study of Lambert and for supplying me with a great deal of valuable source material.

For permission to quote from letters I must thank Mrs Marie MacDermott, Madame Madeleine Milhaud, Mrs Isabel Rawsthorne, Mr Felix Aprahamian, Mr Michael Ayrton, Mr Richard

Buckle and Mr Lincoln Kirstein, Mr Alan Frank, the General Administrator of the Royal Opera House, Covent Garden, Dr Patrick Hadley, Mr Anthony Powell and Mr Humphrey Searle.

Mr Ayrton has kindly allowed me to use material from his book Golden Sections. *I also wish to express gratitude to Constable and Co Ltd for the short extracts from* Count Omega, *by Lord Berners; Peter Davies Ltd, for permitting me to quote one of Charles Ricketts' letters used in the book* Self-Portrait, *edited by Cecil Lewis; Gerald Duckworth and Co Ltd, for some lines from* The Rio Grande, *published in the Selected Poems of Sacheverell Sitwell; Faber and Faber Ltd, for their generosity in allowing me to quote so fully from* Music Ho!; *the Trustees of the Estate of the late Cecil Gray, for extracts from his book* Musical Chairs, *originally published by Home and Van Thal, an extract from* Peter Warlock, *originally published by Jonathan Cape, and part of a letter written by Mr Gray; the General Administrator of the Royal Opera House for the use of extracts from a Covent Garden programme and from Covent Garden Books No. 6; Hutchinson and Co Ltd for the extract from* Tales My Father Taught Me *by Sir Osbert Sitwell; Mr T. B. Radley and Hamish Hamilton Ltd, for some extracts from* The Christ's Hospital Book; *John Lehmann Ltd, for some extracts from* The Fairy Queen; *Macmillan and Co Ltd, for a quotation from* Laughter in the Next Room *by Sir Osbert Sitwell; the Editor of* Opera *for part of an article by Lambert; the Oxford University Press, for allowing me to reprint Lambert's synopses of his own ballets as printed in their scores; and the Rt Hon. Michael Stewart, C.H., M.P., and the Editor of* The Blue *for the extract from Mr Stewart's obituary of Lambert. I am glad to have been able to use extracts from material published in the* Daily Express, *the* Daily Mail, *the* Daily Telegraph, *the* Evening News, *the* Manchester Guardian, *the* New Statesman and Nation, *the* New York Times, *the* New Yorker, *the* Observer *and the* Radio Times.

I thank Mr Michael Ayrton for allowing me to reproduce two photographs, his drawing of Humphrey Searle (in the artist's collection) and his studies for a portrait of Lambert (in the collection of Mr Anthony Powell); Mr Anthony Powell for two photographs and Mr Ayrton's portrait studies; Mrs Maurice Lambert for the reproduction of the bust of Angus Morrison by the late Mr Maurice Lambert; Mrs Isabel Rawsthorne and the BBC Music Library for the manuscript of Salome's Dance; *the Raymond Mander and Joe Mitchenson Theatre Collection for three photographs, including the portrait of Mrs Lambert by Yevonde; Bassano and Vandyk for the study of Lambert at the piano; Roger Wood Photography for the scene from* Tiresias; *and the Victoria and Albert Museum for the scene from* The Rio Grande.

Finally, my thanks to Mr Lewis Foreman for all his help in the preparation of the book.

LIST OF PLATES

Lambert at the piano (1932).   *Frontispiece*

(between pages 112 and 113)

1. Constant and Florence Lambert arriving at Covent Garden for the first night of *Schwanda the Bagpiper* (1934.).

2. (*Above*) Constant Lambert (1933).
   (*Below*) Florence Lambert (1933).

3. *The Rio Grande* at Sadler's Wells, with Margot Fonteyn, Walter Gore and Beatrice Appleyard.

4. Angus Morrison by Maurice Lambert, R.A. (*c.* 1925).

5. (*Above*) "The Five Year Plan": an evocation of life in Soviet Russia.
   (*Below*) Lambert in the character of a jealous husband interrupts a flirtation between his wife and Anthony Powell.

6. Part of Salome's Dance from the incidental music for Wilde's play which Lambert composed in 1931.

7. Lambert and Michael Ayrton working on *The Fairy Queen* (1946).

8. Humphrey Searle by Michael Ayrton (1965).

9. *Tiresias*, Scene I, with Michael Somes and Margaret Dale.

10. Studies for a portrait of Lambert, by Michael Ayrton (1946).

CONSTANT LAMBERT: A MEMOIR

We first met, so far as I remember about the spring of the year 1928, in a crowded pub. Lambert, within a few months of my own age, was then twenty-two. Good-looking in a boyish but distinguished way, he was already getting a trifle fat, though the Christopher Wood picture (now in the National Portrait Gallery) shows him as the comparatively emaciated figure he had been only a very short time before. In this connexion, a favourite theme of his was the lean, rather than fat personage, as typical butt of eighteenth-century jocosity. He would defend this standpoint vigorously. Although his clothes were ordinary, he never looked ordinary. He usually wore an oldish, brownish London suit, a shirt of one fairly deep colour, blue or orange without pattern, a plain tie of another shade. The habit of hatlessness, a shade eccentric at that period, persisted from Christ's Hospital days. Getting into a stiff shirt or "morning clothes" for conducting, one or other form of "tails" outfit required most days, was always likely to threaten apoplexy. Lambert tied by hand the bow of white evening ties, but once caught Sir Thomas Beecham, before the looking-glass in a Covent Garden dressing-room, adjusting his made-up one; for which, to Lambert's great satisfaction, the famous conductor muttered some sort of rather embarrassed apology, a rare reaction.

We got on pretty well from the start. There was a suggestion that Lambert should contribute something with musical bearing to a series of essays by young writers, contemplated (though never brought to birth) by the publishing firm for which I then worked. Writing about this project a day or two after our first meeting, I addressed the letter to "Constantine Lambert, Esqre.", thinking "Constant" a conversational abbreviation of the longer name. Lambert used to assert that —the Russian composer Modest Mussorgsky always excepted—no one had ever been given a less appropriate first name than himself. I am not sure that was absolutely true. In one sense, certainly the way things turned out, constancy may not seem the most pronounced trait in his character; in another, there was consistency in Lambert's life, even his "love life", that had something of constancy about it.

Intellectually speaking, Lambert operated with perfect ease in the three arts, a facility less generously conferred by nature than might be supposed from the way people talk. To appreciate two of the arts in a discerning manner is not unusual; where three are claimed, more often than not, grasp of the third shows signs of strain. With Lambert there was no strain. He always had his own penetrating line on any matter that arose which had to do with either music, painting or writing. He was the first contemporary I ran across whom I found wholly sympathetic in that sphere. This fact is not easy to explain. I lack musical sensibility, and, although, when it came to books and pictures, we had tastes in common, we differed often too. Lambert's approach seemed to me in complete contrast with that of my generation at Oxford, one that produced a fair sprinkling of young men reasonably to be regarded as gifted. I never found myself altogether in harmony with their way of looking at things, especially the arts. Coherent explanation of why that was so again eludes me, but the difference of their outlook and Lambert's can be gauged in a rough-and-ready manner by comparing *Music Ho!* with their own subsequent works of one sort or another, and marking disparity of outlook.

Lambert loved discussing painting, from Böcklin to Braque, Breughel to Brangwyn, especially enjoying putting forward subjects for Royal Academy pictures in the forcible, somewhat sententious manner of the last of these—once much imitated—of which the only two proposed canvases I can remember were *Blowing up the Rubber Woman* and *"Hock or Claret, sir": Annual Dinner of the Rectual Dining Society.* He once described Tchelitchew's work as looking like the winning exhibit in the *Daily Mail*'s prize for the season's best design in the sand at Margate.

We used to meet fairly regularly, drinking in pubs, going for walks, attending from time to time the same rather rackety parties, which for a year or two were such a feature of London of those days; then died away as casually as they had come into being. About a year after getting to know each other, Lambert and I ourselves gave a party together (costing so far as I can remember the steepish sum of ten or twelve pounds) in my basement flat in Bloomsbury, convenient for its three bare rooms. There is reason to suppose this occasion, which began as a cocktail party but extended well into the early hours of the morning, was in the author's mind as prototype of those "cocktail parties given in basement flats", adumbrated in *Vile Bodies* as one of the several elements contributing to the gossip-writer-character's "murky under-world of nonentities".

Lambert used sometimes to lunch, together with a miscellany of other friends and acquaintances, at Castano's in Greek Street. This Italian restaurant, entered through a curtain of coloured beads, ran to about a dozen tables on the ground floor, and stood three or four doors down from the archway leading into Manette Street. It is now no more. When I first knew the place it was called Previtali (presumably after the "Primitive" of that name), and I have heard its frequenters attempt to identify its earlier incarnation with that Restaurant du Vingtième Siècle, where Max Beerbohm consorted with Enoch Soames and the Devil. That cannot be. The *cuisine* of the Vingtième Siècle was specifically French, the tables arranged in a different manner. It is, however, true that George Gissing invited H. G. Wells to dinner at Previtali's in the eighteen-nineties, as appears from Gissing's Letters.

In his biography of Lambert, Richard Shead forces an issue by stating categorically that "Foppa's", a restaurant in my novel *A Dance to the Music of Time*, is Castano's, thereby raising an enormously complicated question on which I am far from anxious to comment, indeed do so most unwillingly. If "Foppa's" is Castano's, is "More-land" Lambert—and are a host of other characters the persons the whim of any reader decides them to be? Without going at length into the diverse methods used by novelists in setting up their puppets, the "short answer" is that "Foppa's", restaurant and proprietor, present as part of the background of the novel a genre picture of naturalistic treatment done from life. "Moreland" is another matter. "Moreland", friend of the Narrator (himself of equally mixed origins), is a musician, wit, sometimes exuberant, sometimes melancholy. Dark, rather than fair, he has the Bronzino-type features of Lambert's "Bluecoat" por-trait by his father. There the resemblance to Lambert fades, invention, imagination, the creative instinct—whatever you like to call it—begins. If I have been skilful enough, lucky enough, to pass on an echo of Lambert's incomparable wit, then "Moreland" is like him; in other respects the things that happen to "Moreland" approximate to the things that happened to Lambert only so far as all composers' lives have something in common. Here and there, as often falls out, a chance bull's eye is registered. For example, until I read Shead's book I never knew Lambert was specially interested in Chabrier. "More-land's" talk about that French composer must seem deliberate to those aware of that, a directly reported aspect of Lambert's musical taste. Such was not so, and in a thousand ways Lambert's career diverges utterly from that given to the character in the novel.

A ludicrous incident that comes to mind is that one night Lambert and I, having dined together, decided to end the evening at the Eiffel Tower, a restaurant treated almost as a club by those who were *abonné* there, on the strength of being connected with the arts, or otherwise well looked on by its proprietor Stulik, but regarded by most young men as too expensive to frequent often. It was fairly late in the evening. Practically the only diners who remained were Augustus John and Irène Dean Paul. Lady Dean Paul (whom I did not know), pianist and composer, mother of the then famous beauty, Brenda, of sad memory, used the name "Poldowski" in its masculine form for professional purposes, but was sometimes familiarly known as "Poldowska". These two invited Lambert and myself to join them. While Augustus John was speaking of the Welsh princes and bards, Lady Dean Paul produced from her hand-bag a small box of pills, which she described as sovereign against the hangover.

It would be idle to pretend that any of the four of us were entirely without all danger of that menace when we woke the following morning, a Sunday.

"They are coated with rubber, which makes them specially efficacious", said Irène Dean Paul.

I cannot recall why that was an advantage, but she took one herself, and handed them round. Augustus, a man of deep experience, refused. I accepted a pill. Lambert, who never did things by halves, took two.

I record with shame what followed. The moment the pill was in my mouth I knew I did not like it. By that time the table had been cleared, and there seemed no way of getting rid of it. I was more than a little overawed at the company in which I found myself. Then I noticed a pot of French mustard remained on the table. I slipped the rubber bullet unobtrusively in, ramming it down with the spoon when no one was looking. Lambert consumed both pills, while he endlessly talked.

The following morning I was woken by the telephone, I suppose about half-past nine or ten. It was Lambert.

"I'm telephoning from the rear", he said. "I've been sitting here since five or six o'clock this morning."

"What's happened?"

"It's those devilish pills Poldowska gave us."

Then I remembered. I was not feeling particularly well myself, but I had at least abstained from the rubber pills. I admitted the disgraceful thing I had done, a Dostoevskian confession.

"Don't spread the story," I cravenly added.

"I won't," said Lambert. "I shan't spread the mustard either—now I must hang up . . ."

Towards the end of his life especially, the laughter and talk of Lambert's lighthearted moods had an obverse side in periodical grumpiness and ill humour. Shead rightly indicates this. Even in his palmiest days there were good friends who could stand only limited stretches of the Lambert barrage of ideas, jokes, fantasy, quotation, apt instances, things that had struck him, not because these lacked quality, on the contrary, because the mixture was after a while altogether too rich. The world on the whole prefers, if not simple, at least less nourishing conversational fare. As with almost every known "good talker", there was also more than a modicum of repetition. Speaking for myself, I very rarely felt the show had gone on too long, but I could see what others meant when they complained it had. Lambert was absolutely prodigal with his wit. He never dreamed of postponing a joke because the assembled company was not sufficiently important. One point should be emphasised. Impatient, at times intolerant, Lambert was also an unexpectedly good listener. He did not in the least insist on holding the floor. In fact he liked nothing better than being himself entertained by the talk of others. He had a mind of extraordinary quickness, beginning to shake with laughter before most stories of any merit were finished, simply because he foresaw how they were going to end. He himself always disparaged those social milieues—again Oxford of my own day comes to mind—where the conventions of a supposedly "amusing" society disallow any development of an anecdote. In such a world, anything like a long story must, by definition, be regarded as a bore. Lambert used to point out that the best, the funniest stories can rarely be told in a sentence. I should not wish support of this view to be perverted into an appearance of exonerating purveyors of prosy *histoires*, but there is a case to be made for unprosy ones that may require a comparatively prolonged build-up for their punch-line. The wit of the 'Twenties, often tempered with self-consciousness, narcissism, and at times a rather childish buffoonery, was on the whole not well disposed to that view.

Although slightly lame—his characteristic movement in walking closely resembled descriptions of the manner in which Byron appeared never to set the heel of his foot on the ground—Lambert was a great walker. One Sunday afternoon in the summer we had tea together, probably at his flat over the Varda Bookshop, afterwards, I can't imagine why, strolling east to have a drink at The Tiger on Tower Hill. This pub of attractive interior stands opposite the gate of the main entrance to the Tower. Licensed premises opening on Sunday only at seven o'clock in the evening, it must have been towards eight, or even later, when we left the Tiger, and continued eastward. The immediate objective was to inspect the bas-reliefs of the Seasons executed by Caius Cibber on the walls of some of the houses in Wellclose Square, beyond the Mint. The sculptor, father of the much mocked eighteenth-century playwright, Colley Cibber, is buried there in the Danish-and-Norwegian church.

By then I have the impression it was already twilight. Having inspected these elegant plaques, we went on through Wapping and Shadwell, Lambert holding forth on the dramatist who takes his name from the latter parish. Dinner was eaten rather late at a Chinese restaurant in Limehouse. In general I found Chinese restaurants only tolerable in Lambert's company, because he justly regarded himself as an authority on Chinese food in London. He had formerly claimed a taste for Chinese wine, but became disillusioned with celestial vintages, making over his Chinese cellar to Tommy Earp, a noted personality of the literary and pub worlds. Earp's high, thin, trembling voice, much mimicked, announced after the first draught: "Rather an aphrodisiac effect." Lambert said he had never noticed that. Earp thought the matter over. "Perhaps it coincides with my annual erection," he said rather sadly.

Continuing our journey, I think there was a visit to The Prospect of Whitby, but cannot be sure—the pub of which Paul Morand wrote that, whenever English people said they would take him somewhere he had never been before, he was bound to end up at The Prospect of Whitby. Certainly several other riverside pubs, less widely known than The Prospect, were included in our survey. Skirting the Isle of Dogs, we crossed the river by the Blackwall Tunnel, in order to make a return journey along the South Bank. By this time it was past midnight, domes and towers of Wren's Greenwich illuminated by the moon. That is something worth seeing, but it would be hypocritical to pretend that the walk back did not become a little exhausting.

Between Rotherhithe and Bermondsey a miracle took place. There was a rattle of wheels on tramlines, and, altogether unaccountably, a tram drew up beside us. Perhaps it was a ghost tram. No one else seemed to be using it for transport, and even at that date its make appeared infinitely antique. Nevertheless, we were grateful. We rode in the tram as far as possible. It turned south before coming to a bridge. We alighted. The spectral tram disappeared into the night. I do not recall where the Thames was recrossed. The hour was past four, when, rather footsore, I descended the steps of the area in Tavistock Square.

There were also long walks during a Christmas spent together in Paris, taking in such outlying areas as the Buttes Chaumont. A visit to Père Lachaise was marred by the keeper at the gate immediately asking if we were looking for the tomb of Oscar Wilde, naturally our goal, but unacceptable in its implications. On that trip to Paris one café visited provided not only an orchestra, but a catalogue of musical pieces to be played on request. Lambert, who used to describe all orchestral players as "arming" (as opposed to "disarming"), took a savage pleasure in demanding those scores most complicated to render. Speaking of orchestras is a reminder of the little wire brush for tapping drums, which Lambert possessed, and used to call "the Sadist's Vade-Mecum".

Several of the Castano's clientèle would from time to time reappear as guests of Gerald Reitlinger, at his house on the edge of the Romney Marsh; later at another house, somewhat larger, in Sussex. Reitlinger—then painter, writer, editor and collector; now oracle of the economics of aesthetic taste—entertained in a manner that was enjoyable, but essentially *sui generis*. Among many who made up his house-parties, when Lambert was present, were John (the Widow) Lloyd, his brother Wyndham Lloyd (who took some of the photographs here reproduced), both expert writers of *bouts-rimés*, and Basil Hambrough, inimitable ex-guardsman. There were also a lot of beautiful ladies. These things have gone with the wind, but some aspects should not remain without any sort of record: the great photographing in costume of the Tranby Croft Case: Hambrough's verbal reconstruction of the Musn'touchit Murder: the roar alleged to have been made by his Commanding Officer: "Stand back, sir, you smell of whisky still."

Lambert used to complain that there was no looking-glass in the bedroom he usually occupied on these visits, and he had to shave in the reflections of a framed watercolour by Meninsky. Although he did not drive a car, he possessed disconcerting knowledge of mechanical matters. During altercations about his host's driving, Reitlinger recalls Lambert snapping out: "Well, I've dismantled a chain transmission drive, and that's a damn sight more than you've ever done."

The game of *Bouts-rimés* was often played at Reitlinger's after dinner. It will be remembered that each player writes down a line of heroic verse which rhymes with the verse before; then turns down the paper, so that the couplet cannot be seen, and writes another line, with which the next player has to rhyme; and so on. Lambert, as at all occasional verse, was adept in building these extempore epics. Other interludes at Reitlinger house-parties were occupied with planchette; the little board equipped with two rollers and a pencil that will sometimes write "messages".

One afternoon when Lambert and I were among the guests, planchette had been "worked" without any result. The pencil had at best merely scribbled about on the paper, usually never moved at all. Lambert had given it up, and sat writing letters at a desk in the corner of the room. Reitlinger and I continued to rest our fingers on the board. Suddenly it began to move. The "influence", transcribed in a long sloping eighteenth-century hand, announced itself as Mozart. Neither Reitlinger nor I were at all associated with music, so we asked Lambert to suggest a question.

"Enquire who was his favourite mistress."

We did so. Planchette wrote the reply.

"*La petite Carlotta.*"

"When did this love affair take place?"

"*A Napoli en 1789.*"

I think that was the date given, but could not swear to the exact year. It was certainly that period, more or less.

"What was she like?"

"*Comme une guenon.*"

The last word had to be looked up, because no one present was familiar with it. The dictionary gave: "she-monkey, ugly woman, strumpet."

Some of the later replies were in English, some in German, the last language known to Reitlinger, but not to myself nor to Lambert, by this time greatly interested, and ceasing to write letters, but playing no tactile part in the manifestation. It certainly looked as if he were in some manner telepathically concerned. Lambert's own subsequent researches produced no information about *La petite Carlotta*, except for the fact that Mozart could not possibly have been in Naples at the time named.

I think it no use pretending that the picture left by Shead's biography is not in some ways a sad one. These foregoing scraps are offered only in an attempt to catch, hold for an infinitesimal flash, those moments of relative content, so much harder to chart in life than their polarity. Although things often went wrong in the course of Lambert's career, it was also in many ways picturesque and extraordinary. To have a blood row with Diaghilev—and stand up to the great impresario —is not the experience of every young composer at the age of twenty. Lambert used to laugh about that, and other of his Diaghilev dealings, but, as in cases of a similar kind when there had been a quarrel, he bore little ill will. He used to say that one of Diaghilev's claims to fame was that he was the sole Russian who liked only one sex; and that his habit of asking a guest "Will you have one [that is 'a'] drink?" always made a depressing start to a meeting. It should also be firmly asserted that both Lambert's marriages linked him with quite exceptional exemplifications of beauty, intelligence and wit—none of which is a quality to be disregarded in a wife.

He had, I think, a touch of genius. The word is unsatisfactory. One envisages a row of lifeless personages, mysterious unapproachable beings, emitting a suffocating leakage of awe; lay-figures riotously carousing in cafés, or lying on truckle-beds in garrets, overcome with despair. Another label is required. One tries again. Lambert inwardly inhabited, often outwardly expressed, a world in which every individual, every action, was instantaneously appreciated in terms of art. Once more the concept falls flat. It is almost worse than "genius". The description suggests a pompous self-conscious aesthete, laboriously evaluating each trivial experience. Lambert could hardly have been further from that too. All the same, those are the lines along which to explore that baffling entity, a personality now gone. What was it Beardsley had? What Apollinaire? Nimrod is lost in Orion, and Osiris in the Dog-star.

After the war, during which circumstances prevented more than an occasional meeting, Lambert took a flat in Albany Street, beside Regent's Park, not far from where we lived in Chester Gate. He and I began to see each other again. In particular, Lambert developed a habit of long telephone calls, made relatively late at night, usually between half-past eleven and twelve, particularly on Sundays, when he would discuss at great length things that had amused him during the previous day or two. A subject to which he was very devoted at that moment, because of the esoteric material there contained, was the unsigned column Sacheverell Sitwell (an old friend) was then writing for one of the Sunday papers, a column very different from most journalism of its kind, no holds barred intellectually or aesthetically. Although a wide field was covered, when Lambert rang up, talk was likely to start with the question: "Have you read Sachie this week?"

Lambert was making these calls two or three times a week, when in August, 1951, I went with my family to the country for a fortnight. We came back to London on Tuesday, the 21st, the day Lambert died. It was announced in the evening paper. The following day two friends dined at our house. I mention them merely as witnesses. At a quarter to twelve the telephone bell rang.

"It's Constant," said my wife.

I went downstairs, and picked up the receiver.

"Hullo?"

There was a click, then the dialling tone.

ANTHONY POWELL

I CHILDHOOD AND SCHOOL

Constant Lambert liked to call himself a Francophil English composer-conductor born to an Australian painter from St Petersburg. The statement was accurate as well as picturesque. George Washington Thomas Lambert, Constant's father, was born in St Petersburg, the modern Leningrad, on 13th September 1873. He was the fourth child and only son of George W. Lambert, an American engineer from Baltimore, and Ann Firth, daughter of Thomas Firth, a British engineer from Yorkshire. Both George W. Lambert and Thomas Firth were employed on the Russian railways. The Lamberts themselves were originally a Yorkshire family.

Seven weeks before young George was born, his father had died in London of heart trouble (25th July 1873). He was only 40. In 1875 Thomas Firth wound up his affairs in Russia, and, taking his widowed daughter and her children with him, went to Esslingen in Württemberg, where he found a post at the locomotive works. In 1881 they all returned to England and settled in Somerset. Shortly afterwards Firth retired, and in 1885 he decided to emigrate to Australia, where some of his family were already living. Ann and her children again went with him. After a short stay in the Sydney area, they went up country to a sheep station called Eurobla, near Nevertire, in the Central Plain well over 200 miles to the north-west of Sydney. This property belonged to Robert Firth, Thomas's brother.

The boy George had no desire to go to school and worked for a while as a stationhand. He was already developing a passion for painting and drawing, but throughout his life he liked to think of himself as a man of action as much as an artist. He was certainly no aesthete: this is made abundantly clear in the book which his wife wrote and published after his death. *Thirty Years of an Artist's Life* is the main – indeed almost the only – source of detailed information about George Lambert's early life. From the literary point of view the book has little merit: as a personal record, written with a devotion not untinged with asperity, it is fascinating. The very artlessness of Mrs Lambert's prose imparts sharpness to some of her anecdotes. Many of Lambert's opinions, faithfully recorded in the book, have a jarringly philistine ring. There are striking examples in his letters from the Middle East during the First World War: his utterances about "lesser breeds without the law" like Egyptians (whom he calls "Gypos") suggest Kipling at his least appealing. He was a man with an excellent opinion of himself; but it is likely that a good deal of his aggressiveness, personal vanity and self-conscious dash was induced by an underlying feeling of inferiority caused by an unsettled upbringing, interrupted education and fierce early struggles for money and recognition.

There is no reason however to doubt that Lambert was sincere in his love of the outdoor life and in his passion for art. His boyhood was not easy: his grandfather was something of a tyrant, and in the late 1880s Lambert found himself living in Stanmore (a district of Sydney which has now become a slum but in those days was respectable though faded) and working as a clerk in a firm of wholesale drapers. Not surprisingly, his heart was not in the job and he was eventually sacked for drawing when he should have been at work. Another clerking post, in the Government Shipping Office near the Harbour, proved a little more congenial, but Lambert hankered for the outback. He had decided he wanted to breed sheep. Finally he "went bush" as a hired hand.

He might never have become a professional artist had not B. E. Minns, a portraitist who worked on the staff of the *Sydney Bulletin*, seen some of his work and advised him to study art in a systematic way. Lambert accordingly enrolled for the evening classes run at the Sydney Art Society by a certain Julian Ashton, and supported himself during the day by doing a grocer's accounts.

At that time a number of Australian artists made a living by contributing black-and-white work to the Sydney illustrated press, and especially to the *Sydney Bulletin*. In the hands of its literary editor, J. F. Archibald, the *Bulletin* became a cultural force as well as a powerful organ of Australian nationalism and republicanism (it was the mouthpiece of the "White Australia" policy). Lambert found that he could sell the *Bulletin* his sketches of bush life and characters. A small oil, *A Bush Idyll*, showing a girl standing among some goats under a group of gum trees, attracted favourable attention and was purchased for a public collection. It is easy enough to mock this type of sentimental pastoral, but the painting was a remarkable achievement for a young and largely self-taught artist and already showed that feeling for the peculiar quality of Australian landscape and light which is one of Lambert's strengths as a painter. Before long he found that he could live by selling his graphic work.

In 1899 a more vigorous and very large painting, *Across the Black Soil Plains*, made Lambert a local celebrity. It showed a team of horses hauling wool clips across open country. The following year, on the strength of three more paintings, Lambert received the first New South Wales Travelling Art Scholarship ever awarded, and set off to Europe with his wife Amy (Amelia Beatrice Absell), whom he had married on 4th September 1900, two days before sailing. They had met in 1898. She had been born in 1872 in Shoreditch, London, but emigrated with her family at the age of fourteen.

The Lamberts arrived in England on 11th November 1900 and re-mained in London until the following February, when they settled in the Latin Quarter of Paris. Their first son, Maurice (a sculptor who died in 1964, the same year as Amy herself), was born in 1901. In November 1902, very short of money, the Lamberts came back to London, where he obtained a studio in Lansdowne House, a block of four studio flats in Lansdowne Road, Notting Hill, belonging to Sir Edmund Davis, a connoisseur, collector and friend of Jacques-Emile Blanche. The top flat was occupied by Charles Ricketts and Charles Shannon, a pair of gentle homosexual artists of mild talent who had been associated with the Decadents of the 1890s (Ricketts had illustra-ted Wilde's poem *The Sphinx*). Lady Davis belonged to a moneyed family called Halford, and both she, her husband and her relative Mrs Arthur Halford gave the Lamberts generous support and financial help during the next few years. From Notting Hill the Lamberts moved to a studio in Chelsea and a flat in Fulham, near the Bishop's Palace. On 23rd August 1905 their second son, Leonard Constant, was born in St Clement's Nursing Home in the Fulham Palace Road.

During these years George Lambert's technical ability and flam-boyant personality were beginning to earn him a certain amount of artistic and social success. He was much in demand as a performer in the pageants so popular at the time. In this connection Mrs Lambert, with the artlessness already mentioned, tells a revealing story about a pageant in which her husband took the character of Lord Thomas Seymour:

I cannot remember the names of many of the other performers, which perhaps is just as well when I recall that the ineptitude of the

lady who played Katherine Parr was particularly irritating to her
stage husband, Lord Seymour, and as I had to take her part at
home rehearsals I always received a slap on the face at the conclusion
to ease the feelings that had to be repressed in public!

Another glimpse of Lambert's inimitable social manner occurs on the
previous page of the book:

> Sunday evening parties were popular. On one occasion, at the
> house of Mrs Arthur Halford, where there was commonly a cosmo-
> politan gathering of many professional artists and musicians, Signor
> Paolo Tosti, even then an old man, yielded to persuasion to sing
> some of his own compositions. His voice failed him in his famous
> "Good-Bye", but Lambert rushed into the breach, catching the
> falling phrase, and continuing to the end with gathering fervour.
> At the conclusion, the composer jumped down from the piano-
> stool, and, seizing the singer by the shoulders, kissed him on both
> cheeks, to the delight of the company.

Doubtless many a merry scene of this kind also took place at the
Chelsea Arts Club, of which Lambert was now a member. He liked a
joke: Alfred Munnings was apt to arrive at the Club in full riding kit,
with spurs, on a bicycle. One day, as he left, he discovered a load of
hay on his machine; it had been placed there by Lambert. But there
were times when things went too far. Lambert used to ride with
R. B. Cunninghame Graham, and painted his friend's portrait with his
favourite mount. The friendship suffered a severe setback when
Graham, not caring for the likeness of himself, painted it out, preserv-
ing only the beast with its Mexican saddle.

Most of those who sat for Lambert were satisfied with the result.
One of his finest oils, a portrait of his friend and pupil Thea Proctor,
was painted in 1903, and he was commissioned to carry out portraits
of Lady Beaverbrook and the Gaekwar of Baroda. Sargent praised his
work. Less ambitious but more charming are the paintings and draw-
ings in which Lambert used his wife and children as models. Maurice
and Constant were very much alike as children, and both were con-
spicuously good-looking. Their father, too, presented a striking appearance with his red beard, and was given to self-portraiture.

Constant was a delicate child, and needed much care. In his mother's
view he probably owed his life to the help provided by Mrs Arthur
Halford when he was very young. Later Mrs Halford paid for his and

his brother's piano lessons; these were given them by Elsie Hall, an Australian pianist who had been hailed on her arrival in London as "the Antipodean Phenomenon". Both boys became pupils at Manor House School, Clapham, where they encountered Christianity for the first time, their domestic education having been conducted on atheistic principles. Despite the commissions, the Lamberts were still in financial straits, and they fell into arrears with the boys' school fees. Revealingly Amy Lambert writes:

> He was always in a state of self-discipline before his vocation. A portrait commission or an unexpected sale never meant studio or home improvement, or investments other than in himself or what he needs must express as occasion arose.

Mrs Lambert, in saying that her husband was prepared to sacrifice not only his own comfort but that of his family for the sake of his art, seems to be implying that he was selfish, as to all appearances he was. But he was completely honest in this matter: in his view an artist's need to express himself took precedence over all other considerations in his life. The grave doubts he voiced when both his sons decided to become artists were due not only to the uncertain rewards of such a life but to his belief that an artist's duty was to put himself and his gift first and that this was likely to create domestic unhappiness.

Before the outbreak of war George and Amy Lambert moved to 25 Glebe Place, Chelsea, a sizeable house in a side turning off the King's Road. It was Constant's home until 1926. When the First World War began the family were staying with Mrs Halford at her house at Cranleigh in Surrey. Lambert wanted to enlist, but he was 40, he had a young family, and he was told that if he wished to join the Australian forces he would first have to go back home. For the moment, then, his life did not change its pattern, except that he became poorer. It was from Cranleigh that Constant went to be interviewed for a place at Christ's Hospital, Horsham, and in his application to the Almoners of the school his father stated that his income was about £200 a year, but that since the outbreak of war commissions for portraits and sales of pictures had practically ceased: he was therefore obliged to ask for help in educating his children.

Constant became a pupil in the Preparatory School for Christ's Hospital on 15th September 1915. He was then ten years old. Writing to his mother in 1945, when his own son Kit was ten, he said:

At Kit's age there were only two things I really detested:
(a) children of my own age
(b) boredom.
Blame me not him if he takes after me.

In any case, the boy had little opportunity to take a normal part in the life of his new school. He had to endure over two years of illnesses. There was appendicitis, and a double mastoid which left him deaf in his right ear for the rest of his life. He appears also to have developed Roseola Infantum (also known as Duke's Disease and Fourth Disease). This was a rash over the trunk, probably caused by streptococcus. Osteomyelitis, or perhaps Brodie's Abscess, followed. Treatment with antibiotics was unknown, and over the next years the boy had some eighteen operations, which left him lame for life. He nearly died: his condition was so grave that his parents stayed for a time in the school doctor's house in order to be near their sick son. Constant was due to move from the Preparatory School to Lamb A House in the winter term of 1916, but was too ill to do so. He returned to normal school life in the summer term of 1918, only to go back to the infirmary after summer was over. These continual sicknesses were expensive, and the Governors of the School bore a great deal of the cost. In later years Lambert was apt to say of Christ's Hospital that "it was a charity school, and they let you know it". It is never agreeable when young and proud, to be dependent on the kindness of others: but he owed the School a debt. On the other hand, the pain he suffered at the hands of well-intentioned doctors left him with a lifelong inclination to avoid the medical profession as much as possible. Morphia was used in his treatment, and at one stage his diet consisted of champagne and burgundy. There was a family theory that this early and enforced intake of alcohol laid the seeds of Lambert's heavy drinking as an adult. The idea seems far-fetched, but his sister-in-law, Mrs Maurice Lambert, remembers that he always "made a face" when drinking, as if he were taking medicine.

His scholastic work suffered. In the summer of 1916, while still at the Preparatory School, he won prizes for English and Drawing, but a year later his position in the form was very low. By summer 1919, however, things had changed for the better, and his leaving report was a good one. The long months in the infirmary gave him plenty of opportunity for reading, and it was due to this – as well as his formal education and his family background – that he became so well-informed while still a boy. His command of English was already remarkable. In 1954, three years after Lambert's death, his Housemaster, the late A. C. W. Edwards, wrote of him:

> It was this (the lameness) which set him apart – a little bitter-tongued and affecting a cynical, unboyish outlook – and forced him, in a sense, to prove that he was superior in other and more important fields. He was very grown-up in his language and ideas. He was a ready speaker with a remarkable quickness of repartee, which he used to amuse, to amaze and often to hurt. . . . He had his admirers and friends, but I would not call him a popular boy. His lameness and maturity of outlook were great handicaps to success in the philistine society of a Public School.

The boy was in continual pain. He could never put the whole of his foot to the ground and had to walk on his toes, with that strikingly individual gait which he retained all his life and which Michael Ayrton has called "bird-hopping". Since his ankles were weak he was obliged to wear boots, which was humiliating for anyone as sensitive and self-conscious in social dealings as Lambert. But though organised games were out of the question (which may not have troubled him greatly), he swam well and enjoyed it, and even boxed, it seems, fiercely. On one occasion he was concerned in some escapade or other, for which the other culprits were beaten, and he escaped punishment, because of his physical condition – a well-meaning forebearance on the part of authority which merely incensed the boy.

As a pianist and composer Lambert made an impact at the School, and he wrote a short operetta for a house concert in 1921. He also asked to conduct the school orchestra. T. B. Radley, who knew him at school and in later life, tells the story:

> I retain a vivid picture of his passing me in the lobby of Big School. We all keep these private picture galleries, I expect, in the attics of our minds; lumber, most of it. But this portrait has turned out to be a master. He had light proud eyes, clouded then with a trouble he was too haughty to share; a pale and handsome face; his hair grew off his forehead slightly wavy, and it gleamed and glinted as if in the sun, as the hair of young people often does. His lips, especially the lower, were rather full, but set into supercilious curves which I knew were already habitual. He stalked past with a kind of stillness

B   33

about him, as though he noticed none of his surroundings. . . . He must have been about eighteen. I remember being somewhat awed by the beauty – no – by the power in his face; but attracted too, and friendly. He passed by.

Within a week or so the music master came as usual to the Big School on Friday evening for the choir practice. He was evidently much put out, nor could he keep the reason of his disquiet to himself. After reducing us to silence by rattling his keys he told us, in tones of irritation and shock, that Lambert had actually requested to conduct the school orchestra. The music master got what he needed: we laughed. A *boy* to conduct the orchestra, what a nerve; and I do not recollect that our laughter was sycophantic, as boys often are. We were in our fashion as shocked as the music master.

Michael Stewart, the Labour politician, was a fellow-pupil with Lambert in Lamb A House. He remembers a happier moment:

At the age of sixteen, or even earlier, he had the mind and interests of a well-informed adult . . . in his company one was apt to be frequently and sharply reminded that outside school there was a real world, with manifold problems and interests, and that school life, however enjoyable, could not be more than a preparation for reality. This doesn't mean that he was a solemn person at all – he was an adult, but a gay, almost boisterous adult. . . . My dearest memories of him belong to his last term, the summer term of 1922. I have a particularly vivid mental picture of a small group . . . hurrying across Lamb A pitch to the Baths for "early dip" with Lambert among us, reciting his own poems, or explaining the works of Ibsen or occasionally listening to what the rest of us had to say, but always a figure full of life and enjoyment.

Meanwhile, through the influence of Sir Alfred Mond, George Lambert had obtained a post as Works Officer supervising the felling of timber for military purposes, and he and his wife lived for a time at Haverfordwest in Pembrokeshire. This work continued until Lambert became an official war artist: on 29th December 1917 he set out for the Middle East with the task of recording the part played by the Australian Light Horse in the Palestinian campaign. He enjoyed this, flinging himself into the work with enthusiasm and making a great impression, not only by his artistic ability (a quality which the members of the Australian Light Horse, truth to tell, were hardly fitted to assess) but by his dash, his gifts as a mimic and storyteller, and his horsemanship. Amy Lambert remained in England to look after the boys, run the house, and keep the creditors at bay. Her husband returned to Britain in July 1918, but after only a short period he went back to the Mediterranean, this time to Gallipoli.

Constant spent some of his holidays at Chilham Castle in Kent, which Sir Edmund Davis had bought. He had installed Ricketts and Shannon in a house known as "the Keep" in the castle grounds, and in September 1919 Ricketts wrote as follows to his friend Mrs Muriel Lee Mathews:

> Young Lambert is here and lives at the Keep. He has grown and is very intelligent. I am threatened with two compositions of his on the piano at the house when the house-party is away. He is less Stravinskiesque and seems genuinely interested in Weber and Liszt, the names least mentioned in recent years. . . . Judging from young Lambert, it would seem as if the young realised the need of movement and climax in music, the two things Debussy and his school tabooed.

It is worth noting that at the age of fourteen Lambert had already gone through a "Stravinskiesque" phase, and that he was expressing a fondness for Liszt, whose music he loved all his life. Ricketts was very interested in the Diaghilev Ballet, and may well have talked about it to the boy, who was destined to be associated throughout his career with the world of dance.

In the absence of Australian models and landscape George Lambert was having difficulty in completing the official work he had been commissioned to carry out, and in November 1920 he sailed for Australia on a concession passage. He never saw his sons again. His wife stayed behind in Chelsea and did not rejoin her husband until 1926. Even then she returned to England in 1929, and was there when George died. It seems unlikely that the painter had any further influence on the development of his sons, who were accustomed to complain that he spent the money he should have been sending back to England on scent for his beard.

George Lambert rapidly established a dominant position in the artistic life of Sydney and Melbourne. Robert Hughes refers to him as "the Boldini of Point Piper and Toorak" (fashionable districts of Sydney and Melbourne respectively). It was his custom to spend half the year in his studio; then he would emerge, take a suite in a Sydney hotel and give party after party before returning to work when the year was up. He was hailed as a great painter, and was for a time, so to speak, both the Orpen of Australia and its John. However, as Lionel Lindsay put it, he was "possessed of a Renaissance ambition to excel in all media". This took the form of an ill-advised decision to embark on monumental sculpture, a field in which he encountered many personal and technical problems which he had not solved when he died suddenly at the age of fifty-seven on 28th May 1930. He left £300. A Lambert Memorial Society was formed, with the support of Dame Nellie Melba and other prominent Australians, to acquire his works for national collections, and the prices asked were unusually high for the work of an Australian artist in the middle of the Depression.

Aggressive, swashbuckling and selfish, George Lambert was not altogether a sympathetic character, and Constant had far more respect for his mother, whom in any case he knew far better than he did his father; but in the breadth of his interests at least George resembled his younger son, who became not only a composer but a conductor, speaker, author, journalist and wit.

In 1922, Constant Lambert won a composition scholarship to the Royal College of Music. He left Christ's Hospital on 3rd August and began his musical studies a month later. His teacher for composition, his main study, was Ralph Vaughan Williams, with Herbert Fryer for piano and eventually Malcolm Sargent for conducting. Later he studied composition also with R. O. Morris, Vaughan Williams' brother-in-law and an authority on polyphony, and with George Dyson. Lambert established a rapport with Morris and respected Vaughan Williams, although he never greatly cared for the English folksong school: he even – with some unspoken reservations – dedicated a work to his former teacher. For Dyson, on the other hand, he had no sympathy, and it is easy to see why: despite his academic skill Dyson represented everything in British music which Lambert regarded as faded and provincial.

Vaughan Williams saw at once that he had acquired a brilliant pupil. In an appreciation of Lambert the scholar Edward J. Dent recalled a meeting with Vaughan Williams at that time:

> It was Vaughan Williams who first discovered his marvellous musicianship. . . . He called on me one day at Cambridge glowing with excitement to show me Constant's first attempt at a fugue, written without any previous knowledge of the rules. It was a most unorthodox fugue on a most unorthodox subject, but there could be no doubt that it was the product of an original and highly intelligent mind.

Lambert found at the College a number of students who shared his wide interests – in painting, literature, the cinema and the theatre as well as music. Among them were Humphrey Procter-Gregg, musician and opera producer, Gavin Gordon, later composer of the highly successful Hogarth ballet *The Rake's Progress*, and Leslie Heward. Heward was one of a trio of brilliant conductors whose early deaths were a great loss to British music, the others being Lambert himself and his friend Hyam Greenbaum.

Angus Morrison, the pianist, whose sister Olga later married Lambert's elder brother Maurice, was a particularly close friend. He lived with his parents in Oakley Street, Chelsea, very near the Lamberts' house in Glebe Place. The two young men often went to the theatre and the cinema together, and played innumerable piano duets, familiarising themselves in this way with the ballets of Stravinsky, Debussy and Ravel, then still enticing novelties.

One joint visit to the theatre was crucial in Lambert's development. In May 1923 C. B. Cochran presented a show with the title *Dover Street to Dixie* at the London Pavilion. The first half, representing "Dover Street", was a collection of songs and sketches which fell below Cochran's usual high standard, but the second part, "The Plantation", was a very different matter. It gave London its first sight of the troupe of coloured artists who achieved sensational fame three years later as the "Blackbirds". In 1923 the main attractions were the singer Florence Mills and Will Vodery's "Plantation Orchestra". Few of those who acclaimed the same artists in 1926 recognised their merit at this time, so that the show was not a great success and ran for only about three months. But some who went to the London Pavilion were completely captivated, among them Lambert, seventeen years old and highly impressionable. Angus Morrison writes:

> Without a doubt this performance was one of the key experiences in his life, beginning not only his long preoccupation with jazz and the possibility of fusing and blending many of its rhythmic inventions and subtleties into the texture of more serious music, but also moving him in a far deeper way emotionally than any other music he had hitherto heard. Later he went (often in my company) very frequently to see and hear the same players in "Blackbirds", but by then his interest in jazz was more conscious and formulated; fully aware of all the complex technical processes and determined to master them for his own uses. The early experience was the truly formative one. I am convinced that the first time he saw "The Plantation" was a moment of true inspiration – a moment he sought to recapture over and over again in his own music – in *The Rio Grande*, the slow movement of the *Piano Sonata*, the *Piano Concerto*, the *Elegiac Blues* and even that exquisite piece written many years later, *Aubade Héroïque*. Similar in some ways to the experience in the life of Delius, described by Cecil Gray in his autobiography, *Musical Chairs*, when Delius heard negro voices singing in the

38

distance during the summer night on his orange grove in Florida, and analogous to Proust's immortal description and analysis of subconscious memory and the moment of illumination when it is recaptured at the beginning of *Swann's Way*.

The arresting start of the whole performance was a sort of fanfare on the tune of *Carry me back to old Virginia*. The Delius-like harmonies were made to sound even more lush and glowing by the clear ininhibited playing of this magnificent negro band. It was indeed the memory of this opening flourish played by the superb first trumpeter, Jonny Dunn (described in the programme as "the Creator of Wa-Wa"), that remained with Constant all through his life. Its echo can be heard somewhere in almost all his works, and there is no doubt that the first phrase of the chorus in *The Rio Grande* was a conscious attempt on his part to reproduce the same effect – that irresistible blend of blatancy and sweetness that had stirred him so deeply when he first heard it.

This was the memory of a specifically musical impression; a particular sequence of notes and a special quality of sound in the orchestration that he tried so often, both consciously and unconsciously, to reproduce in his own music.

The other strong impression made on him by the performance, exerting an influence more all-embracing and with even deeper emotional repercussions, was the incomparable personality of Florence Mills herself. After the earlier show, the later "Blackbirds", with its greater sophistication and far more conscious sense of "presentation", was in some ways a disappointment, and it was Florence Mills, alone of all the company, who still retained the essential simplicity and childlike quality that had made "The Plantation" so utterly endearing.

Mr Morrison goes on to describe Florence Mills' first entrance in "The Plantation":

After the pungent, yet softly caressing timbre of the coloured voices had plunged one straight into the right atmosphere with an opening chorus of peculiarly haunting charm, she made her first entrance, dressed (rather like a pantomine Dick Whittington) in conventional stage rags, with a bundle on her shoulder, singing of the "sleepy hills of Tennessee". With the same effortless ease of Charlie Chaplin revealing an unexpected vein of pathos in some perfectly ordinary event, Florence Mills brought tears to one's eyes purely by the quality of her voice and the sincerity of her acting.

Lambert's sympathy for the American negro was partly a musical thing: he loved jazz, and regarded Duke Ellington as a talented and interesting composer, as important as Kurt Weill and far more so than Hindemith. The fondness Lambert expressed for the hymns of John Bacchus Dykes was not due only to the frequent risibility of the words, but to the fact that Dykes was one of the first musicians to make popular use of extreme chromaticism. The harmonies of hymn tunes such as his were absorbed by the negroes into their own music, and they reappear, filtered by a major composer's creative imagination, in the works of Delius, which in their turn influenced Ellington and other jazz musicians.

The impact of Florence Mills' personality on Lambert was so great that it appears to have set a pattern which recurred throughout his life. A few years later he experienced the same feeling of passionate admiration for the film actress Anna May Wong, and Lambert's first wife (also called Florence) was of partly oriental ancestry. There were other, more fleeting relationships, with coloured women. Lambert's intense romanticism and passion for the exotic produced striking and beautiful music from him, but it was not a recipe for domestic happiness, which eluded him until the last years of his life.

It took some time for the influence of jazz to find its way into Lambert's scores: the works he wrote as a student reflect two other enthusiasms, French and Russian music. He was not alone in these: for many of the musical young the 1920s were a time of emancipation from the domination of the Austro-German classics and romantics, and the most glamorous forces in the cultural world were the Ballets Russes of Diaghilev and the scores of Diaghilev's greatest composer, Igor Stravinsky. Lambert's penchant for French and Russian music remained with him all his life, though it did not prevent him from liking composers like Schumann, Liszt, Delius and Sibelius. The works he chose to conduct as a student at the Royal College included movements from the symphonies of Borodin and a suite Lambert himself selected from Glinka's *Ruslan and Ludmilla*, an opera he discussed perceptively in his book *Music Ho!* In July 1925 he wrote to M. Montagu-Nathan, the author of books on Glinka, Mussorgsky and other Russian composers, and in later years a colleague of Lambert's in the Camargo Society:

Next Tuesday I am conducting at the R.C.M. a suite which I have arranged from *Ruslan and Ludmilla*. As it was your excellent little book which drew my attention to the opera, I should be very pleased if you could come. I have not had enough rehearsal to ensure a really finished performance but I hope to give a good idea of the work. Included in the suite are the 5/4 chorus, the Persian chorus, etc.

Several sizeable student works date from this period in Lambert's life. *Green Fire*, an orchestral rhapsody, was played at a Royal College Patrons' Fund Rehearsal on 28th June 1923, and startled audience and critics with "its excessively high spirits . . . like a panegyric to Rimsky-Korsakov, chiefly *fortissimo e con fuoco*". The score appears to be lost. There were a number of smaller pieces, some of them incorporated into scores published later, but the main surviving works are three ballets and a piano concerto.

Prize-Fight, a "Realistic Ballet in One Act", was written in 1923–4 and revised and rescored in 1925. It requires a small orchestra including cornet and harmonium. It is unpublished and appears never to have been performed in public. The manuscript has a synopsis written in by Lambert, as follows:

A boxing ring (in confusion). A noisy group enters. The referee attempts to announce the programme and to obtain silence (in vain!) The referee makes wild efforts to silence the crowd and eventually succeeds. He introduces first the white man (a popular figure), then the negro (a man of sullen disposition). The old attendant places a placard with the figure 1 on his pole. The bell sounds. The boxers proceed gingerly from their corners. (N.B. During the round the blows on the stage are registered off stage by machines making the sound of breaking glass, horses' hooves, motor horns etc. ad lib.) The white man claims a foul. Undue excitement of a certain section of the audience. The referee gets into the ring. The nigger drives the white man into a corner. The white man falls. Bell!

Saved by the bell! During the rest the seconds attempt to revive their exhausted champions with fanning, massage, sponging, dry shampoo, revolving hair brushes, cups of Bovril, bottles of champagne etc. A drunkard with a concertina mounts into the ring and starts playing. He is ejected by the referee. The drunkard, undaunted, again mounts into the ring and plays but is again ejected by the indignant referee. He falls down in front. An attendant in white clothes rolls the floor of the ring with a light roller. The drunkard plays a furtive solo. Someone whistles. The attendant places a placard with the figure 13 on his pole. The bell sounds.

The boxers stagger from their corners and proceed to fight with great caution. So much so, that not a single blow is exchanged during the whole round. A member of the audience flings a ham-bone into the ring. The old attendant holds up a placard with "No Ball" on it. The nigger in avoiding the white man falls through the ropes, an attendant holds up a touch-flag, and the referee throws him back. A group enter the ring and start a derisive dance. The referee attempts to remove them, but in vain. More people join the dancers and complete chaos reigns. The boxers, goaded to desperation, attack the referee, who produces a police-rattle and waves it. The drunkard, mounted on the light roller, is wheeled round the ring in triumph, playing wildly. Entry of Mounted Police, who attempt to quell the disturbance, and get into the ring, which under so great a weight groans and collapses. The old attendant holds up a placard with the words "Grand Slam".

Those familiar with the stage works of Jean Cocteau and "Les Six" will have no difficulty in perceiving the source of Lambert's inspiration in this piece. The title recalls Honegger, whose ballet *Skating Rink* appeared in 1922, the sub-title Satie, who described his *Parade* as a "ballet réaliste", and the action of the work the farcical happenings in the Cocteau-Milhaud *Boeuf sur le Toit* with its negro and its comic policeman who is decapitated by a fan. The instrumentation of *Prize-Fight*, with its suggestions of the music-hall, is another homage to the aesthetic of Cocteau and Satie, as is the use of stylized "noises-off". The music of the ballet, which is continuous, mingles the modality of Lambert's teacher Vaughan Williams with jaunty music-hall tunes and occasional Gallic touches. Lambert already shows a fondness for irregular metres. The work is worthy of performance for its deftness and professionalism, but it has no great personality of its own: it is obviously written by a talented student with a lively interest in the musical and aesthetic fashions current at the time.

Mr Bear Squash-You-All-Flat, a one-act ballet based on a Russian children's tale, is scored for wind, piano and percussion and was finished in June 1924. There have been no public performances. The scene is a glade with a fallen, hollow tree-trunk in the background. A series of animals enter, dance and go into the trunk: Mr Frog, Mr Mouse, Mr Hedgehog, Mr Duck (whose dance is a tango), Mr Samson Cat (who enters to music marked *moderato maestoso e marziale*), Mr Donkey and finally Mr Bear. Mr Bear, needless to say, sits on the trunk, which is the end of it and also of the ballet. In this work the modality derived from Vaughan Williams is tinged with Russian touches, but the ballet is less impressive than *Prize-Fight* though not without charm.

Adam and Eve marks an advance, but since the greater part of it was incorporated into Lambert's first published work, *Romeo and Juliet*, it will be considered later. The *Piano Concerto* (not to be confused with Lambert's later and mature work, the *Concerto* for piano and nine players) was written out for two pianos in 1924 and probably never scored. It is in four linked movements, all based on the same thematic material: *Allegro risoluto*; *Presto*; *Andante* and *Allegro*.

Lambert's studies did not prevent him from making many new friends at this time. This is easily understood, for despite a certain shyness which he never completely lost he had a captivating personality, great charm and radiant good looks. Those who saw him only in later years, when ill health and excessive drinking had left their mark, may find this hard to believe; indeed he himself was accustomed at one stage to carry around a photograph of himself as he once was, and would occasionally take it out of his pocket and contemplate it in a melancholy way.

Among his new friends were the Sitwells, Edith, Osbert and Sacheverell. He had invited the brothers to attend a performance of his settings of two of Sacheverell's poems, *Serenade* and *The White Nightingale*. They were also neighbours of his in Chelsea: Osbert and Sacheverell lived at 2, Carlyle Square, on the corner of King's Road and very near Glebe Place. They already knew certain other musicians, among them Bernard van Dieren, whom a small band of enthusiasts, Philip Heseltine and Cecil Gray to the fore, regarded as a master. But their particular protégé was the young William Walton.

Sacheverell Sitwell had met Walton at Oxford, where both were undergraduates. The Sitwells recognised Walton's precocious talent – a remarkable achievement since Walton at that point had written little of consequence – and the following year, 1920, the brothers took him on holiday with them to Italy and Sicily. When Walton left Oxford he came to live at Carlyle Square, where he remained for some ten years. While friendly with the Sitwells, Lambert never became a protégé, and it was not until 1925 that he first stayed as a guest at Renishaw, the Sitwell house in Derbyshire, as part of a house party presided over by the eccentric Sir George and also including Walton and the writer Peter Quennell.

Comparison between Walton and Lambert is inevitable. They were friends, and during the late 1920s and early 1930s they were generally regarded as the most interesting and promising young composers working in Britain. And yet they were most unlike each other in many respects. Lambert's interests were multifarious, his life in later years increasingly disordered. Walton was before all things a composer, and a greater one than Lambert: no single work of Lambert's is of the calibre of *Belshazzar's Feast* (on the other hand very few works written in this century are on that exalted level). A musician who knew both men well wrote in 1930:

> Walton's work improves at every hearing. He is the best musician this country has produced for a long while. Lambert is perhaps more talented, but I do not feel that music is his ultimate mode of expression. His keen observation, sensibility, wit and critical intellect seem rather to point to literature as his medium, whereas Walton is specifically musical or nothing.

This may not be completely true: yet it seems probable that Lambert, had he so wished, could have made a career for himself as a writer of books rather than music, while Walton had no such alternative. On the personal side, it is futile, when comparing the two men, to lament the fact that Lambert did not enjoy Walton's good fortune in finding rich and generous patrons willing to ease the process of composition. Lambert's temperament was never attuned to the role of protégé, and he lacked entirely that ruthlessness in the pursuit of circumstances favourable to creation which is the hallmark of many major artists. In the later 1930s and the 1940s Walton's stock as a composer rose, and Lambert's declined. Walton had concentrated on composing, Lambert had not. Walton was achieving a freedom from money worries that eluded Lambert. Lambert quite lacked the occasional pomposity which allowed Walton to declare at the time he produced his *Viola Concerto* that "my music is becoming more melodious and mature". Yet in truth Walton showed a gradual development lacking in Lambert, who wrote

44

most of his best music between 1926 and 1931. After 1940, it is true, Walton began to repeat himself, and his music acquired an "official" ring which caused Lambert to refer to him as "the late Sir William" long before Walton was knighted (1951). However, the two composers remained friendly and to this day Walton regards Lambert as the greatest influence on his own development as a musician.

The musician whose perceptive comparison of Lambert and Walton has been quoted was Philip Heseltine (Peter Warlock). In the 1920s he was nearing the end of his brief life. He lived in a cottage at Eynsford in Kent which he rented from Hubert Foss of the Oxford University Press (Heseltine's and later Lambert's publishers). Walton and Lambert used to visit Heseltine for convivial evenings, as did many other young men at that time. Lambert and Heseltine had several features in common: a fondness for writing limericks, a passion for cats, a basic pessimism and an interest in early music. Heseltine and his friend Cecil Gray had rediscovered the curious and sinister Prince of Venosa, Carlo Gesualdo, in whom Stravinsky interested himself forty years later. Lambert read a paper to the Royal Musical Association[1] on Thomas Roseingrave, the extravagant admirer of Domenico Scarlatti, who went mad from an excess of frustrated passion for a female pupil. Lambert was intrigued by Roseingrave's strange life and the experimental quality of much of his music. No doubt under Heseltine's influence, Lambert also took up the neglected figure of William Boyce, edited some of his works and scored them for strings and wind, omitting the continuo in a way which today would be considered stylistically incorrect but which sounds well enough to the lay ear and at least had the effect of getting the music performed. Naturally Lambert stood to gain financially from this work but he was genuinely enthusiastic about Boyce, as an article he wrote for *The Listener*[2] makes plain. He later used some of Boyce's music for his ballet "The Prospect Before Us" (1940). A further Heseltine influence on Lambert may be seen in the latter's fondness for the use of archaic musical terms in his scores (Coranto, Brawles, Rigadoon, hautboy, etc.).

If Heseltine's influence on Lambert had been confined to cats, limericks, William Boyce and the self-consciously archaic, no harm would have been done. But there was more to it than that. Heseltine was a deeply unhappy man. His drinking was carried to almost insane

---

[1] *LVIII*, 1932.   [2] 16th January 1929.

lengths, and he eventually gassed himself, having carefully put his beloved cat out first so that the animal should not have to share in his death.

Unhappily he did not show an equal consideration for his friends. There is a character in Anouilh's play *La Répétition* who says: "J'aime casser". Heseltine was of this type: he was a destroyer. This characteristic could take such comparatively harmless (though irritating) forms as attempting to disrupt a concert of music by his friend Christian Darnton by singing obscene songs; it could also take the form of teaching young men how to drink. There can be little doubt that Heseltine did much to confirm Lambert in a course that led to destruction. It is possible that Lambert never completely recovered from the shock of Heseltine's death. The blackest of all Lambert's works, the *Piano Concerto*, is dedicated to Heseltine's memory, and in many ways Lambert seems to have done all he could, short of suicide, to rejoin his friend at the earliest opportunity. Bernard van Dieren, friend of Heseltine, Gray and Lambert, appears also to have exerted a baneful influence on Lambert and others, and in much the same way. Lambert once said "I will never, never forget what I owe to Bernard". It is impossible to know what he meant, for while he greatly admired van Dieren's scores they had little if any direct influence on his own work. He may have been referring to the fact that van Dieren, like himself, had wide interests, which included literature and sculpture (he wrote a book on Epstein) as well as music. But it is also relevant to point out that van Dieren appears to have subsisted on tumblers of neat gin for a great deal of the time. Lambert was fond of pointing out, accurately, that because of the cultural "time-lag" between the Continent and England musical nationalism had struck Britain at a time when it was going out of fashion elsewhere. A case could be made for saying that the same geographical phenomenon caused the "doomed" romantic movement of the mid-nineteenth century, with its overtones of diabolism, to reach England belatedly in the early twentieth century. In this sense van Dieren, Heseltine, Lambert and others are best understood by reference not to their contemporaries on the Continent but to Nerval and Baudelaire.

While Walton also knew van Dieren and Heseltine, he was not affected by the atmosphere of their circle in the way that Lambert was. And the work with which he first attracted wide attention, the entertainment *Façade*, was very much of its own time. *Façade* had created something of a sensation at its first public performance at the Aeolian Hall in London on 12th June 1923 (there had already been a private performance at the Sitwell house in Carlyle Square on 24th January 1922). In 1923 it had a largely hostile reception, but when it was given again, in revised form, at the Chenil Galleries in Chelsea on 27th April 1926, it enjoyed a triumph. It even received the accolade of a laudatory notice from Ernest Newman, then firmly entrenched as the arbiter of musical elegance in England. The audience was packed, elegant and enthusiastic. Diaghilev was there. Not long afterwards the Sitwell brothers arranged a luncheon at Carlyle Square for the Russian and his entourage (his secretary Boris Kochno and his *premier danseur* and friend Serge Lifar). There was only one piano in the Sitwells' house (the upright on which Walton composed); so after the meal the party moved to Angus Morrison's house in Oakley Street, where there were two. Walton and Morrison played Diaghilev parts of a projected ballet score by Walton, but the impresario courteously turned it down, saying that one day Walton would "write something better". The ballet was later recast as the *Sinfonia Concertante* with solo piano. While at the Morrisons' Diaghilev noticed a portrait of one of the Lambert boys by their father, and admired it, thereby demonstrating a certain magnanimity, for reasons that will shortly appear. No Walton ballet ever entered the repertoire of the Ballets Russes, though both *Portsmouth Point* and a suite from *Façade* were played as interludes.[1] Unlike Lambert, Walton has never again been greatly drawn to write for the ballet stage. *Façade*, in its orchestral form, later achieved great success in the theatre, but Walton's only original composition for the dance, *The Quest*, is one of his few comparatively undistinguished works. In his early career Walton seems often to have been anxious to cap the achievements of other composers. His *Piano Quartet* followed hard on the heels of Herbert Howells' essay in that medium, much praised when it appeared. Walton's desire to place a work in the Diaghilev repertoire may also have been due to a desire to "go one better" than his English confrères. At all events, having failed in this aim, he turned to the concert hall, where he has scored his greatest successes.

The reciters at the Chenil Galleries were Edith Sitwell herself and

---

[1] The Interludes played at the Russian Ballet, usually under conductors of the calibre of Roger Desormière and Eugene Goossens, show a fascinating and eclectic musical taste at work: Diaghilev's own.

Lambert. An actor called Neil Porter had been going to share the programme with the poetess, but in the event Lambert took his place. Of
Lambert as a reciter Osbert Sitwell wrote:

> In Paris, the Hague, London and Siena, Constant Lambert, posses-
> sor of so many rare gifts, has proved himself to have yet one more:
> to be the perfect instrument of this performance, a speaker *sans
> pareil* of the verse, clear, rapid, incisive, tireless, and commanding
> vocally an extraordinary range of inflection, from menace and the
> threat of doom to the most debonair and jaunty inconsequence.

Lambert wrote to his mother from Paris in May 1926:

> *Façade* was great fun just before I left. I ended up by doing about
> half the programme. The house was very crowded and most
> enthusiastic.

Façade is dedicated to Lambert, and the printed score acknowledges
him as a collaborator in No. 14 ("Four in the Morning"), the first
eleven bars of which were written by Lambert. The form of Walton's
"entertainment" seems to have changed a good deal between the 1922
and 1923 performances, and again between 1923 and 1926. Its final
shape (21 numbers grouped in threes) was conceived, at Lambert's
suggestion, as a deliberate allusion to, or parody of Schoenberg's
Pierrot Lunaire, "three times seven poems of Albert Giraud".[1]

Shortly before the triumph of *Façade*, a remarkable piece of good
luck brought Lambert, still only twenty, on to the international scene.
The artist and book illustrator Edmund Dulac, a friend of Ricketts,
Shannon and Sir Edmund Davis, introduced Lambert to Diaghilev.
Lambert and Angus Morrison played the Russian the suite dansée
Adam and Eve, which they had jointly conceived: Diaghilev com-
missioned a ballet from Lambert.

---

[1] Lambert and Edith Sitwell recorded eleven numbers from *Façade*. See
Appendix II.

III

It was a great honour to be invited to compose a ballet for Diaghilev. In order to understand the prestige of Diaghilev's Russian Ballet and the fascination it exerted it is necessary to put out of one's mind all thoughts of the ballet troupes of today. One does not go to the Royal Ballet, the Danish Ballet or the New York City Company, still less to the Bolshoi or the Kirov, to be shown what is newest and most exciting in contemporary artistic thinking – be it in painting, music or literary ideas. All these companies can boast fine dancers and good ballets, but by no stretch of the imagination could any of them be described as an intellectual and artistic powerhouse. This is precisely what the Diaghilev Ballet was. At times the quality of the choreography and the dancing suffered, but not to the degree that some writers have pretended. Any company which can produce in the space of ten years *The Three-Cornered Hat, La Boutique fantasque, Les Biches, Les Noces, Apollon Musagète* and *Le Fils Prodigue* cannot be accused of choreographic poverty. The result was that in the 1920s (and to some extent in the 1930s also, after Diaghilev's death) there was far more contact between the ballet world and the literary one than is the case today. Indeed it was Bloomsbury (in the person of Keynes and his friends) which, by founding the Camargo Society, bridged the gap between the collapse of the Ballets Russes in 1929 and the establishment of the Vic-Wells Ballet. The de Basil and René Blum Companies of the 1930s, full though they were of superb dancers, lost this artistic vitality. In this respect Diaghilev's heirs were the Camargo Society, the short-lived" Ballets 1933", Vic-Wells and Sadler's Wells in their earlier days (and to some extent until Lambert's death), and the Ballets des Champs-Elysées. This last company, which flourished briefly after the Second World War, was largely the creation of Diaghilev's former secretary, Boris Kochno.

Diaghilev was always on the lookout for new creative talent, and he possessed a remarkable "nose" for it. Why did he choose Lambert? He certainly recognised the young man's ability, and to commission a ballet from an unknown English student was a way of attracting useful publicity. Lambert had charm and good looks, and Diaghilev liked masculine charm and good looks, though he rarely allowed his sexual tastes to impair his artistic judgment. Nevertheless the fact that Lambert had a winning appearance as well as ability clearly did him no harm with the Russian. His youth, too, was no disadvantage. Diaghilev was never averse to employing the young, for a variety of reasons. Exciting novelties were the lifeblood of his Company. He liked to bring the young men in whom he was emotionally interested before the international public who attended his seasons. And there was yet another factor, during the last years of his career: the young, or most of them, did as they were told. Earlier collaborators of his like Stravinsky and Cocteau were now too established and too influential in their own right to dance to Diaghilev's tune, and some of them, like Cocteau and Léonide Massine, had already committed the sin of working for rival organisations like the Ballets Suédois or the "Soirées de Paris" of Count Etienne de Beaumont.[1] Younger artists, if well chosen, could be relied upon to be sufficiently overwhelmed by the honour of working for the Ballets Russes to obey the instructions they received. This was especially important when Diaghilev was in one of his modish moods and intent on presenting what came to be known as a "cocktail ballet", in which the main point was the deliberate incongruity between the component parts of the enterprise.[2] The majority of the young artists

---

[1] Both the "Soirées de Paris" and the Ballets Suédois (under the control of Rolf de Maré) produced worthwhile results and presented for a time a real artistic and commercial threat to Diaghilev. de Beaumont and de Maré shared Diaghilev's sexual tastes: the Swedish Ballet was a vehicle for de Maré's friend the dancer and choreographer Jean Borlin, while de Beaumont, though married, was attached to Massine, his chief choreographer. Both impresarios lacked Diaghilev's flair, persistence and professionalism, and neither enterprise lasted long.

[2] A case in point is *La Chatte*. The music for this ballet was by Henri Sauguet, who in later years wrote some fine operas and at least one excellent ballet score, the Kochno-Bérard-Lichine work *La Rencontre, ou Oedipe et le Sphinx*, which will be remembered for its stunning trapeze-like décor and the electrifying dancing of Jean Babilée and Leslie Caron. The vapid and Gounodesque music Sauguet provided for *La Chatte* passed unnoticed in view of the proceedings on stage. These comprised Serge Lifar posturing in a heroic manner, a plot of stupefying absurdity, a clockwork mouse that became so unreliable that it was discarded as "inartistic", sets and costumes made of talc, and a stage littered with objects "looking as though they might conceivably separate milk from cream".

concerned in such ventures obligingly suppressed such professional consciences as they possessed and meekly complied with Diaghilev's wishes. As Lambert himself put it:

> Diaghilev was far more than a mere impresario. Though not, strictly speaking, a creative artist, he had very much more genius than many of the artists who worked for him, and it hardly seems worth while examining the work of such minor composers as Dukelsky, Sauguet, Nabokov and others, apart from their connection with Diaghilev. They were merely the gunmen executing the commands of their Capone, who, like all great gangsters, never touched firearms himself.

There was a particular reason for Diaghilev to commission a ballet from an English composer. He was short of money (a normal condition for him) and in 1925 he had still not recovered from the financial disaster of his *Sleeping Princess* of 1921. One of the greatest ballet productions of all time, it had played to half-empty houses at the Alhambra Theatre in London and had never been seen anywhere else. Diaghilev was trying to persuade Lord Rothermere to underwrite his London seasons, and it seemed tactful to include some English works in the Company's repertory. Diaghilev chose for this purpose not only the unknown Lambert but a more established composer, Lord Berners.

Gerald Hugh Tyrwhitt-Wilson, Lord Berners, was a friend of Lambert's from the 1920s to his death in 1950, a year before Lambert himself. He was a novelist and painter as well as a musician, but better known to the general public as one of the last of the English eccentrics. He is the original of the character of Lord Merlin in Nancy Mitford's novel *The Pursuit of Love*. He created a considerable stir by dyeing the pigeons at his house in Faringdon in Berkshire, and building, also at Faringdon, the last folly to be erected in England, to the designs of Lord Gerald Wellesley.[1] Berners' fondness for musical and practical jokes caused him to be dubbed "the English Satie". There was some

---

[1] Lieutenant-Colonel Lord Gerald Wellesley was born in 1885 and died in 1972. He became seventh Duke of Wellington in 1943. He was a contemporary of Berners at Eton, and, like him, served in the Diplomatic Service in Rome and Istanbul. For a time he was a professional architect. He was Surveyor of His Majesty's Works of Art from 1936 to 1944. He wrote several books about the first Duke of Wellington as well as a travel book, *Desert Journey*. His wife, Dorothy Wellesley, was a poetess.

point in the comparison: both men were shy, both had a highly developed sense of humour, both were fundamentally unhappy. But Berners could no more have conceived the controlled ferocity of *Parade* or the classical passion of *Socrate* than could Satie the "penny-plain-tuppence-coloured" Victorian cosiness of *The Triumph of Neptune*. Much of Berners' painting was done in Italy (he had houses in Rome and London as well as at Faringdon), and he exhibited in London in the 1930s. He published two volumes of autobiography, *First Childhood* and *A Distant Prospect*. The latter, as its title suggests, is about Eton. Surprisingly, perhaps, in view of Berners' shyness, he appears to have been one of the few English artists who positively enjoyed their schooldays. His literary output was completed by a series of short, witty novels, among them one with the title *The Girls of Radcliff Hall*.

He began to write music seriously when he was an attaché at the Embassy in Rome, and both Stravinsky and Alfredo Casella gave him advice and help. By 1925 he was an established composer, and thus a far more obvious choice for Diaghilev than Lambert. Berners' one-act opera *Le Carrosse du Saint-Sacrement* had been produced at the Théâtre des Champs-Elysées in Paris in 1924 (Lambert later arranged an orchestral *Caprice péruvien*, based on this work). Berners' *Fantisie espagnole*, a parody of "Spanish" mannerisms in music, had been played as an interlude at the Russian Ballet. The score he now wrote for Diaghilev, *The Triumph of Neptune*, an "English Pantomime" with a book by Sacheverell Sitwell, was produced after Lambert's – at the Lyceum Theatre in London on 3rd December 1926.[1] It was a success. With commendable tact, the composer dedicated his score to Lord Rothermere. The newspaper peer had agreed to back Diaghilev's

---

[1] It was rare for the Russian Ballet to give a work its first performance in London. The usual practice in the 1920s was to try the ballet out at the Company's base, Monte Carlo, and then show it to Paris before bringing it to lesser cultural centres, like London. Of the ballets presented by Diaghilev (some seventy in all) only seven were first danced in London. These were the full-length *Lac des Cygnes* in 1911; *La Boutique Fantasque* and *The Three-Cornered Hat* in 1919; *The Sleeping Princess* in 1921; *Barabau* in 1925; *The Triumph of Neptune*; and *Les Dieux Mendiants*, which was put together hastily to please Beecham in 1928 (he had been conducting for Diaghilev) and proved an unexpected success. *Barabau* and *Les Dieux Mendiants* (renamed *The Gods Go A-Begging*) were later taken into the Vic-Wells repertory.

gence, which fastened on to everything that was mentioned with immediate understanding and quicksilver rapidity of mind. Wood appears to have been to some extent Lambert's Steerforth – there was an element of hero-worship in the composer's attitude to the painter, and Lambert's only son was named Christopher, with the intention that he should be called Kit, as Wood had been. Wood's death, probably by suicide (he fell under a train at Salisbury on 21st August 1930) – came a matter of months before Philip Heseltine's suicide in December.[1]

Trouble on the new ballet began well before Lambert's arrival at the Diaghilev headquarters in Monte Carlo. The leading parts were to be taken by Diaghilev's brilliant young protégé Serge Lifar and the very much older Tamara Karsavina, making her return to the Ballets Russes after some time. It was during Nijinska's own absence from the Diaghilev circle that Lifar had established a dominant position in the Company and in the affections of Diaghilev. The choreographer insisted that Lifar, being so young, should audition for the part of Romeo – a suggestion that was not well received by Lifar, never the most modest of men. However, Diaghilev prevailed upon him to comply, and he did so, dazzling, he tells us, all those fortunate enough to be present. After the première it was Diaghilev's turn to become distraught: he thought that his young friend was growing too attached to Mme Karsavina.

Clouds were also looming on the artistic front. Diaghilev, with that oriental capriciousness which was one of his most marked characteristics, had decided that *Romeo* was going, after all, to be a "cocktail ballet". In the first place it would be not a direct telling of the story: rather it would be about a company rehearsing *Romeo and Juliet*. In the second place Wood's designs would not be used. Though talented, he was not as newsworthy as the two surrealists Max Ernst and Joan Miró. The commission was transferred to them.

The "scenery", such as it was, took the form of "scenic adjuncts" by Miró (such as an enormous blue disc like a gramophone record, which represented the Moon) and two drop-curtains by Ernst. Adjuncts and curtains bore little or no relation to what was happening on stage. Some composers today would no doubt be delighted to have Miró and Ernst as collaborators, but the two surrealists did not enjoy the reputation in the 1920s that they do now, and there was in any case no real collaboration whatsoever between the painters on the one hand

---

[1] Lambert himself died twenty-one years to the day after Wood.

and Lambert and Nijinska on the other. At one point Diaghilev had considered doing without décor altogether. It remained to be seen how the unknown young English composer would react to these changes when he arrived. Would he accept them without demur, as other composers had in similar circumstances?

By the time Lambert appeared on the scene, Nijinska had finished her work and gone. Lambert told the story of subsequent developments in a long letter he wrote to his mother shortly afterwards. Amy Lambert had just rejoined her husband in Australia. Her son began his letter on 24th May, when he was staying with friends at Giverny, between Paris and Rouen, and finished it the following day at the Hôtel du Panthéon in Paris. It is a precious document, since Kochno's account of the business is sketchy and misleading,[1] while the references in books by Ninette de Valois and Lydia Sokolova are incomplete (de Valois and Sokolova were members of the Company but not personally involved in the rows that preceded the première). Lambert begins:

> When I arrived at Monte-Carlo I found that the 1st performance was in 2 or 3 days time and that far from doing the ballet without a décor Diaghilev had chosen two 10th-rate painters from an imbecile group called the "surréalistes". I cannot tell you how monstrous the décor is, both in itself and as an accompaniment to my music and the choreography of Nijinska. As you know, I am not academic in my point of view about painting but never in my life have I seen anything so imbecile.
>
> Not only that, but Diaghilev has introduced disgraceful changes in the choreography, altering bits that Nijinska declared she would never be induced to change. For example, at the end of the 1st tableau, instead of the dance of 3 women which Nijinska designed, the lovers (who are supposed to be dragged apart) return and do a

---

[1] Boris Kochno, who was Diaghilev's secretary at this time, has given a quite different account of the genesis of *Romeo and Juliet*. According to him Diaghilev heard some of Lambert's early works at a concert, called, Kochno thinks, "Promenades", presenting new composers. If Kochno means Henry Wood's Promenade Concerts (and he can hardly mean anything else) it is relevant to point out that no work of Lambert's was played at these until 1929, three years after the first performance of *Romeo*. Kochno's account of subsequent developments in the creation of *Romeo* differs substantially from the one given here.

pas-de-deux, with all the rest staring at them. Can you imagine anything more stupid and vulgar? Of course I sent Nijinska a telegram immediately. I was so upset by all this that I asked for and with great difficulty obtained an interview with Diaghilev. Instead of giving it to me alone he had Kochno and Grigoriev (the stage manager) with him. To frighten me, I suppose. He started off by saying that my letter to him was so rude that he didn't wish to speak to me, but as I was young he would pardon me. After a short pause in which I did not thank him I asked why he had rejected Kit Wood's décor. He became very angry and said "I forbid you to say a word about the décor". I then tried to speak about the choreography but he said "I have known Madame Nijinska for 20 years and I forbid you to mention her name in my presence". I naturally lost my temper and said I would withdraw the music entirely. I'm afraid it was rather a dreadful scene but then it is impossible to remain calm with a man like that. The next morning I went to see a lawyer in Nice, who told me that unfortunately there was no way out of my contract. I went back to Monte-Carlo, quite calm by now, and went into the salle d'orchestre to listen to the only rehearsal for orchestra alone. To my surprise, they tried to stop me getting in, and when at last I "effected an entry" I found all the orchestra waiting but no music put out. After about half an hour a sort of military funeral came in with the score and parts, and all during the rehearsal there were 2 concierges on each side of me to see I did not tear the work to pieces. After the rehearsal the parts were collected, carefully corded and sealed and taken up into a strong room! This ridiculous business has gone on ever since, and now Diaghilev has spread the report that I went quite insane at Monte-Carlo and had to be watched by 2 detectives! The orchestra were so annoyed by all this that they made a special point of cheering me at the dress rehearsal and at the 1st performance. It went down quite well at Monte-Carlo, but everyone I met thought that the décor spoiled everything, as indeed it does. It is not only a gross mistake artistically, but a most dreadful blunder from the business point of view, as it will be detested in England, particularly as everyone knows that Kit's scenery had been accepted.

It must have taken great strength of mind for an unknown English music student to speak his mind to the dictator of the Russian Ballet in this way. Lambert, though shy, inexperienced and only twenty years old – he had obtained leave from the Royal College to go to Monte Carlo – had a mind of his own. At this distance in time all the fuss may seem slightly absurd, and Lambert himself joked about it in later years. But for a young composer being given his first big chance before an international public it was very disillusioning. There was little that Lambert could do, and the ballet received its first performance on 4th May 1926. Karsavina and Lifar led the cast, with Lydia Sokolova as the Nurse, Woizikovsky as the Nurse's servant, Peter, and Danilova, Doubrovska, Gevergeva, Savina, Markova, Slavinsky, Tcherkas, Pavloff and Hoyer in lesser parts. The conductor was a certain Marc-César Scotto. The ballet was described (despite the contributions of Ernst and Miró) as "a rehearsal, without scenery, in two parts". The synopsis was as follows:

1. The action takes place in the class-room of a ballet. Enter the premier danseur and the première danseuse, who, seeing that they are late, quickly change their clothes and get ready for the class.

    The professor teaches them a pas de deux, during which, forgetting their proper steps, they make no secret of their affection. The lovers are separated by their scandalized friends, who carry them off to the theatre where a rehearsal is due to start.

2. The stage is being prepared for a rehearsal of scenes from Romeo and Juliet.
    (a) The first meeting of Romeo and Juliet at the ball.
    (b) The nurse and the servant.
    (c) The duel between Romeo and Tybalt.
    (d) The balcony scene.
    (e) Paris enters, accompanied by musicians, and searches for Juliet, his fiancée.
    (f) The death of Juliet.
    The curtain falls and the enthusiastic audience imitates and applauds the principal actors. The curtain rises, but Romeo and Juliet are not there to take their call. The spectators rush on to the stage and vainly search for the lovers, who elope by aeroplane.

One cannot help wondering whether it was all as foolish as it sounds. Are ballet dancers so easily scandalized? If it is a rehearsal, why is there an audience? How does the audience "imitate" the principal actors? The modified dance suite *Adam and Eve*, which served as the accompaniment to this piece of ill-digested Pirandello, fell into a series of short numbers. The first tableau comprised a Rondino, Gavotte and Trio, Scherzetto, Siciliana and Sonatina; the second tableau a Sinfonia, an Alla Marcia, a Toccata, a Musette, a Burlesca, an Adagietto and a Finale.

Lambert's letter continues:

> After the Monte-Carlo performance, Kochno came to see me and asked if I had any music for an entr'acte as they thought it would be more "vivante" if there was a passage of dancers from the classroom to the theatre. I was very annoyed at their trying to spoil Nijinska's work any more, so I said I would give him music for an entr'acte but only on the understanding that not a note of it was to be danced. So they have now added a sort of comic march-past of the characters (without music) in very dubious taste and in a style which is the complete opposite of Nijinska's. It is really too sickening about the ballet – at one time it was going to be the best since *La Boutique Fantasque* or *Tricorne* but now it is just a dismal failure as far as I am concerned. What annoys me is for people to tell me that I am very lucky to have it done at all and shouldn't worry about anything else except the mere notes! When I get back to England I want it to be publicly known that I tried to withdraw the ballet on account of the décor and the changes in the choreography. I don't want people to think that I associate willingly with 10th-rate incompetent charlatans like Max Ernst and Joan Miró (the "surréalistes").

There was more trouble in Paris. The first night took place at the Théâtre Sarah-Bernhardt on 18th May. The opening ballet on the programme was the Massine-Stravinsky-Picasso *Pulcinella*, which had such enormous influence on young composers of the period, Lambert included, and the evening closed with Auric's *Les Matelots*. The conductor was the twenty-seven-year-old Roger Desormière, who had worked for the Swedish Ballet and the "Soirées de Paris" before coming to Diaghilev. In the middle came *Romeo*, with Nikitina opposite Lifar, rather than Karsavina, No sooner had the curtain risen than . . .

> about fifty men got up and blew on pea-whistles while others threw down thousands of leaflets from the roof. For three movements not

a single note could be heard. It soon developed into a free-fight, the most extraordinary scene you could imagine; eventually the police were called in and managed to throw most of the rioters out. Everybody yelled out "Recommencez" so they started again, but this time the leader of the surréalistes jumped up and started a speech from one of the boxes. The only word I could hear was "Merde" at the end. The performance didn't really quiet down until the 2nd tableau. Naturally the ballet was cheered at the end, but that was chiefly reaction. If the protest against the scenery had been because it was bad I should have heartily sympathised, but as the motive was a purely political one I was furious, particularly as the protest, being of an aural nature, merely spoilt the music and left the scenery untouched. At the second performance everything went quite calmly; the orchestra (under Desormière) were much better than at Monte-Carlo, where Marc-César Scotto, who conducts like a porpoise in a rough sea, didn't help matters much.

The riot of the first night was directed by Louis Aragon from the gallery and André Breton from the stalls. The surrealists, motivated at that time as much by political as by artistic considerations, were incensed because two of their party had gone over to the enemy and collaborated with the hated "capitalist" Diaghilev by providing what passed for scenery. There had been a similar though rather less violent scene two years before, at the first performance of the Massine-Satie-Picasso ballet *Les Aventures de Mercure* at the "Soirées de Paris". There is no reason to think that Diaghilev was in any way upset: "All Paris will flock to see the ballet which caused a riot" wrote the *Sunday Referee,* and so they did – and a product like *Romeo* was so far removed from Diaghilev's private aesthetic taste (which ran to *Tristan* and the *Pathetic Symphony*) that it is highly improbable that he thought anything remotely worth while had been spoiled. And indeed, while one can understand Lambert's original enthusiasm for the project, it is hard to agree that *Romeo* could ever have been "the best since *La Boutique Fantasque* or *Tricorne*": *Les Biches* and *Les Noces* had come between. But with sets by Wood, intact choreography by Nijinska, and a straightforward retelling of the story, it might have been a very respectable work, and an interesting one.

There was no riot when the ballet reached His Majesty's Theatre in London on 21st June, with Eugene Goossens in the pit and Karsavina, the darling of the London public, as Juliet once again. The ballet got a good reception, but the regularity with which the English newspapers commented on the disparity between music and décor suggests that Lambert had carried out his intention and made his disapproval public. *The Times* liked the score but wished that Diaghilev had seen fit to entrust the scenery to an English artist. *The Sphere* regretted the fact that the Russian Ballet seemed to have abandoned the idea of ballet as a collaborative effort and went on:

> In the present case he [Diaghilev] has, I understand, taken the music written by Mr Lambert in order to express something entirely foreign from the *Romeo and Juliet* ballet, and used it as an accompaniment to scenes and emotions that have probably surprised nobody more than the young composer himself.

The *Daily Telegraph* voiced the same thought:

> As one listened to the young Englishman's music one felt that it bore but the remotest, if any, sort of relationship to the décor. Indeed, one would not be surprised to learn that to Mr Lambert the whole setting was antipathetic, that as a youngster he had done his bit, so to speak, in an operation over which he had no control.

The *Yorkshire Post* told its readers that Lambert's

> modesty is such that he was unable to obtain a seat at the theatre for the first night of his own ballet, and it was from "Standing Room Only" that he came after repeated calls for the composer to take his share of the applause.

As he did so, he "blushed like a schoolboy", according to the *Daily Express*. It must have been an uneasy moment.

Despite Lambert's later scornful words about some of the composers who worked for Diaghilev, his own Diaghilev ballet is a minor piece. He was only twenty when he wrote it, and he was acutely aware of all that was going on around him. It is reasonable to suppose that up to the time of his actual dealings with Diaghilev the young musician was as mesmerised as were most of the intelligent young by the glamour of the Ballets Russes, and *Romeo* displays the neoclassicism fashionable in ballet scores of the time. In later years, ironically, Lambert wrote in harsh terms of "the movement sometimes dignified by the name of neo-classicism" and mocked the fondness for pastiche which could lead to a score being praised because in it "se retrouvent les grâces étincellantes de Scarlatti". There is plenty of Scarlatti in *Romeo*. Lambert attacked Georges Auric for writing strings of boy scout tunes with an acid harmonic accompaniment, and here he was on even more dangerous ground, as David Drew, no lover of Lambert's critical writing, has been quick to point out. For example, on pages 31–2 of the published piano score of *Romeo* there occurs a fanfare-like theme in C major, strongly suggestive of the Boys' Brigade, which is saddled with an accompanying figure in G flat major. This extremely and mechanically dissonant passage occurs twice, framing a contrasting section harmonised with blameless conventionality and providing a perfect example of the kind of music Lambert himself derided for "oscillating disturbingly between the pretty-pretty and the ugly-ugly". As a very young man Lambert was affected as much as most of his contemporaries by what he called "the exigencies of vogue". In this connection Angus Morrison has written:

> *Romeo and Juliet* was almost entirely influenced by what was then fashionable in Paris, all derived from the works written by Stravinsky in the ten years immediately following *Le Sacre du Printemps*, and most particularly by the first of his consciously conceived musical pastiches, the ballet *Pulcinella*, based on the music of Pergolesi and produced by Diaghilev for the first time in 1920. Perhaps it was just because Constant at first was so exclusively influenced by that mode of composition, or rather copied its mannerisms so closely and skilfully in his first published work, that later when he wrote his book he discredited so unmercifully the whole of that post-1918 period. I cannot help feeling, in spite of the immense brilliance of the writing and the logic of his arguments, that the whole section called "Post-War Pasticheurs" in *Music Ho!* has too much of the exaggerated indignation of the reformed sinner castigating his own erstwhile lapses, and that in repudiating the early influence of Stravinsky with so many ardent protestations he did not draw on his own mature judgment but merely succumbed with equal blindness of personal vision to the influence and opinions of his admired and close friend Cecil Gray.

There are however traces of the mature Lambert in *Romeo*, in the Rondino, the Sinfonia and the Finale. This last movement, though Scarlattian, contains melodic and harmonic turns of phrase that are prophetic of *Pomona* and *Horoscope*, and it is full of a triumphant youthful gaiety which is most appealing. The pas de deux for the lovers is a Siciliana, a dance which Lambert loved and which appeared in his last ballet, *Tiresias*, as well as his first. But as a whole *Romeo* is little more interesting in itself than a number of other scores written for the Diaghilev Ballet in its silver age and now almost completely forgotten. For a balanced view of the music as it struck a professional musician at the time one cannot do better than turn to André Messager, the distinguished composer and conductor:

> La musique de M. Lambert ne pèche pas par l'absence de clarté, loin de là. Elle est remplie de promesses qui se réaliseront sans doute, le jour où ce tres jeune compositeur aura conquis une personnalité et échappé à l'influence par trop directe de quelques-uns des compositeurs de notre jeune école. Il y a déjà beaucoup de dextérité dans la manière de traiter l'orchestre; il doit, maintenant, s'efforcer de mettre ses idées a l'hauteur de son habileté.

The *Romeo* affair laid the foundation for Lambert's animosity towards Diaghilev and much that he stood for – an animosity that found powerful expression eight years later in the pages of the book *Music Ho!* But it was only certain aspects of Diaghilev's complex character – notably his reckless pursuit of chic at this later stage of his career – that aroused Lambert's dislike. For Lambert, as for many of his contemporaries, the Diaghilev Ballet at its best was something to be admired and emulated. In his preface to the 1948 edition of his book Lambert wrote:

> My criticisms of Diaghilev were aimed at his later artistic policy and were in no way an attack on his genius as a producer, least of all were they meant to foreshadow the present school of ballet critics who, alas, are unacquainted with his living work.

Lambert adhered all his life to the concept of ballet at its best as a union of three arts, a concept he learned from Diaghilev. It was an idea Lambert found peculiarly sympathetic, loving good choreography and design almost as much as he did good music. It pervaded his own later ballets; it was behind all his thinking as the Musical and later an Artistic Director of Sadler's Wells; and it is diametrically opposed to the Maryinsky aesthetic, which is enjoying a new lease of life today, and in which the balletic equivalent of "canary-fancying" reigns supreme. In one specific respect Lambert resembled Diaghilev himself: in the days of the Vic-Wells Ballet he did all he could to develop the minds and personalities of promising dancers. When the young Robert Helpmann arrived from Australia in 1933, Lambert helped him by suggesting books he should read, pictures he should see and music he should listen to, and later discussed with him what he had read, seen and heard. Margot Fonteyn also benefited from Lambert's guidance in this way. He played a most important part in the mental development of both, with results that may still be seen and enjoyed today. In this sense what Diaghilev was to Massine, Lambert was to Fonteyn. It is good, therefore, to be able to point to some sort of rapprochement between Lambert and Diaghilev later on. In 1929 the composer conducted one of his works as an interlude during the Russian Ballet's last London season. But he never conducted ballet for the Russian impresario or wrote another work for him.

1926 was a vital year for Lambert: from then onwards he was known to the general public as the young man from whom Diaghilev had commissioned a ballet, and his name was already associated with the world in which he was to live most of the rest of his life.

IV

THE LATE 1920s AND *THE RIO GRANDE*

In April 1926 Amy Lambert rejoined her husband in Australia, where she remained for three years. On Constant's return to London from France he and his elder brother stayed on for a few weeks in Glebe Place, but on 27th July Maurice married Olga, Angus Morrison's sister, and the Chelsea house was given up. Maurice, an accomplished and successful sculptor in later life, was very different from his brother and conscious of his seniority. He had inherited all his father's pugnacity, and his well-meaning but hardly tactful attempts to restore order in Constant's life (an almost impossible task) led to family quarrels. The "official' wing of the Lambert family, represented by Amy and Maurice, disapproved deeply of Constant's way of life, both his wives and many of his friends, and feared, quite justifiably, for his health. But they were unable to exert much lasting influence on him.

On his brother's marriage Lambert went to stay in the house of a Mrs Travers Smith, who lived nearby in Chelsea. She had a consuming interest in the occult: just as in our own day Debussy, it is said, appears from time to time in Balham to dictate a piano piece to Mrs Rosemary Brown, Oscar Wilde materialised in Chelsea to communicate an entire play to Mrs Travers Smith. This novelty from beyond the grave reached the stage, but the general verdict was that Wilde had been below his best on this occasion, or else there had been communication problems; at all events the play has never been revived. Mrs Travers Smith was also a friend of the poet Yeats. A fellow-resident with Lambert in her house was Thomas McGreevy (1894–1967), a poet and acquaintance of Yeats who became Director of the National Gallery of Ireland from 1950 to 1963. Lambert found that he was expected to spend hours at the ouija board, where his sense of humour was apt to undermine the solemnity of the proceedings. Lambert found the atmosphere of the house unsympathetic and soon moved. Probably he had always intended to live on his own after his mother had gone, but refrained from saying so to avoid an argument. In the autumn of 1926 he took two rooms at 59 Oakley Street, Chelsea, almost next door to the once-celebrated Pier Hotel, now demolished but in its day a haunt of the bohemian, the raffish and the queer. Lambert stayed in Chelsea for about another year before moving to Bloomsbury.

Throughout the 1920s he was short of money. He had no regular income at all until he became conductor of the Vic-Wells Ballet and music critic of the *Sunday Referee* in 1931. He made some sort of living by playing the piano for dancing classes (an experience which left him with a lifelong loathing for Schubert piano pieces), by occasional conducting engagements, rare at first but steadily growing more frequent, and journalism. This was not necessarily musical in nature – he wrote a good deal of film criticism – but he soon began to contribute articles on music to various magazines and newspapers. As early as October 1926 the magazine *Apollo* published an article on Chabrier, who was misunderstood and underestimated in Britain at that time: Lambert was beginning his battle on behalf of composers he thought undeservedly neglected – a battle that continued in the columns of journals and newspapers as well as in the concert hall, until his death.

Despite Lambert's obvious promise, no more commissions for musical works came his way. Clearly there was nothing to be expected from Diaghilev. George Lambert's doubts about the wisdom of his son's choice of an artistic career must often have seemed abundantly justified. Lambert badly wanted to conduct. "I wish I could do some more conducting", he wrote to his mother; "if only I had someone to back me I could give such interesting concerts". Few opportunities occurred until 1928, when the BBC gave him some work. That year too (10th July) he conducted a small ballet arranged to music by Gluck and called *Leda and the Swan* which received a single performance at the Apollo Theatre. The choreographer, Frederick Ashton, was about to go to France to join Ida Rubinstein's Company. This was the first time Lambert collaborated with his future partner in the Sadler's Wells Ballet.

Despite his financial problems Lambert was not unhappy: he had many friends and he led a busy social life. There were many parties to attend, and he had begun to frequent the Café Royal, the Fitzroy Tavern in Soho and – when he had some money in his pocket – the Eiffel Tower Restaurant in Percy Street. At the first of these he found one of the few examples in London of the kind of café society that was commonplace in France, and he used it throughout his life. The Fitzroy, in the 1920s and the 1930s, was a bohemian meeting-place popular with such figures as Augustus John, Wyndham Lewis and Nancy

Cunard (later it became a homosexual bar and a resort of prostitutes before sinking into total anonymity). Osbert Sitwell has written of the Eiffel Tower, with its rows of Tokay bottles and its eccentric proprietor, Stulik. Lambert loved such places: he was completely urban in disposition, and could, as the mood took him, dominate a group by his wit and turn of phrase or cut himself off completely and achieve among a press of people a more complete solitude than would have been possible for him at home.

Over the next few years Lambert wrote more music than he ever did in later life. Apart from *Romeo*, two works of his were performed in 1926. The first of these, a pastoral movement called *Champêtre*, was given at the Aeolian Hall on 27th October under Guy Warrack. The second was a *Divertimento* in seven movements (of which *Champêtre* became the first) which Anthony Bernard and his London Chamber Orchestra played at the Chelsea Music Club on 16th November. This was the one and only performance of the *Divertimento* in this form. It had been written in Chelsea and at Renishaw during 1926. After the November performance Thomas McGreevy drew the composer's attention to the old legend of Pomona and Vertumnus, and suggested that it might make a good theme for a ballet. Lambert agreed, and the Divertimento, with the addition of a Passacaglia from *Adam and Eve*, became the ballet *Pomona*. The synopsis printed (in French and English) in the published score reads:

Intrata. At the rise of the curtain Pomona, goddess of fruits, and her nymphs are discovered in an orchard in a wood near Rome, the nymphs in little groups, Pomona apart.

No 1. **Corante.** The sound of hunting horns is heard. The god Vertumnus and his train of immortals, all wearing hunting attire, enter. Vertumnus makes attempts to gain favour with Pomona but she repulses him and then, frightened by the bolder advances of Vertumnus and the immortals she and her nymphs fly into the wood. Vertumnus watches her departure; then, disgusted with the failure of his disguise expresses his chagrin in a dance. But it is with new decision that he leads his train away.

No 2. **Pastorale.** Pomona comes back timidly and expresses her sense of isolation in a dance. She goes.

No 3. **Menuetto.** The nymphs re-enter timidly but are disappointed to find the hunters gone and dance with melancholy.

They are interrupted by the return of the immortals who, having discarded their hunting attire, make a gentler entry this time. Pomona comes back quietly, and unnoticed, looks on while the immortals succeed little by little in gaining favour with the nymphs and leading them away, one by one. At the end she is again alone.
No 4. **Passacaglia.** Vertumnus returns disguised as a lady of uncertain age. He endeavours to comfort Pomona. He succeeds. They go.

(It should be pointed out that there is rather an amusing mistranslation here: the French text for this number reads: "Rentrée de Vertumne, déguisé en femme d'un certain âge".)

No 5. **Rigadoon.** Divertissement danced by the nymphs and immortals.
No 6. **Siciliana.** Vertumnus having put aside his disguise comes back to the orchard with Pomona. They dance a pas de deux expressive of their love for each other.
No 7. **Marcia.** Joyous return of nymphs and immortals. Nuptial dance. Procession. Solemn entry of Flamen Pomonalis, who gives the nuptial benediction and receives as a precious relic the woman's costume worn by Vertumnus. Curtain.

Pomona marks a distinct advance over *Romeo*. Like that work, it shows many affinities with the French school of the 1920s, in its neo-classicism, clean, economical scoring, occasional harmonic astringency and general aesthetic, but the music is far more lyrical and of a more personal cast. Angus Morrison writes:

In *Pomona* Constant shows for the first time what Ernest Newman so aptly described as "musical fingerprints", and nowhere can this be more clearly seen than by comparing the two Sicilianas. Constant was always very fond of the Siciliana. One of his favourite pieces of music was the slow movement of the Mozart A major *Piano Concerto*, K. 488, and especially the almost Puccini-like melody with which the orchestra enters at the end of the long opening phrase for the solo instrument. The strange sadness of the characteristic 6/8 rhythm, as well as the poetic associations and overtones of the name itself, had always a particular fascination for him, and in both ballets he used this form for the emotional core of the whole work (equivalent in a ballet to the love duet in an opera): the central *pas de deux* for the two leading dancers.

The one in *Romeo* has quite a charming, slightly acid flavour, but it seems composed in unrelated snippets and the harmony, apart from one or two attractive touches, is static and lacking in a sense of progression, especially in the Coda, which peters out in a most unconvincing and pointless manner. The Siciliana in *Pomona*, on the other hand, is a real gem, with a haunting melancholy in performance far greater than the extreme simplicity of its appearance on paper would lead one to expect. The lyrical interest grows and evolves out of itself from the first bar to the last, and the Coda is a real emotional climax in which all the different musical strands are gathered up and finally resolved. One hears for the first time certain melodic shapes which were to appear in various forms and disguises all through the rest of his music, and nothing is more utterly personal to his style than the phrase of three notes descending from the seventh that comes twice right at the end of the piece. The proportions are quite flawless, while the obvious debt to Scarlatti is perfectly assimilated and no more incongruous in its surroundings than the ruins of an antique temple in the landscape of a romantic painter. Constant himself had always a very special affection for this piece, and when I was asked to play pieces by Lambert and Walton at a musical party he made an exquisite little transcription of it for two hands as a companion piece to the Waltz from *Façade*, arranged by Walton also for the same occasion.

Lambert made a private recording of the Siciliana from *Pomona* and his *Elegiac Blues* on a 78rpm disc. His performances are marked by *rubati* so exaggerated that one might be inclined to criticise them if the composer were not at the piano. They leave Lambert's innate romanticism in no doubt. Talking of Debussy and Mozart in *Music Ho!*, Lambert wrote:

> Through his capacity for investing an apparently insignificant and light-hearted tune with an almost tragic significance, Debussy stands very close to Mozart. We find the same quality in, for example, the Siciliana that forms the Finale of the D minor quartet – a simple dance tune into which and its variations Mozart seems to have compressed the emotional experience of a lifetime.

Nijinska was still at the Colón Theatre, and Lambert's talent and his personal loyalty to her during the *Romeo* affair had made an impression on her; it was at the Colón that *Pomona* was first performed as a ballet, on 9th September, 1927, with Nijinska's choreography.[1] The other artists concerned – the designer, Rodolfo Franco, the conductor, Aquiles Lieti, and the principals, Leticia de la Vega and Eugene Lapitsky – are mere names today. Though the BBC broadcast the music in June 1929 and Anthony Bernard gave a concert performance in February 1930, it was not staged in Britain until late in 1930.

The lyricism of parts of *Pomona* finds moving expression in Lambert's *Eight Poems of Li Po*, the greater part of which was written also in 1926. They are settings of the eighth-century Chinese poet in a translation by Shigeyoshi-Obata published by E. P. Dutton and Co. of New York. Originally written for voice and piano, they were scored in 1929 for a small chamber ensemble. They are among Lambert's finest shorter pieces. Like the words, the music has a cool fragrance and delicate melancholy; at one point the songs celebrate the pleasures of drinking, at another they lament a lost lover. Perhaps the most beautiful of all is the shortest (occupying only one page in the piano score), *On the City Street*:

> They meet in the pink dust of the city street.
> He raises his gold crop high in salute.
> "Lady," says he, "where do you live?
> There are ten thousand houses among the drooping willow trees."[2]

The tender epilogue is utterly personal to Lambert. The predominant mood of the whole cycle, as with much of the composer's best writing, is elegiac and nostalgic. He dedicated the songs to Anna May Wong, the film actress. Though he had not yet met her, he became infatuated with her beauty and drank quantities of Chinese wine in her honour; a tribute indeed, as the result was severe constipation. A fictional character partly suggested by Lambert (Moreland, in Anthony Powell's novel *A Dance to the Music of Time*) says of himself that he suffers from a "princess lointaine" complex; but when the princess ceased to be distant the results could be disillusioning. In March 1929 Anna May Wong came to London to take the lead in *The Circle of Chalk* at the New Theatre. Lambert attended the first night and met his idol, but Miss Wong made it painfully clear that enthusiasm, good

---

[1] Pomona is often described as a Diaghilev ballet. This is not so.

[2] From the book *The Works of Li Po*: The Chinese Poet done into English verse by Shigeyoshi-Obata. Copyright, 1922, 1950 by E. P. Dutton and Co. Inc., publishers, and used with their permission.

looks and talent were not enough in an escort: money was necessary as well. Lambert was always susceptible to the glamour of the stage: during the 1920s he also conceived a passion for Angela Baddeley, who was the dedicatee of *Pomona*, and in later years he had a long affair with a leading ballet dancer.

Music for Orchestra, which Lambert composed in 1927, is one of his few pieces of "abstract" music. It is a symphonic movement in two parts: a short, slow introduction based on two main themes, the first heard on muted violins, the second on horns, and an *Allegro risoluto* ushered in by a sudden crescendo chord on the brass and introducing new themes which are combined at the end with those of the introduction. It had to wait two years for its first performance, but thereafter enjoyed a certain success for a time. Lambert himself was fond of it, and it is a solidly written work showing its composer's grasp of contrapuntal techniques, but it cannot be called one of his most interesting or attractive pieces. With one conspicuous exception, the *Piano Concerto*, he was never at his best without a literary text or a stage spectacle as stimulus to his imagination.

The other pieces Lambert wrote in 1927 were connected with his enthusiasm for jazz. In September 1926 the "Blackbirds" returned for a season at the London Pavilion. Florence Mills was again the star, but Will Vodery's "Plantation Orchestra" had been replaced by the Pike Davies Orchestra, composed entirely of American negroes. This time the coloured artists were rapturously received: they were not only very popular with the general public but immensely fashionable among the artistic intelligentsia, and there was a rash of "Blackbird parties" in Chelsea and Bloomsbury. Lambert went to see the show on several occasions, and he was at the last night, on 14th May 1927. When Florence Mills died prematurely young he wrote in her memory an *Elegiac Blues*.[1] The piece exists in two versions, one for solo piano and the other for a small orchestra. It ends with a reminiscence of the "Plantation" fanfare which had so impressed and moved Lambert in 1923.

The other jazz-inspired work dating from 1927 became the most famous composition Lambert ever wrote. This was *The Rio Grande*. In later years the success of this work often irritated its creator, who was accustomed to refer to it as a millstone round his neck. He believed that certain of his other works – the *Piano Concerto* and *Summer's Last Will*

---

[1] November 1927.

71

and Testament, for instance – were superior to it. *The Rio Grande* was for Lambert what *Bolero* was to Ravel and the C sharp minor *Prelude* to Rachmaninov, but while the Ravel and Rachmaninov works rank fairly low in their creators' output, *The Rio Grande* is one of Lambert's most perfect and finished works and possibly his best. It is easy to understand the composer's desire not to be pigeon-holed as a composer of "jazzy" music, but one does not have to know *The Rio Grande* very well to realise that it contains as much nostalgia as it does exuberance and a brash jazziness is very far from being the dominant mood.

A setting, for solo piano, chorus and an orchestra without wood-wind, of a poem by Sacheverell Sitwell first published in a collection called "The Thirteenth Caesar and Other Poems" (1924), it evokes a South American seaport on carnival day. There is nothing in the text to require the introduction of North American jazz or negroid elements into a musical setting. The text was a convenient "peg" on which Lambert could hang his musical ideas. The words are used for their evocative character rather than their precise meaning (not in any case a quality for which Sacheverell Sitwell's verse, with all its charm, is re-markable). Lambert implied as much in a letter he wrote to Alastair Royalton-Kisch, then with the British Council in Athens, on 3rd December 1945:

> I am so glad to hear that you are conducting so much, and that you are doing an interesting concert in Athens. What language are they going to sing *The Rio Grande* in? There is actually, although not printed, a French translation by myself, which makes considerably more sense than the original English, if I may say so. I will ask the Oxford University Press to send it out but perhaps by now, owing to the influence of the late lamented Conservative Government, the Greeks can sing in English."

When *The Rio Grande* became a ballet Lambert devised a scenario about the amorous adventures of a Creole girl. This bore no relation to the words of the poem, and Lambert stated in a programme note that "the theme is suggested by the music".

The work opens with an insistent rhythm on strings and percussion which leads to the entry of the chorus on the words "On the Rio Grande they dance no sarabande". After a climax the opening phrases return and there is a piano cadenza of great brilliance, with interjec-tions by side drum, tambourine, castanets, Chinese Block, tom-tom, cow-bell, triangle, tenor drum, bass drum and cymbals. A quiet section in habanera rhythm follows, beginning with the words "The noisy streets are empty and hushed is the town". This is succeeded by a scherzando passage led by the piano and a further climax. After a second piano cadenza, shorter than the first, a solo alto voice rises out of the chorus and brings the piece to a quiet end, with the piano gently and nostalgically recalling the opening theme.

The Rio Grande is an extremely original piece, quite unlike anything by other composers. It is also one of the very few successful attempts to use the language of jazz in concert music (others that spring to mind are the ballet *La Création du Monde* by Lambert's friend Darius Milhaud and *Die Sieben Todsünden* of Weill, a work much admired by Lambert). This is not to deny that the work shows influences, and not only the obvious ones like jazz, Spanish military marches and tangos, Stravinsky in the rhythms and Delius in the harmonies. Liszt, too, is an influence. The "free fantasia" form of this dance rhapsody is itself Lisztian; and on three occasions Lambert refers to a particular passage in Liszt – bars 188 and 189 of the "Gretchen" movement in the *Faust Symphony*. Lambert was obsessed with these bars from Liszt's masterpiece, but his allusions to them in his own work are so skilfully integrated into the surrounding texture that one would be hard put to it to recognise them without forewarning.[1] The first reference to the Liszt passage is at the words "By the river music gurgling thin", the second towards the end of the long piano cadenza, and the third (the closest to Liszt's original) at the marking *Molto espressivo e rubato*, where Liszt's idea is metamorphosed into a haunting habanera: this is the passage leading from the final climax, the loudest of all, and linking it to the closing section of the work. "Would it be too fanciful", writes Angus Morrison, the work's dedicatee,

> to suggest that some part of the intense inner compulsion Constant felt about this special passage derived from its original identification with the character of Gretchen? By incorporating it into his own music did it thereby become the symbol of a central female figure, as necessary to him as Gretchen was for Faust: some coloured Marguerite, glimpsed every now and again amidst the thronging crowds and revealing herself finally in the single alto voice that rises out of the chorus to sing so movingly the closing words of the

---

[1] The author's source for this information is Mr Angus Morrison.

poem. It is here, surely, that he gives expression more completely than anywhere else in his music to the passionate longing he always felt for exotic beauty, and his perpetual sense of the beckoning wonder of distant and unattainable horizons.

In an interview reported in *Everyman* on 16th October 1930 Lambert told Derek Patmore:

> I want to do *The Rio Grande* with a negro choir. I have always had negro voices in mind for this piece, as the idea for the music came from seeing Florence Mills in *Dover Street to Dixie* and from some of the music in "Blackbirds".

Details, too, recall "The Plantation": there is the "wa-wa" of Jonny Dunn's trumpet at the words "and fright the nightingales" and the negro show's opening fanfare at the very first entry of the chorus. Christopher Palmer has pointed out the recurrence of upward-thrusting pentatonic triplet figures not only in the "Plantation" fanfare (reconstructed from memory by Angus Morrison) and in *The Rio Grande* but also in the music of Duke Ellington and a great many works by Delius. He has also drawn an interesting parallel between the final passage of *The Rio Grande* and the great choral entry towards the end of Delius' *Appalachia*, both works concerned with the American negro. He points out that both Delius and Lambert use a solo voice rising from within the chorus to carry the burden of a passage of highly charged emotion.

There is a sense in which *The Rio Grande* may be regarded as almost an autobiographical piece, and in this autobiography the piano is the central character. In Morrison's words:

> It was always Constant's idea that the piano should be like the "I" of a novel, a central narrator interpreting and reflecting upon the varied episodes that occur in the course of the work and binding them all together into one single subjective experience. This is the main artistic reason for the long cadenza accompanied by percussion, which is such an important and almost unique feature of the work. Unlike all other extended cadenzas, which come near the end of a movement as a penultimate climax, this one occurs much earlier and introduces one theme of paramount importance in the pattern of the work. Ravel, in his *Introduction and Allegro*, places a cadenza echoing passages from the *Introduction* just before the return of the *Allegro*, with the most magical effect, but Constant

introduces his much sooner, at a point corresponding roughly to the end of the exposition. Formal symmetry and conventional procedure have been sacrificed in order to produce a particular dramatic and psychological effect, and the experiment, like everything else in the work, comes off with unqualified success.

The cadenza accomplishes two extremely important things. Firstly it establishes the solo piano in its dominating place right in the centre of the picture, and secondly it bridges the wide gap between the highly contrasting moods of the two main sections of the work, linking the strident brilliance of the climax "Tireless while all others tire" with the muted intimacy of "The noisy streets are empty and hushed is the town". In poetry transitions are quickly made. On the printed page those two lines, following each other with no more than a blank space in between, carry the reader from one contrasting image to the other with all the ease and swiftness of thought. In music, on the other hand, it is an entirely different matter. Musical ideas take far more time to establish and develop themselves and most real contrasts of mood require considerable change of dynamic intensity as well.

It seems to me that nowhere does Constant show more clearly the sustained state of inspiration in which he composed *The Rio Grande* than in the way he solved this particular problem, making the cadenza not only a brilliant showpiece of dazzling virtuosity and bravura (which always seems to issue from the preceding trombone *glissandi* with the force of a rocket projected into space) but also a sort of journey in which the player as narrator seems to take the listener by the hand and guide him through the streets and squares of this imagined city.

Edwin Evans said of the work that "if it were French one would call it a blend of the nostalgia of Baudelaire with the festive glamour of Debussy's *Fêtes*". It is a composition in which Lambert never puts a foot wrong; one of today's most brilliant musicians, Richard Rodney Bennett, has said in conversation that he regards it as a masterpiece without a single superfluous note.

Between the composition of *The Rio Grande* and its first performances Lambert left Chelsea and went to live in Bloomsbury, at the Varda Bookshop, 189 High Holborn. Presiding over this establishment was Dorothy Varda, a striking blonde. She was usually known as "the Beautiful Varda", having been billed as such in earlier days, when she was one of C. B. Cochran's "Young Ladies". The ground floor comprised the bookshop itself, and beyond it a lavatory, where those who used it were greeted by the neat if repulsive legend:

Ici s'écroulent en ruines
Les triomphes de la cuisine.

To the rear of the building was a dark and noisome yard where various women of the area were in the habit of relieving themselves after the public houses had shut their doors. On the first floor Varda herself lived; on the second Lambert; on the third the writer Peter Quennell. The raffishly bohemian atmosphere of the Varda establishment, more literary than musical, suited Lambert well enough: he was always as much at home with writers, painters and mere *flâneurs* as he was with other musicians. In his rooms he installed an upright piano, on top of which there stood earthenware jars containing the Chinese wine which Lambert, joined sometimes by a rather doubtful Quennell, continued to drink in honour of Miss Wong. New acquaintances included Boris de Chroustchoff, who owned an antiquarian bookshop near the British Museum, and E. Powys Mathers, an admirer of the Beautiful Varda and the translator of Mardrus' French version of *The Arabian Nights* into English.

Lambert was anxious to arrange a performance of *The Rio Grande*, but there were problems. It was not the kind of piece English choral societies of the period were accustomed to singing, and for this reason Lambert approached the BBC to see if they would give the work a hearing. Later, when *The Rio Grande* became a very popular item in concert programmes, it was sung by many choirs who found it hard to capture the right style. In particular, the closing passage was usually marred by the presence of a contralto, resplendent in evening gown and all too obtrusive, on the platform beside the conductor. It would be fascinating to hear the work sung by negroes, as Lambert wished, or failing that by one of today's small crack groups of professional singers; large amateur choirs have neither the precision nor the sound quality that the piece demands if it is to make its full effect. There was also the question of the soloist. One evening in the winter of 1927–8 Lambert dined with Harold Rutland and then went back to Rutland's flat in Cheyne Walk, Chelsea, where he played the new work to his host. Rutland asked if he had anyone in mind as the pianist, and to his surprise Lambert mentioned Edyth Baker, then delighting audiences, with her white piano, at the London Pavilion. However, the first professional performance of *The Rio Grande* took place at the BBC's Savoy Hill studios on 27th February 1928, with the composer conducting and Angus Morrison at the piano. There had already been a private "chamber" performance at Hubert Foss's house, where all the singers had been boys. Given the somewhat erotic flavour of the music, the sensuality of the words and the timbre of boys' voices, the effect must have been curiously Firbankian. The BBC repeated the work on 23rd July in a programme of jazz-inspired music quaintly entitled "Blue on the Boulevard" The note in the *Radio Times* referred to the gaiety of a simple people, the homesickness of the captive slave and the barbarous rhythms of jungle civilizations (the rest of the programme was composed of music by such artists as Auric and Satie). It went on to remark that "the price of the white man's domination of the Blackamoor is the tribute which is being paid to Negro influences by Western poets and musicians".

Ten days earlier Lambert heard Puccini's *Turandot* at Covent Garden. It became almost his favourite opera, and one of the few he ever conducted in the theatre. In September he was in Siena, where the Festival of the International Society for Contemporary Music was in progress. Walton and the Sitwells also attended, and at the Teatro dei Rozzi there was a morning performance of *Façade* with the composer conducting. Lambert recited the words through a handsome new curtain designed for the occasion by Gino Severini. All went well until the Tarantella, when the Italian audience, thinking the piece was a calculated insult to their national dance, grew restive and had to be soothed. Sir Osbert Sitwell wrote many years later about a special performance of the Palio, the Sienese horse-race, arranged in honour of the Festival:

> I recall that just before the Palio was due to start, William and Constant, plainly after a very good luncheon, walked with dignity, though with a slight but telling lurch, across the Piazza del Campo, the centre of which had now been cleared for the imminent horse-race, and that their stately intrepidity won them a resounding cheer from the great crowds.

Life was not always as amusing as this for Lambert. His *Piano Sonata* (1928–9) is a dark, rather savage work, a new departure for him. He wrote it in London and Toulon. Lambert was very fond of Toulon and Marseilles, having probably first visited them when he was in the south of France for the production of his first ballet. A book, or at least a substantial essay, could be written about the attraction of seaports – particularly Mediterranean seaports – for the artists of the 1920s. Lambert himself provided a perceptive analysis of this fascination in the section of *Music Ho!* dealing with the exotic in relation to "low life". The fascination was not the same for everyone. For homosexual drug-addicts like Jean Cocteau and Christian Bérard it was largely a matter of the ready availability of opium and sailors. For others, like Lambert, there was the heat, the proximity of the sea, and above all the picturesqueness and variety of these ports, where one could watch almost any aspect of the human comedy being acted out with a complete lack of inhibition.

Naturally the artists who thronged to these towns expressed their affection for them in their work. There are many instances. Relevant ones, apart from Lambert's own *Sonata* and the later *Concerto*, are the paintings of Edward Burra and the little opera by Cocteau and Darius Milhaud, *Le Pauvre Matelot*, whose wheezy javas recall the sound of the mechanical pianos which so delighted Lambert in waterfront bars. Burra was an excellent choice as designer when *The Rio Grande* became a ballet, and it was intelligent of someone in the Sadler's Wells Ballet (probably Lambert) to think of him at the planning stage of Helpmann's *Miracle in the Gorbals*.

The antics of some of the other visitors amused Lambert a good deal, as may be seen from a letter he wrote to Anthony Powell (whose own novel *What's become of Waring?* is largely set in the south of France) on 1st May 1930, while at Marseilles between conducting engagements at two spas of unimpeachable respectability, Bath and Bad Homburg:

> Au rendezvous des Nauséabondes
> Rue Crapoule
> Vieux Port
> Marseille

My dear Tony,

As I write I am surrounded by so many negros and dwarfs that I can hardly believe I am not in the heart of Old Bloomsbury. In fact the only real difference between Marseille night life and a Gt. Ormond St. party is one of expense. One feels that at any moment the homely figure of Dick Wyndham may emerge from a bordel or that Wadsworth will be seen trying to retrieve his hat from some old hag or other. All the female whores look like Greta and all the male ones like Brian Howard. There is an exact replica of * * * * who dances a solo charleston outside one of the homosexual bars – a cosy place whose principal attraction is a monkey that picks pockets and a boy with only one leg and one arm.

I expect that you are by now dressing for David Tennant's Mozart-cum-bottle party. I meant to suggest that you should go as a character from the Magic Flute – there is a dragon in the 1st Act and 2 men in armour later on. 3 people between them could more or less finish off the Watteau atmosphere. I suppose Harry Walker will go as Leporello and Stephen as the Queen of the Night. You will excuse the shaky handwriting I'm sure – it's all I can do to hold a pen these days. My obsessions are becoming more pronounced I'm afraid but not quite so narrow. I feel rather like Walt Whitman – all races, all colours, all creeds, all sexes etc.

I find smoking Maryland has had an aggravating effect on my vomiting – fortunately nobody minds a bit of retching here.

I leave for Toulon tomorrow where I may see Willie.

Yours 666 puzzle – find the goat!

Some explanation is needed: the Vieux Port of Marseilles, destroyed during the Second World War, was famous for its picturesque squalor, but the address is, of course, a joke. Dick Wyndham was a wealthy amateur artist, in later years often Lambert's host, who was killed in Palestine after the War. Wadsworth is Edward Wadsworth, the painter. Fancy dress parties were very popular in London at this time. "Willie" is Walton; and the signature is an allusion to Aleister Crowley's habit of referring to himself as "The Beast 666". The passing reference to Brian Howard is interesting as an instance of the impact that strange and rather sad creature made even on contemporaries as unsympathetic to him as Lambert. Recently the subject of a heavy book, his principal interest is that to some extent he suggested the characters of Anthony Blanche and Ambrose Silk to Evelyn Waugh.

The *Sonata* which Lambert wrote amid such surroundings is very urban music, tense and jagged. If *The Rio Grande* has the gaiety of jazz, the Sonata has its melancholy and outbursts of violence. It is in three movements. The first, *Allegro* changing to *Presto*, is in free sonata form with many fugato passages and jazzy syncopations. It ends

79

with a *lontano e capriccioso* reminiscence of the opening theme. The second movement, a nocturne in rondo form, is pervaded with mysterious gloom. The steady tread of the opening theme, *lento e lugubre*, is interrupted from time to time by fast jazz interludes. If one were given to analogies, one might say that the movement suggests a walk down a long, dark city street at night; there is no one about, but occasionally one passes an open, brightly lit window from which come the strains of a gramophone playing jazz. According to Louis Kentner, this was Lambert's favourite movement of the three. The Finale opens with a slow introduction, again marked *lugubre*. The theme is virtually the same as that to which the solo baritone sings the words "Adieu, farewell earth's bliss" in the Saraband of *Summer's Last Will and Testament*. Lambert had already sketched a setting of these words by Thomas Nashe at the time he was writing the *Sonata*. The slow tempo changes almost at once to *presto*, with a theme, first heard in octaves, which dominates the body of the Finale, perhaps to an excessive degree. The "Saraband" theme returns at the end. Cecil Gray wrote perceptively of the work's "dark, black Célinesque quality", inspired, he said, by "long, cat-like, nocturnal prowlings through the suburbs of Paris". It may have been Paris as well as Toulon; it hardly matters. From the musical point of view the *Sonata* is interesting because it shows Lambert using a similar language to that employed in *The Rio Grande* for completely different expressive purposes. The use of some of the mannerisms and turns of phrase of jazz did not bind him in any way to a particular mood or emotional atmosphere; in other words he used jazz rather than allowing himself to be dominated by it. The work should attract virtuoso pianists more than it does, though the later *Concerto* is a more accomplished and successful attempt at conveying a similar state of mind. The *Sonata* was dedicated to Thomas Earp, a friend and drinking companion of Lambert's who also knew Heseltine and Cecil Gray well. Earp shared with Lambert a fondness for nineteenth-century French literature – he translated some works of Stendhal into English – but was probably better known as a bohemian and art critic.

Lambert's musical career took a sharp turn for the better in 1929. *Music for Orchestra* received three performances: on the air under Leslie Heward on 14th June; at Covent Garden under the composer[1] and

---

[1] During the Diaghilev season. *Le Sacre du Printemps* was also in the programme, with the result that Lambert's work was inadequately rehearsed.

at the "Proms" on 29th August. The latter was a "British Composers Concert" at Queen's Hall, and Heseltine also appeared to conduct his Capriol Suite. Lambert's work had a mixed press. The *Telegraph* said that the audience were "obviously impressed with the efficiency and assurance of the young man at the conductor's desk", and the second part of the work was described, in terms that probably set the composer's teeth on edge, as "a jolly essay in fugato writing, syncopated rhythms and the newer counterpoint".

On 19th September Ashley Dukes' dramatisation of Feuchtwanger's *Jew Süss* opened at the Duke of York's Theatre with Matheson Lang and Peggy Ashcroft in the cast. Lambert wrote some interludes and arranged a Scarlatti ballet, *Mars and Venus*, for Act II. This was later taken into the Camargo repertory. The production ran well into 1930, and provided a small but useful income for Lambert, who conducted the music each night. *Jew Süss* was later seen in New York with Lambert's music.

The little *Mars and Venus* ballet, of no great consequence in itself, was one of the first of many instances of Lambert's gift for assembling agreeable and danceable ballet scores from the music of other composers. This was an important contribution to the early success of the Vic-Wells (later Sadler's Wells) Ballet. It was Lambert's habit to use hitherto little-known works by such composers as Boyce, Couperin, Auber, Meyerbeer and Liszt for this purpose, thereby encouraging a revival of interest in their music as well as doing the ballet company a service.

On 30th October Gordon Bryan played the *Sonata* in public for the first time, at the Aeolian Hall. The programme also included the *Li Po Poems* in their instrumental version (another first performance), and music by Lambert's friends Walton and Patrick Hadley. Lambert conducted when necessary. Press reviews were good, though some found the *Sonata* too percussive, and the work was repeated at a BBC Contemporary Music concert at the Central Hall, Westminster, on 3rd March the following year. Morrison was the soloist on that occasion, and Lambert and Edith Sitwell recited *Façade* under the direction of Leslie Heward.

But the most important event of 1929 for Lambert was the first concert performance of *The Rio Grande*. This took place at Manchester on 12th December, with Lambert conducting the Hallé Orchestra and the Orchestra's conductor, Sir Hamilton Harty (who had fallen in love

with the work) at the piano. The following day the same artists repeated the work in Queen's Hall.

SUDDEN FAME
FOR
YOUNG COMPOSER.

QUEEN'S HALL IN A FRENZY.

JAZZ CHANGED INTO MUSIC OF GENIUS.

... said the *News*. Other papers told the same story less sensationally.
"A new work of great genius" said the *Daily Express*; "an extremely
clever and attractive work" agreed the *Chronicle*; the *Telegraph* said
that it was "a work of great fascination" and its creator "a conductor
born to conduct". It had been received "with prolonged acclama-
tions". In the *Manchester Guardian* Neville Cardus compared *The Rio
Grande* with Křenek's *Jonny spielt auf*, greatly to the former's advantage, and he too called Lambert's piece "a work of genius"; "Mr
Lambert", he said, "transfigures jazz into poetry". It was the kind of
critical and public reception composers dream about. The *Express* returned to the subject on 17th December:

> There are only two composers who have anything to say just now.
> One of them is Constant Lambert, whose *Rio Grande* is as fine a
> piece of work as this syncopated age has heard. . . . At the Queen's
> Hall the other night . . . just before the music began, the other
> young-man-who-has-something-to-say came up and said: "Don't
> miss a second of this. It's great. Much better than I have ever
> written." That man was Mr William Walton.

While no doubt both Walton and Lambert winced at reading this sort
of journalese, it was useful publicity for both, and Walton's words, if
accurately reported, are interesting: his *Viola Concerto* had appeared
on 3rd October.

More performances of *The Rio Grande* followed swiftly, in Britain and overseas. It became a "Prom" standby, festivals such as those at Brighton and Eastbourne hastened to perform it, and in early 1930 a record was issued with the original artists. It was given in New York in January 1931 by the Schola Cantorum under Hugh Ross with Colin McPhee at the piano, and prompted the *New Yorker* to write:

> It has remained for a young Englishman, Constant Lambert, to employ Jazz so that the general effect isn't that of someone lecturing in French after having had two lessons on the radio.

When Koussevitsky conducted it at Boston in April 1931, during the 50th Anniversary Season of the Boston Symphony Orchestra, the reception was ecstatic. The following day the *Boston Herald* wrote that

> Mr Lambert's *Rio Grande* is not only full of life that is contagious; it brings near far off scenes, and this without the borrowing of real or spurious "folk-songs". No one knows what "Isle joyeuse" Debussy had in mind when he wrote his piano piece. This *Rio Grande* flows through a country as undefined and empties into a harbour unsounded, unknown to any pilot. Therefore the audacity of Mr Lambert's fancy makes captive the hearer. Seldom in Symphony Hall has there been so instant, spontaneous, so prolonged, so tumultuous recognition of an unfamiliar composition signed with an unfamiliar name.

Lambert had enjoyed a triumph of a kind denied to all but a few composers. It would never happen to him so dramatically again. Ernest Newman shook a warning finger in his direction soon afterwards:

> This young man will have to be careful. It is fatal, in a world so stupid as this, for any composer to be a thinker and writer in addition; and when a young composer thinks as soundly and writes as brilliantly upon music as Mr Lambert does, the chances are a thousand to one that the crowd will refuse to believe in him as a composer.

That was one danger – the British public of that time was apt to distrust brilliance and versatility, and preferred their composers solid and worthy. There was another: a sensational success like this, achieved at the age of twenty-four, was hard to follow satisfactorily; and failure to do so could lead to disappointment and boredom. To hail a man not yet twenty-five as a genius is not necessarily to do him a service.

V THE FOUNDATION OF THE VIC-WELLS BALLET

In April 1929 Amy Lambert returned to London from Australia, and Constant went to live with her at 42 Peel Street, off Kensington Church Street. It was a surprising thing for him to do, though his prime motive may have been financial. Lambert was fond of his mother, and held her in some awe: friends remember that he always tried to be on time when lunching at her house. When *Music Ho!* was published the family discovered that it was dedicated to his mother, which surprised them a great deal. Amy Lambert was proud of her brilliant son, even when he was at his lowest ebb, but he cannot have found it easy to live the kind of life he wished to live while staying at Peel Street.

Before Mrs Lambert's return an important event in Lambert's personal life had occurred. He was lunching one day with Anthony Powell at Castano's in Greek Street, Soho, an establishment that has now found its way into literature as "Foppa's" in *A Dance to the Music of Time*. Lambert had to go that afternoon to see a Russian pianist called Elsa Karen who lived in St John's Wood. When he arrived, the door was opened to him by a girl of striking beauty, little more than a child. Her features revealed her partly oriental ancestry. Lambert seems to have been completely bowled over. Florence Chuter (or Kaye) had been brought up in an orphanage, and was now working as a housemaid. She was probably about fourteen when Lambert first set eyes on her. He began to see her regularly. One day she came to tea with him over the Varda Bookshop, and when she was about to leave, and he was helping her on with her coat, he kissed her – but was immediately overcome with remorse because, he explained, he was "in love" with Anna May Wong. The incident seems absurdly romantic, but Lambert was romantic to a degree, despite the glitter of his conversation and the abrasiveness of his wit. There is little doubt that he fell in love with Florence very quickly, although it was at least two years before he introduced most of his friends to her. His normal tendency to keep the various parts of his life in watertight compartments was intensified on this occasion by the fact that the circles in which he moved could not fail to be hard going for a bewildered child with great charm but little education.

Meanwhile more conducting engagements came his way. There was a Contemporary Arts Festival at Bath in late March and early April 1930, where he recited *Façade* and conducted *Pomona* and the *Elegiac Blues*. After a holiday in France he travelled to Germany, where an English Music Week was being held at Bad Homburg. The highlight of this event was a concert by the combined orchestras of Bad Homburg and Radio Frankfurt on 16th July (broadcast by the BBC as well as Frankfurt). Harriet Cohen was the soloist in a programme of music by Bliss, Bax, Lambert, Moeran and Walton, conducted by Lambert. The day after the concert he wrote to Anthony Powell:

> The concert went quite well. . . . The platform was draped with the flags of the British Mercantile Marine, most of them upside down. A week with Harriet Cohen is like being put next to one's *bête-noire* at school lunch and knowing you have to wait until the end of term. Shall recuperate in Paris – I need a little colour in my life.

More employment, of a very modest kind, came from a different source. Diaghilev had died in 1929 and his Company collapsed at once. Marie Rambert and Ninette de Valois had already begun their pioneer work in England, and Lambert's friend the dancer Marie Nielson (later the wife of Cecil Gray) introduced him to de Valois:

> Ninette wanted some music for a ballet orchestrated and as none of the conductors at the Vic could be bothered with ballet asked me if I thought that young man, Lambert, would do it. If so would I give her an introduction? I said that he was playing for the Rambert ballet at Hammersmith that week[1] and if we went to a performance we could go round in the interval. Both Constant and I were exceptionally shy in those days so muttering something I put her into his room and fled. She joined me a few minutes later looking rather worried and when I asked if Constant would do it said "I don't know, a very vague young man. Says he is busy for ten days but will do it after that!" I said, "He'll do it if he says he will." At the end of the week she said, "You see, nothing from that young man." I pointed out that he had said ten days, and I thought she would hear from him then. "H'm, I'll be very cross with you if I don't. I

---

[1] They were performing the *Mars and Venus* ballet arranged for *Jew Süss*.

think I should have got someone more reliable". Of course, Constant did phone to make the appointment and after the interview Ninette was beaming – "A most efficient young man – he's going to conduct for us too!" And that was the beginning and *making* of the Ballet because if Ninette had got someone else it would have been just another English ballet and not the living thing Constant made it.

The ballet Lambert orchestrated for the Old Vic was Mozart's *Les Petits Riens*.

About this time a group of ballet-lovers in Britain formed the Camargo Society, whose purpose was to arrange occasional performances of ballet in London. For the smaller rôles and the corps de ballet they drew on the nucleus of dancers forming round Rambert and de Valois. Lambert was the natural choice as conductor. The Society's first programme was given at the newly-built Cambridge Theatre on 19th October 1930, and the highlight of the evening was the first English stage performance of *Pomona*. The ballet had new choreography by Ashton and sets and costumes by John Banting; Anton Dolin danced Vertumnus, the American dancer Anna Ludmila, Pomona. There were abundant administrative and financial problems, but the Society had got off to a good start.

From the private point of view 1930 was a year of deaths for Lambert. His father died in Australia on 28th May; Christopher Wood in August; and worst of all, for Lambert, Philip Heseltine gassed himself on 17th December. On the 27th Lambert wrote to Marie Nielson:

> I was very upset and had to look after someone who was even more so. . . . I came to Paris on Sunday hoping to avoid the gloom of London. Not altogether successfully. Still I enjoy going for interminable walks in the more sinister and uncharted quarters of this town. . . . As for the Camargo – when I think of returning to it I am tempted to change my name and run away to sea.

The "someone" was Cecil Gray. Lambert took part as conductor in the Peter Warlock Memorial Concert at the Wigmore Hall on 23rd February 1931. The concert, which was broadcast, was financed by Delius, Keynes, Shaw, John, Anthony Asquith and the Hon. Evan Morgan (later Viscount Tredegar). Bax accompanied the songs. A packed hall heard a programme whose emotional climax was Heseltine's Yeats setting, *The Curlew*, one of the most desolate pieces of music ever written.

It was at this time that Lambert was writing his *Piano Concerto*. This tribute to Heseltine's memory shows its composer at his most bitter and disillusioned, but he did not lose his sense of humour about it. In a letter to Patrick Hadley he wrote:

> My musical St Vitus dance gets worse and worse. My new concerto has now got out of 11/8 only to get into 13/8. However after this I am going to turn over a new leaf and in future my works will be noticeable for their morbid introspection, their extreme length, the paucity of notes to a bar and the remarkably deliberate tempo in which those few notes will be played.
>
> The Captain told me a good story against myself which I feel you would be the first to appreciate. He played over one of my *Façade* records to his aunt who said when asked for an opinion – "Yes, my dear, I'm sure it's very pretty once you're used to it, but you know I've never cared for records in dialect!"
>
> Your idea about the Carlyle Square Fagging Suicide kept me happy for some time . . .[1]

The *Concerto*, which was partly written in Marseilles, is in three movements: Overture, *Intermède* and Finale. Lambert again used the melodic and rhythmic patterns of jazz, elaborated and refined so that his music has a rhythmic complexity and harmonic subtlety seldom found in "pure" jazz. Blues-like passages occur side by side with others marked by jagged rhythms, violent harmonic clashes and pungent instrumentation. The work is scored for solo piano and an ensemble composed of six wind players, cello, double-bass and percussion, and this choice of instruments makes for an abrasive sound which Lambert makes no attempt to soften.

---

[1] "The Captain" was Osbert Sitwell. William Walton had now been living for some ten years as the guest of Osbert and Sacheverell Sitwell at Carlyle Square. About this time the newspapers carried an item about a boy who had committed suicide because he "couldn't stand the fagging" at his school. Friends visiting the Sitwells had noticed that from time to time Osbert would say, "Oh Willie, do fetch that book for me" or something of the sort, and hence they sometimes teasingly referred to Walton as "Osbert's fag". Hadley appears to have suggested the possibility that the "fagging tragedy" might be duplicated in Chelsea.

The Overture (*Allegro*) begins restlessly in 7/4 with a repeated alternation of two notes a semitone apart. The piano introduces a theme in 11/8, and the work develops by way of a brilliant cadenza for the soloist which forms the emotional and technical climax of the movement. A long coda based on the opening two-note motive with its pronounced rocking motion closes the Overture, which ends suddenly and unexpectedly in a remote key. The *Intermède* (*Andante recitando*) is built on similar lines to the central movement of the Sonata, with elements both of slow movement and of *scherzo*. It has a slow, melancholy, ruminative opening, with a blues tune on the trumpet, followed by a quiet passage for clarinets and cello. The mood is broken abruptly when the piano enters with a fast, restless passage in constantly varying metres. In the course of the movement the blues theme reappears, growing increasingly sardonic in character up to its final statement *fortissimo*, punctuated with beats on the tom-tom. There is a brief, rapid coda. When Lambert wrote to Hadley about "getting out of 11/8 only to get into 13/8" he touched on a characteristic of this work which is at once a source of rhythmic interest and a technical weakness: an unusual and irregular metre which begins by pleasing and intriguing the ear can become a rhythmic straitjacket, and there are moments in the concerto where this seems about to occur.

By contrast the cortège-like Finale maintains a steady beat throughout its course. It is marked *lugubre*, like the last movement of the *Sonata*, but while the latter rapidly grows animated there is no such change in the concerto. After a heavy descending chordal phrase on the piano, with *fortissimo* interjections by the other instruments, and a few quieter bars marked by the hollow sound of the temple blocks, the piano gives out the main theme, which is marked *con stanchezza* (wearily). The clouds do not lift for a moment, and after a tragic climax and *fortissimo* reiteration of the main theme the music begins to die away inconclusively and darkly. This movement is probably Lambert's most profound: in its acute grief and measured tread it recalls, not Delius nor Heseltine nor even Kurt Weill, but – though in technical terms the two are poles apart – the blues singing of Bessie Smith.

The Camargo Society continued to function in 1931, with Lambert (despite the sentiments expressed in his letter to Marie Nielson) still at the musical helm. There were plenty of annoyances and irritations, and M. Montagu-Nathan told Foss that he and Lambert would often exchange furtive glances at Camargo committee meetings on observing the reaction of the dancer-members to Edwin Evans' suggestions of appropriate music for ballet purposes. But in his heart Lambert knew that the enterprise was worth while, and in any case he was in no position to refuse work. About this time the Alhambra, then a music-hall, offered him its conductorship, and he seriously considered taking it, but in the end decided to struggle along and await developments in the musical and balletic fields. *Façade* and *Mars and Venus* were taken into the Camargo repertory, and a great stir was created by the first stage performance of Vaughan Williams' *Job* in a version for theatre orchestra which Lambert made. The last interesting première of the year was at the Savoy Theatre on 29th November, when *The Rio Grande* was staged as *A Day in a Southern Port* with sets by Edward Burra and choreography by Ashton. Angus Morrison was at the piano. The principal dancers were Markova as a Creole Girl, William Chappell as a Creole Boy, Walter Gore as a sailor and Lydia Lopokova as "the Queen of the Port". Burra's drop-curtain – depicting a waterfront scene with tarts leaning out of their windows – was considered very daring, and Ashton arranged a brilliant solo for Gore to the long cadenza for piano and percussion.

Lambert was also concerned in a smaller-scale theatrical venture at the Gate Theatre, which was a club and therefore able to present plays that were considered too immoral to be exposed to the delicate sensibilities of a public theatre audience. One of these was Oscar Wilde's *Salome*. On 27th May 1931 a production of this piece in Lord Alfred Douglas' English translation opened, with Margaret Rawlings, then an unknown, in the lead. Robert Speaight was Herod, Flora Robson Herodias, John Clements Jokanaan. Esmond Knight and Norman Shelley played smaller parts. John Armstrong designed the sets and Ninette de Valois addressed herself to the task of choreographing the *Dance of the Seven Veils*. The incidental music – for clarinet, trumpet, cello and percussion – was by Lambert, and the small group who played it were placed on a shelf above the dressing-room. The cast had to get in early and shut the door so that a ladder could be propped between stage and orchestra; Lambert mounted the ladder and conducted while perched on one of the rungs. "A nerve-racking experience if one knew his habit of stepping backwards", wrote Marie Nielson. Alan Frank, now of the Oxford University Press, was the clarinettist, and Lambert's friend "Bumps" Greenbaum presided over the percussion. The play ran for thirty-two performances.

Lambert's score, completed on 3rd May, is in nine movements, all very short except for the Dance. For this piece Lambert, like Strauss, wrote a fast, loud opening to attract attention; then the music became slow for a while and gradually gained speed until a hectic final *presto*. The climax of the Dance includes a trumpet phrase (C sharp – F sharp – C sharp – G natural) which he later used with striking effect in the *King Pest* movement of *Summer's Last Will and Testament*.

Lambert's music figured in the I.S.C.M. Festival at London and Oxford in July 1931. He conducted the newly-formed BBC Symphony Orchestra at Queen's Hall in his *Music for Orchestra*, and *Pomona* once again at Oxford. Aaron Copland, who was present at the London concert, took Lambert for an academic, not realising that *Music for Orchestra* was far from typical of its composer and that it had already been followed by other compositions of a most unacademic nature. The French magazine *Comœdia*, in a summary of the whole Festival published on 23rd August, made the same mistake. The writer liked *Pomona*: "la musique est charmante avec une certain gaucherie désinvolte qui rappelle à s'y méprendre la manière de Francis Poulenc. Il existe entre ces deux musiciens une certaine parenté spirituelle et j'aime dans les premières oeuvres de Constant Lambert à retrouver cette fraîcheur naïve qui est un des éléments du charme de Poulenc." But as for *Music for Orchestra*! "Déjà le terrible académisme, héritage de Mendelssohn, plaie de la musique anglaise, perce ou même éclate dans ses oeuvres. Le voici, à vingt-six ans, déjà mûr pour une brillante carrière officielle. Il y trouvera honneurs et profits . . . je pense qu'on pouvait espérer mieux de lui." One does not know whether to be glad or sorry for Lambert's sake that this forecast proved so wide of the mark.

On 6th November Lambert conducted his first opera, Purcell's *Dido and Aeneas* at Sadler's Wells, with Joan Cross. On 18th December his *Concerto* was played at the Aeolian Hall under BBC auspices, with the composer conducting and Arthur Benjamin as the soloist. The work received good notices, expecially the following in the *Manchester Guardian*:

A curious and interesting feature of the work . . . is the way in which it begins in the highest spirits and gradually becomes gloomier and gloomier as it goes on. In this respect it suggests . . . a symbolical representation of the spiritual experience of the post-war generation to which he belongs. There is something exceedingly sympathetic in the way in which he deliberately refuses to supply the orthodox "happy ending" in the shape of the rollicking finale prescribed by tradition and convention, although it is certain that the popularity of the work must suffer on this account.... The melodic and harmonic material of the work come recognisably from the pen that wrote *The Rio Grande*, but with an added maturity and an astringency which will probably prevent it from ever becoming as popular. It is nevertheless, in my opinion, a very much more interesting work in every respect.

It was an intelligent and sympathetic review, though the "high spirits" of the opening are more apparent than real and it is likely that the work's melancholy sprang at least as much from personal grief as from some sort of nebulous collective experience shared by Lambert's whole generation.[1] The reviewer was completely right in one respect: the work has never become popular as *The Rio Grande* did, partly because of its mood and partly because the general musical public prefers large orchestral and choral works to chamber concerti: Falla's *Harpsichord Concerto* has never attained the popular success of *Nights in the Gardens of Spain*.

During 1930 and 1931 Lambert and Florence Chuter were seen together a good deal, and her unusual beauty and his talent made them good material for the gossip columnists. "I have often seen Mr Lambert and Miss Florence Chuter together" gushed the *Evening News*, "and they are an arresting couple – he bare-headed, broad and almost burly, yet using a silver-mounted walking stick; she no taller than his shoulder, and *petite*. She usually wears a little knitted hat on the back of her head, and the hair is drawn back from an interesting brow mantling wide brown eyes. Twenty-five and eighteen they are: and Constant Lambert is likely to attain further distinction. . . . Yesterday I found Mr Lambert deep in a discussion on the ground floor while Miss Chuter was drinking iced coffee under the roof." Twenty-five and eighteen they were not: Miss Chuter was probably no more than sixteen at this time. During summer 1931, at a party in Anthony Powell's

---

[1] Similarly, the evident tensions of Walton's *First Symphony* were once construed as a reflection of political conflicts in Europe and an intimation of the struggle to come. The composer has since said that the work sprang primarily from his own personal concerns.

flat in Bloomsbury, Lambert went down on his knees to Florence and proposed marriage. He was accepted. There was £25 for the honeymoon and £25 for the wedding breakfast, which was to be at the Eiffel Tower Restaurant.

The wedding was fixed for 5th August. Lambert collected Florence from St John's Wood in a cab, but, noticing that she had no flowers, stopped at a florist's and emerged with some carnations. The photograph of his bride, still carrying the carnations wrapped in their original paper, appeared in that night's *Evening Standard*. They drove to Kensington Registry Office, where they were married in the presence of April Gordon (Gavin Gordon's wife) and Tommy Earp. The groom put his hand into his pocket in order to pay the fee only to discover that he had lost his wallet, presumably while buying the carnations. There followed frantic efforts to recover the wallet from police stations, and when these were fruitless a stern decision to proceed as planned to the Eiffel Tower, get Stulik drunk on his own Tokay, and then drop the bombshell by admitting that no one was in a position to pay. The tactic worked, and the "mariés de la Tour Eiffel" returned to Peel Street to prepare for their honeymoon in France. On the train Lambert ordered a bottle of wine, which the waiter proceeded to empty over his one respectable suit.

When they returned there were several pieces of good luck. Charles Laughton and Elsa Lanchester, about to leave for America, let the Lamberts have their flat at 15 Percy Street; it was far from chic, being situated over an Indian restaurant, but it was a beginning. The wallet had been recovered intact. Lambert accepted a job as music critic for the *Sunday Referee* at a salary of £7 a week. And he was offered, and took, the post of conductor and musical director to the newly-formed Vic-Wells Ballet. He was to hold the post until 1947. Stability of some sort seemed possible: his wife was still very young; they were vastly different in background and intellectual training; but for a romantic of Lambert's stamp this was unimportant.

For the next sixteen years the ballet dominated Lambert's life. He gave it all he could, and the most menial and boring musical tasks were not beneath him. In the early days he would often sit up all night orchestrating music he had selected for balletic use and copying out the parts himself if necessary; during the Second World War he played one of the two pianos which accompanied performances when no orchestra was available; he conducted night after night; and he advised not only on musical matters but on all artistic affairs, for his breadth of knowledge of all the arts far outshone that of his colleagues.

So much for his contribution to the ballet; what did the ballet do for Lambert? His work there undoubtedly gave him great satisfaction, for he loved ballet and valued it as an art form. But he never again achieved the density of creative activity in the field of composition that he had attained in the late 1920s. This was at least as much due to his preoccupation with the affairs of the Sadler's Wells Company as with poor health and excessive drinking. There is no doubt that the bulk of the best music Lambert left behind him dates from the period 1926 to 1931. But the fact that the years 1931–1951 yielded only four or five works of consequence does not necessarily mean that his inspiration failed him and that he had little more to say: he may have failed his inspiration, in the sense of being unprepared to take advantage of it when it came. The technical fluency acquired by concentrated composition in the 1920s had to be regained each time after months or even years of neglect. It is significant that *Horoscope*, an extremely polished work from the technical point of view though not one of Lambert's most original, was written at a time of comparative calm when he had broken free from an emotional situation that had become intolerable and time-consuming and acquired more leisure in which to think and work. The combination of grindingly hard days at the theatre and a tempestuous emotional life too often caused Lambert to drink to excess and dissipate his remaining energies on trivialities.

At first things were not too hectic. Performances in London averaged no more than three or four a fortnight during the long winter season, and this comparatively leisurely curriculum allowed Lambert time for other activities. But the stress and fatigue of wartime conditions made inroads into his vitality and physical well-being from which he never recovered. Other former members of the van Dieren-Heseltine circle were as hard-drinking as he was; but some of them had private incomes and none was obliged to lead the gruelling life of a ballet conductor and pianist. It would be pleasant, though probably unrealistic, to think that his sacrifice is appreciated by those on both sides of the footlights who profit from the ballet today.

It was not only Vic-Wells for whom Lambert conducted at this time. In January 1932 he made successful appearances with the Scottish Orchestra in Glasgow and Edinburgh, and the Camargo Society continued to function, although in early 1934 it made over its resources and sets to Vic-Wells. One of the ballets presented in 1932 was *Adam and Eve* with choreography by the young Antony Tudor. This used Lambert's *Romeo and Juliet* score for its original subject. The Camargo first night at the Savoy on 6th June attracted a fashionable audience in which Mayfair jostled with Bloomsbury. They were there to see *Job* under Lambert, the second act of *Le Lac des Cygnes* under Beecham, and a new ballet, *High Yellow*. This last was danced to a jazz score written by Lambert's friend Spike Hughes, who conducted the London Symphony Orchestra, augmented for the occasion by nine dance-band players. Vanessa Bell was responsible for the sets, and the choreography was a collaborative effort between Ashton and a negro dance-arranger called Buddy Bradley. It was an ephemeral piece, but not without a certain chic – not an easy quality for inexperienced dancers to achieve. M. Montagu-Nathan recalled that during the season the first Mrs Lambert "used often to join me in the Secretary's Box. She possessed what appeared to be the smallest hands in London, but they were so powerful that between us we often succeeded in transforming a mere favourable reception into a veritable ovation".

After the season was over Lambert and his wife escaped to the south of France. On 26th July he wrote from Toulon to Anthony Powell:

I have just torn up a cheaply sensational letter I wrote you in which I said that there simply wasn't a single white settler in the whole town. Alas, my pen was too optimistic. As I was sealing the envelope a grisly cortege headed by Baby Bera and * * * * passed along the quay. Still the hotel is amazingly free from pests and smells more of ozone than opium.

Milhaud has just left Toulon for Aix, Reynaldo Hahn is at Cap Brun, Bera at les Sablettes, Cocteau at St. Mandrier, Kochno's at Tamaris, the snail's on the thorn etc.

I can honestly claim to be the only English party goer in the whole town and can also congratulate myself in rather a Bellocian fashion on being the only intellectual here who is not a teetotal Jew. I feel some distinction should be awarded me. If not the Legion of Honour perhaps the 3rd Class Agricultural Palms.

The exchange is apt to sting one a bit as all prices seem to have gone up about 50% quite apart from only getting 88 or so to the pound.

Mechanical pianos seem to be on the wane but there are a thousand and one electric gramophones of unbelievable force. They are so loud that one just has to order drinks in dumb-show.

The only event of international interest here has been a "Grand Concours de Pyjamas". The whole town is so quiet in fact that the whores just hang about in bunches in the street without even troubling to accost one. Wherever we go we have to take one of Patrick Hadley's wooden legs with us as he can't make up his mind which fits him best.

I expect I shall be home soon as money seems a bit short. Cedric Morris disguised as a beggar has just passed playing the ukelele. Everyone here looks like Cedric Morris or D. H. Lawrence. It is most depressing.

I am getting nostalgic for the hectic life of old Bloomsbury (district of laughter, district of tears).[1]

In September the same year Adeline Genée and Geoffrey Toye, with the assistance of the Danish and British Governments, organised a

---

[1] "Baby Bera" is Lambert's way of referring to Christian or "Bébé" Bérard. He first attracted attention as a painter, being associated with Tchelitchew, Léonid and the latter's brother Eugène Berman, in a group known for a time as the Neoromantics. Later he became France's leading stage designer, contributing sets and costumes of great elegance to the productions of Jouvet and Barrault, and the ballets of Kochno, among others. "Cedric Morris" refers to Sir Cedric Morris, the painter and horticulturist.

series of appearances by a small troupe of English dancers at Copenhagen. Lambert, who was to share the conducting with Toye, went
ahead to rehearse the Danish orchestra. According to Marie Nelson:

> The Company were, to say the least of it, "snooty" about Florence
> and he asked me to stay with her in Percy St and bring her with me
> to Copenhagen. She was very charming and shy, and I remember
> read Conrad's *Typhoon* on the crossing until we were both ill.
> Constant met us in the early morning at the station in very good
> spirits.

Certain kinds of unconventional union are more acceptable in a ballet
company than others, and the somewhat tight-lipped bourgeois attitude stemming from on high which was in a way one of the strengths
of the Wells and may have saved it from disruption had its disadvan-
tages for an adventurous and uninhibited personality like Lambert's.

Before he left Lambert had written to Powell:

> I have just received my sailing directions and they read very like
> the more depressing patches in *Venusberg*. I go in a small boat
> which takes about 3 days and arrives in the small hours. The right
> Nordic note is struck, I think, by the sentence "Captain Nellemose
> – whom you will know by his scarred face – will meet you".[1]

The performances went well enough, but, according to Marie Nielson,
Lambert

> found Copenhagen "clean and characterless" and not his cup of
> tea. After one of the performances a number of us were invited to
> the most fashionable night club – a very dignified place. Constant
> suddenly said "I'd like to ask you to dance but I can't do these
> dances – I could if they played Sousa". Without thinking I said
> "Well ask them to", and the next minute he was threading his way
> across the ballroom to the band. The conductor recognising him
> beamed but his expression changed when he was asked if he knew
> Sousa and if so would he please play *The Double-Headed Eagle*.
> However he did and we set off. The other dancers were completely
> bewildered but probably out of courtesy to the English one by one
> joined in, sedately marching round while Constant charged down
> the ballroom doing a sharp turn at each corner and charged back

---

[1] Powell's second novel, *Venusberg*, published in 1932, deals with life in a
small city on the Baltic.

again. He actually asked for and got an encore. We missed one of the official functions because he insisted that a Laurel and Hardy picture in the suburbs was not to be missed.

The first main project at the Wells in 1933 was a revival of *Pomona* on 17th January, with new sets by Vanessa Bell, revised choreography by Ashton, and Anton Dolin and Stanley Judson alternating in the part of Vertumnus. This production had the useful effect of attracting a fashionable audience, eager to see Dolin. On 7th February there appeared a product of Lambert's enthusiasm for Purcell, *The Birthday of Oberon*, with choreography by de Valois and sets by John Armstrong. There were thirty dancers and a sizeable chorus. The ballet was founded on the Masque of the Seasons from Act IV of *The Fairy Queen*, with additional music from other parts of the work. The press liked it, but it did not survive for very long in the repertory, partly because it was expensive to mount and partly because the public was lukewarm. Marie Nielson was now in America, and Lambert wrote to her about the season on 22nd April:

> I am so sorry not to have written before but life has passed in a dreary whirl and I never seemed to have a moment. My beastly book which is now half done has kept me busy and the fact that Malcolm Sargent has had an operation and Uncle Geoffrey has dislocated his arm has given me extra work to do.
>
> Are you still functioning in Radio City and how is The Dance in America? When do you come back? Soon I hope.
>
> The Camargo is at present following a policy of masterly in-action owing to the usual low funds. There is vague talk of a season after the opera but I very much doubt it.
>
> *Adam and Eve* was quite mild fun, with some good choreo-graphy by Antony and some very post-war decor by Banting. I wrote some very devotional music for the angel and the music on the whole sounded better in its old form than in *Romeo*. Freddy re-did *Pomona* for the Vic-Wells getting much more shape and defini-tion into the ensembles. Excellent decor by Vanessa Bell. Pat over-acted disgracefully as the Widow Twankey and Stanley, who is coming on tremendously this season, was really much better in the part.
>
> The best ballet this season has been *The Birthday of Oberon* with Purcell music and a chorus of 40. Very good straightforward

choreography by Ninette (much better than *Origin*). People objected to the chorus being in masks but, as I said, had they seen them without? It had excellent notices but wasn't a success after the first night.

The season rather fell off after that but was pulled together by *Coppelia* with Loppy (who was superb). Uncle Geoffrey was to have done it but ran into a car and only just escaped with his life so I had to do it at short notice.

The old Copenhagen gallop is to be revived for the last night after which I shall be out of a job unless I can get in with the Monte Carlo Ballet which I hear is coming to the Coliseum in June.

Stanley was excellent as the fool in Rimsky's *Snow Maiden* and Hedley was magnificent as the old man in *Coppelia*.

I am getting very bored with London and hope to get away when my book is finished and do some composing – I have about 40,000 more words to do though. How are you enjoying New York? Are you still at the same address? Are you drinking beer or gin? What is the feeling about the Scottsboro' trial? (I have subscribed a wretched pound towards the defence so I expect I shall be stopped at Ellis Island if I ever go to New York).

Do you go to Harlem? Is there anyone there better than Ellington? Have you met my New York bores Van Vechten and Max Ewing? Answers please.

The book of which he speaks was, of course, *Music Ho!*. "Uncle Geoffrey" was Geoffrey Toye, conductor and composer of *The Haunted Ballroom*; "Pat" was Dolin, "Stanley" Judson. The other de Valois ballet Lambert mentions was *The Origin of Design*, to music by Handel. "Loppy" was Lydia Lopokova's nickname, and the "old Copenhagen gallop" was a divertissement to music by Glinka arranged to give everyone an opportunity to shine during the Danish season. Lambert did not get a conducting job with the Monte Carlo Company (the troupe of Colonel de Basil) though he was employed by a rival company, the "Ballets 1933" that summer. "Hedley" was the dancer Hedley Briggs.

The reference to the Scottsboro' Trial is a revealing one. The "Scottsboro' Boys" were a group of young negroes accused of raping white girls in Alabama. Their case created a great stir among European intellectuals, and not only among those, like Nancy Cunard and indeed

98

Lambert himself, whose interest in the coloured races was at least partly sexual in nature. So far as politics went, Lambert was impressionistic: in some ways he was a romantic reactionary, in others a romantic revolutionary. Certainly he had many close friends of left-wing opinions – people like Tom Driberg, Randall Swingler, Alan Rawsthorne and Christian Darnton. And where the ill-treatment of coloured people was concerned his attitude was unambiguous: it incensed him. Curiously enough, his one and only visit to America (in 1949) was not arranged without difficulty.

In June Lambert went to Holland to conduct Walton's recent choral work *Belshazzar's Feast,* with great success. The "Ballets 1933", for whom he conducted that summer, was a short-lived but brilliant company backed by Edward James[1] and starring Tilly Losch, the Viennese dancer who was James' wife at this time, and the very young Tamara Toumanova. The choreographer was Balanchine. Lambert shared the conducting of the Brecht-Weill "ballet with song" *The Seven Deadly Sins* (known as *Anna Anna* in London and starring Losch and Lotte Lenya) with Maurice d'Abravanel (now in charge of the Utah Symphony). Lambert admired this piece, and wrote about it with understanding and sympathy in the book on which he was working. Indeed he was one of the very few English musicians of the period to take Kurt Weill seriously – and precisely at a point when Weill was going out of fashion and entering on that unsettled period of his life from which he emerged as a composer of Broadway musicals. It is worth remembering Lambert's perception in cases such as this when reading

---

[1] The "Ballets 1933" were only one of the enterprises for which Edward James has been responsible. His James Press published fine books in the 1930s, including *The Next Volume,* a collection of poems by Mr James himself containing some of the most important of Rex Whistler's work. One of Poulenc's best compositions, the suite for chorus and orchestra *Sécheresses,* is a setting of poems by Mr James in a French translation. His collection of modern paintings, notably canvases by the surrealists and neoromantics, is outstanding, and many of them have been exhibited at the Tate and other public galleries. In 1964 Mr James established a Foundation under whose auspices West Dean, near Chichester (the house which Mr James inherited, one of the largest flint-faced mansions in Britain, started in 1804 by James Wyatt and completed by Wyatt's son Benjamin), was opened in 1971 as a residential college to promote traditional arts and crafts and develop them in relation to modern design and technical development.

99

statements like that by the late Colin Mason that "so keen a mind was so infallibly wrong about almost everything that mattered".

In September, Lambert was appointed Professor of Conducting at the Royal College of Music, and the following year (1934) he received the Collard Fellowship of the Musicians' Company. This award was worth £300 a year tax free for three years – a sum worth having in the 1930s – and it was intended to encourage those who received it to compose. During the period from 1932 to 1935 Lambert was engaged on his most ambitious work, *Summer's Last Will and Testament*, but he was still obliged to augment his income by musical journalism, for which he had a great talent. His mastery of English and enthusiasm for neglected or misunderstood composers stopped his articles from degenerating into hack work. From 1930 onwards he was music critic of the *Nation and Athenaeum*, while W. J. Turner, a poet of sorts who felt impelled to commit his thoughts about music to paper, wrote for the *New Statesman*. Turner and Lambert engaged in controversy over the Courtauld-Sargent concerts, whose success, while others were in low water, had been hailed by Turner as "the writing on the wall". Lambert retorted that far from being the writing on the wall it was merely "the writing in the cheque-book". Then the two magazines merged, and Montagu-Nathan was the first to tell Lambert of this development "which signified that he would lose, and W.J.T. would get, the *Statesman* job. Instead of groans he greeted this with peals of mirth. When he had been some time on the *Referee* he told me that the proprietors had sent for him to enquire whether this Wagner chap, to whom they thought he'd been rather rude, was still alive." In fact Lambert went on contributing record reviews and other articles to the *New Statesman* for most of the decade. He also wrote for the *Radio Times, The Listener, Apollo, John o' London's Weekly, Figaro, The Saturday Review, The Daily Chronicle, The Daily Telegraph* and other papers and magazines. When he was appointed as music critic of the *Sunday Referee* Cecil Gray told the paper's readers how lucky they were. Gray was a partisan, but nonetheless accurate: Lambert's articles however idiosyncratic, were consistently entertaining – it was the same man who later remarked that while many composers write at the piano Brahms wrote at the double-bass. Those who bought the *Referee* on 13th March 1932 were treated to an attack on the English translation of the Requiem Mass which Sargent had used when performing Verdi's setting: "It is time something was done about the translation. To refer to Dies Irae as a 'day of trouble' is to reduce it to the level of spring cleaning and to translate 'Tuba mirum spargens sonum' as 'hark the trumpet sounds appalling' shows more aptitude for musical criticism than for versification." The "Venusberg Music" from *Tannhäuser*, said Lambert on 29th May, was "like the Nordic view of a weekend in Paris". Lambert was in particularly acid vein when reviewing the first performance of Professor Tovey's long *Cello Concerto*, which Casals played at a BBC Symphony Concert on 17th November 1937:

> I am told by those who had the moral, physical, and intellectual stamina to sit it out to the end that Professor Donald Tovey's *Cello Concerto* lasts for over an hour. This I cannot vouch for as, like several other musicians, I was compelled to leave at the end of the first movement, which seemed to last as long as my first term at school, but was probably a little shorter in point of fact. I therefore find myself in the melancholy position of not being able to delight my readers with an account of the work as a whole. All I can say is that the first movement is the most completely null and void piece of music I have ever heard in Queen's Hall. (And I have had some gruelling experiences in my day.)

Lambert's writing was by no means consistently destructive; he found room to praise much that was unfashionable. Nor did he hesitate to embark on musical battles on behalf of others. At the end of 1932 he engaged the formidable figure of Ernest Newman on the matter of Hamilton Harty's performance of Sibelius' *Second Symphony*, which Lambert liked and Newman did not. At the end of his life Lambert again crossed swords with Newman, on the occasion of the first visit of the Company of La Scala to Covent Garden after the Second World War, when under the baton of Victor de Sabata they gave performances of *Otello* and *Falstaff* which electrified their audiences. The English critics, headed by Newman and Eric Blom, carped and cavilled, to such a degree that in December 1950 the magazine *Opera* printed a number of opinions as a corrective to the provincialisms of the London press. Lambert, one of those who contributed, attacked

> the carping and niggling of the London critics when faced with the fullbloodedness and all round excellence of La Scala. After some of the most memorable and breath-taking experiences in my musical life it was indeed shocking to find that the critics next day were damning it with faint pseudo-academic praise, but it was not to me

surprising. For the reason that I have, in the past, had to earn my living by that melancholy trade and realise all too well that the average English critic is a don *manqué*, hopelessly parochial when not exaggeratedly teutonophile, over whose desk must surely hang the motto (presumably in Gothic lettering) "Above all no enthusiasm".

As a critic Lambert never carped, never niggled: when he disliked something he could be withering, when he admired something he communicated his enthusiasm in generous terms. In his writing, much of it done for money and for no other reason, he made both enthusiasms and dislikes crystal clear in sharp, astringent phraseology. It was for this reason that his book *Music Ho!*, published in 1934, had so wide-ranging an influence on a whole generation of readers. The views he expressed in it were ones he held for the rest of his life. When it was reprinted in 1948 he inserted a short preface in which he gave his reasons for leaving the text alone. He made two qualifications, however: in the first of these he explained his "apparent lack of enthusiasm for the works of Bartók" and expressed his admiration for that composer's later music; in the second he qualified his criticisms of Diaghilev, as already noted.

There is nothing like *Music Ho!* in the whole literature of music. Some of the views it contains may also be found in two books by friends of Lambert's: Cecil Gray's *Survey of Contemporary Music*, published in 1924, and Bernard van Dieren's collection of essays, *Down Among the Dead Men*, which appeared the year after Lambert's study. But a similar attitude towards certain composers is all that these have in common with Lambert. Gray's book is written in the same heavy, overloaded style that marks, and mars, his book on Philip Heseltine and his autobiography (Lambert once affectionately called him a "Caledonian * * * *", and his style is certainly heavy-handed), while whatever may be the merits of van Dieren's music (about which it is hard to speak, since it is so seldom played) his prose style is clotted to a degree. Neither book reads well today, while *Music Ho!* seems as fresh as when it first appeared.

But Lambert's brilliance has probably made the book as many enemies as it has won it friends. The very qualities of wit, sparkle and encyclopaedic knowledge lightly worn that make the book "compulsively readable" have aroused distrust among the musical establishment. Musicians are not expected to be witty when they turn from notes to words, and the average writer on musical subjects loyally abstains from startling his *confrères* by flashes of brilliance. One might be forgiven for thinking that dullness is not only inevitable but in some way desirable. To provoke a yawn is to prove one's worthiness and reliability, to cause a smile is to arouse distrust. To be serious one must be solemn. Many people in Britain are apt to assess music in the same way: even today it is often considered that *The Magic Flute must* be a greater work than *Cosi fan tutte,* because of its subject-matter. How unreliable, how "quirky", therefore, must be a writer who can say, in the course of a book about music:

> Oriental daydreaming has suffered a slight setback since American travelogues, emancipated potentates and shoals of scrutable Indian students have brought the East unromantically near, but America, in destroying the romance of other countries, has created a romance of her own and the "gangster's moll" has overthrown the "veiled houri" of the nineties. Unable to find exoticism in the strange and distant, we force ourselves to dive down into the familiar, and what is conveniently called Low Life provides the exotic motive for the post-war artist. The grubby gamins and snotty little brats that haunt the pages of Gide and Cocteau have taken the place of Pierre Louÿs's pitiless courtesans; and Swinburne, were he alive today, would write about a very different sort of queen.

Apart from the fact that the average British musician would be unlikely to be sufficiently familiar with the writings of Gide, Cocteau and Swinburne, let alone Pierre Louÿs, to perceive the truth of this statement, the whole tone of the passage is not the sort of thing one expects to find in a book on music. Lambert understood that it was neither possible nor desirable adequately to consider twentieth-century music out of its social and artistic context; but his irreverent wit, joined with his Franco-Russian leanings, was bound to arouse hostility. His attacks on Stravinsky might have pleased many English musicians; but the fact that he took Kurt Weill seriously, praised Liszt, Balakirev and Glinka, and denigrated Brahms was certain to give offence. Lambert's withering attack on the English folksong school made him many enemies, and his analysis of the Jewish element in jazz, convincing and pungent as it is, upset certain members of that understandably sensitive race. Indeed, very near the end of Lambert's life, one Jewish composer who was very lucky at that stage to achieve any hearings at all in the concert hall refused to be present at the performance of a work of his because the conductor was Lambert. Join to these considerations Lambert's championship of neglected figures like Bernard van Dieren, despised ones like Puccini, allegedly frivolous ones like Satie and jazz composers like Ellington, and even his exaggerated reverence for Sibelius could not save him from being branded as an iconoclast.

The title of Lambert's book is taken from *Antony and Cleopatra*. The relevant passage reads:

> *All:*   The music ho!
>   (*Enter Mardian the Eunuch*
> *Cleopatra:*   Let it alone; let's to billiards.

The sub-title is "A Study of Music in Decline". The implication, clearly, is that Cleopatra may well be forgiven for preferring billiards to music, the more particularly as the music offered her is to be provided by a eunuch.

Lambert's main argument, much compressed, is as follows. Neither the aristocratic classicism of the eighteenth century (typified by *The Marriage of Figaro*) nor the romanticism of the nineteenth (*Tristan and Isolde*) nor yet its nationalism (*Boris Godunov*) will serve today. The delicate social balance that supported the first has collapsed, the ardent idealism of the second has evaporated, and the genuinely national (as opposed to political) differences reflected by the third have disappeared. Artificial attempts to cultivate a "national" style (like the English folk-song school) are false and ludicrous. The great revolutionary upheaval in music which took place before the First World War, and in which Debussy and Schoenberg played crucial parts, is over; consolidation is less exciting than revolution, and few composers even try to consolidate. The majority prefer to fall back on devices like pastiche (Stravinsky in his neoclassic period, together with his followers) or on "mechanical romanticism" (like Honegger's *Pacific 231*) or on facile note-spinning (Hindemith and his "Gebrauchsmusik", which so far as Lambert is concerned consists in providing music of little or no value in the hope of supplying a need which does not exist). Everywhere one goes one is exposed to a continual stream of music, and the art is suffering from this "appalling popularity". It is futile to expect the general public ever to be as deeply responsive to newly-composed concert music as it once was, and the "middlebrow" composer is a disappearing phenomenon. In the future composers will be either un-popular and sophisticated highbrows, like Alban Berg, or popular and sophisticated lowbrows, like Cole Porter and Kurt Weill. The only hope for music lies in the kind of composer who, unconcerned with fashion, goes his own way, working out a musical style that pleases himself (rather than a coterie) and paying attention to the dictates of form rather than to those of mode. And Lambert gives Sibelius, Busoni and van Dieren as examples.

It is still too early to say whether Lambert was "right" or "wrong" about the figures he discusses. Many of the composers concerned – even towering figures like Stravinsky and Schoenberg – are not com-pletely beyond controversy. All that can be done is to look at Lambert's opinions in the light of current assessments. It is worth pointing out that there are considerable differences – apart from stylistic ones – between Lambert's book and Cecil Gray's. They are united in rating Sibelius, Busoni and van Dieren very highly, in admiring the early works of Bartók but not his so-called "middle period", and in respect-ing certain works of Elgar. Neither cares for Strauss. Gray reveres Delius, while Lambert, though thinking very highly of some of his music, believes that eventually Delius sacrificed too much to harmonic interest. In common with most musicians of the time, Gray regards Debussy's later works as showing a decline in inspiration and vigour, while Lambert anticipates the views held today by such authorities as Edward Lockspeiser and Pierre Boulez and believes that works like *Jeux* and *En blanc et noir* are among the composer's finest pieces. Gray dismisses Ravel apart from *Daphnis et Chloé*: Lambert is far from doing this, though he does not greatly care for Ravel's later works. Gray patronises Puccini: Lambert takes him very seriously. The two greatest differences between the two men lie in Lambert's view that jazz is capable of producing good music and perhaps also of providing a useful *lingua franca* for present-day composers (he instances Milhaud and Weill) and in the fact that for Lambert ballet is an important art form, while for Gray it is merely a sophisticated pantomime, unworthy of serious consideration.

Lambert follows Gray in denigrating Stravinsky – though not all the way: Lambert writes with great understanding about *Les Noces*. Angus Morrison's views on the psychological reasons which led Lambert to attack Stravinsky's neoclassic manner with such venom have already been quoted. The sheer brilliance of *Music Ho!* has led some readers to miss the elements of personal prejudice that creep in here and there. Lambert's diatribe is inconsistent with the fact that the first bars of *The Rio Grande*, to take an obvious instance, are clearly influenced by the percussive style of Stravinsky, just as other parts are influenced by jazz and Spanish marches and tangos. And while Lambert broke away from Gray in his high estimate of Alban Berg he followed his friend's line on Schoenberg.

Obviously it will not do to give Lambert the credit for all the views expressed in his book which now seem "right" while blaming all that seems eccentric on the unfortunate Gray. It is undeniable that by the light of the 1970s Lambert appears very misguided about Stravinsky and Schoenberg, and, while the period of foolish denigration of Sibelius is now, it appears, happily past, it is hard to follow Lambert in seeing him as a guiding light for the future. Rather does he appear as an important late nationalist with a remarkable grasp of symphonic form. But Lambert's views on a number of individual composers are very much in tune with current thinking: on Weill; on Satie; on Debussy; on Berg; on Hindemith (though to mention Hindemith and storm troopers in the same breath was unfair: Hindemith, though open to criticism on grounds of musical dullness, was of unimpeachable anti-Nazism); and Lambert's analysis of nationalism and exoticism in music remains masterly. And can one question Lambert's main theme? Is the intelligent man in the street really responsive to the "serious" music being written today, apart from that of isolated and conservative figures like Britten and Shostakovich? Do the works of Birtwistle, Boulez and Nono make much impact on any but coterie audiences? In one passage Lambert seems even to anticipate the nihilistic dadaism of such men as John Cage:

> When the mentality of the spoilt child who kicks his meccano to pieces out of boredom is valued above that of a man with the skill and patience involved in building a bridge, it is clear that some examination not only of the methods but also the impulses of the modern artist is gravely needed.

The reader with an intelligent but unspecialised interest in the arts and an awareness of what is going on around him can still derive from *Music Ho!* a clearer understanding of the ways in which twentieth-century music has developed than he would ever obtain from most other books on the subject, which tend to pay less attention to the social developments of which music forms a part. Like all composers, Lambert has his blind spots, and is wont to argue from time to time from his own practice: but who would expect an unbiased view of Britten from Stravinsky, or of Malcolm Arnold from Peter Maxwell Davies? And Lambert can throw a new and striking light on composers he admires and loves.

On Debussy:

> The magnificent orchestral *Images* are free from any superficial "artiness", but we do not require to be told that Debussy was an ill man when he wrote them to realize that they represent not the extrovert's enjoyment of present activity, but the introvert's half-recollected, half-imagined fantasia round action. Chabrier's valses are like Chabrier himself valsing with the utmost gusto, but Debussy's *Gigues* is like a Proustian synthesis of the emotion drawn from some jig danced on the Breton coast, a jig in which he himself could never genuinely take part.

On Weill:

> Weill is almost the only composer who can evoke in music the odd, untidy, drably tragic background that is presented to us so forcibly by William Faulkner in *Sanctuary* and *Light in August*.

On the *Création du Monde* of Darius Milhaud:

> Milhaud . . . represents the primeval incantations of the gods Nzamé, Mébère and Nkwa by a three-part jazz fugato over a percussion accompaniment. The rhythm and inflections of the fugue subject are clearly derived from jazz arabesques, yet, at the same time, the subject is an admirable one from any save the most crusty academic view. Crudely and naively analysed, the percussion background provides the necessary barbaric atmosphere, the jazz inflections of the tune suggest a stylized negro speech, the counterpoint provides the element of mingled and growing effort, while from the objective point of view the passage, theatrical atmosphere apart, is an excellent and logical "arrangement of notes".

"Crude and naive" analysis of this sort has the effect of making the reader want to hear the music at once; and, curiously, this often applies to the scores Lambert attacks as well as those he praises. He was not all praise where Milhaud was concerned, incidentally:

The mechanical imposed polytonality of Milhaud's earlier works, which jump sharply from the most academic euphony to the most startling cacophony, remind one of a host who having forgotten to put gin in the first round of cocktails puts methylated spirits in the second round to make up for it.

Milhaud seems to bear no resentment, for Madeleine Milhaud writes that "Milhaud a toujours eu une grande admiration pour C. Lambert qu'il a vu diriger plusieurs fois – qu'il considérait comme compositeur d'une grande sincérité."

Denis ApIvor, the composer, was a young student when he first read *Music Ho!* Of its impact on him he writes:

The influence of Constant's work and personality on myself is bound up with the historical fact of the emancipation or Europeanisation of British music, the liberation from the folky and the homespun, from the academicism of Leipzig and the emasculate decencies of Hubert Parry. Van Dieren's intellectual attitude was Germanic, but his taste was utterly un-German and his admiration was reserved for Liszt, Berlioz or Donizetti. We know that Constant was interested in the Russians like Borodin almost from his schooldays, and that Philip Heseltine was a friend of Bartók. It all adds up therefore to a sort of orientation towards the Latin, the Slav, the Russian, as opposed to the age-old influence on British music of German music and German composers. The historical peculiarity of works like *The Rio Grande* and *Belshazzar's Feast* lies in their utterly un-Germanic character and their utilisation of the technical advances of the revolution in musical composition going on in Europe at that time, specifically excluding the influence however of the work of Schoenberg and the Second Viennese School. With the true composer's genius for arguing from temperament to prove points which are valid for himself Constant proceeds to hammer home this French-Slav-Russian departure in *Music Ho!* But what an effect this book had when one first read it! – the encyclopaedic knowledge of recent musical developments all over the world, the wit, the social observation and satire, the sensitivity to painting, the experience of ballet from the inside. Here was a musician who was in the best sense of the word a European as well as an Englishman.

VII FROM *MUSIC HO!* TO THE OUTBREAK OF WAR

Under the guidance of de Valois, Ashton and Lambert, the Vic-Wells Company developed on satisfactory lines during the 1930s. In 1934 they enjoyed a major triumph with their first production of the complete *Lac des Cygnes*, Markova taking the parts of Odette and Odile and the young Robert Helpmann that of Siegfried. Shortly afterwards Markova left the Company, and a new star had to be found. On 26th March 1935 *A Day in a Southern Port*, now re-named *The Rio Grande*, entered the Wells repertory, with a girl not yet sixteen in the part created by Markova: this was Margot Fonteyn. Other important events in the ballet field were the first performance of the de Valois-Gavin Gordon-Rex Whistler *Rake's Progress*, suggested by the paintings of Hogarth (20th May 1935) and the introduction of *Façade* into the repertoire (8th October). For the 1935–6 season the orchestra was enlarged, and it was now possible to perform *Job* in its original scoring. Under Lambert's direction musical standards continued to improve.

By far the most frequently performed work of Lambert's at this time was *The Rio Grande*, but his *Piano Concerto* was given at the Biennale in Venice in September 1934. Lambert and his wife were present. The audience in the Fenice Theatre were partly hostile to the work, and Mrs Lambert, incensed, took an active part in the demonstration. It was in Venice that the Lambert's only child was conceived: a son, born on 11th May 1935 and given the name Christopher. By now the Lamberts had moved from Percy Street to 7 Park Row, and later they lived in Trevor Place, also in the Knightsbridge area. The course of the marriage had not been smooth, and there had been frequent rows; but there seemed to be no danger of a permanent rift at this time.

It was to his wife that Lambert dedicated the ambitious composition he worked on intermittently from 1932 to the end of 1935. This was *Summer's Last Will and Testament*, a "Masque" for orchestra, chorus and baritone solo to words by the Elizabethan poet and dramatist Thomas Nashe. Nashe, who died in his early thirties, wrote the first important picaresque novel in English, *The Unfortunate Traveller*, and a number of extremely scurrilous pamphlets which at one point in his brief career caused him to be consigned to the Fleet Prison. The title of the "pleasant comedy" from which Lambert chose his texts contains a punning reference to the name of Henry VIII's jester, Will Summers. An uneven work, the play contains some magnificent lyrics, and it was these that Lambert used. The words are ostensibly concerned with the seasons, but their underlying theme is the precariousness of life in Elizabethan London and the ever-present danger of Plague. When the work was revived in 1965 Felix Aprahamian wrote in the *Sunday Times*:

> The "bitter-sweet unity" conferred by the undercurrent to this Masque of the seasons (the "temporality of existence seen under the shadow of the Plague") now, in retrospect, seems to have autobiographical overtones: Lambert was one of an ill-fated and tragically short-lived group of native composers.

Though the dominant mood of the work is extremely sad, and the harmony has a richness reminiscent of Delius, the scoring (about which Lambert consulted his friend Hyam Greenbaum) ensures clarity of texture and there is ample evidence of the rhythmic vigour typical of Lambert. The three fast movements – the Coranto, the Brawles and the Rondo Burlesca – make an effective contrast with the slower movements. There are seven sections, of which two are orchestral. The first movement is an orchestral Intrata in the form of a Pastorale and a Siciliana; the opening theme pervades the whole work. The first choral movement, a "Madrigal con Ritornelli", is set to the words "Fair Summer droops, droop men and beasts therefore . . ." It is an appeal to Summer, "bright soul of the sad year", not to leave the world. Autumn was not only melancholy for Elizabethan Londoners, as it is for everyone else: it was also dangerous, for it was then that the risk of Plague was greatest. The verses of the Madrigal use a semi-chorus, the refrain the full choir. A vivace coda, using ideas from the Siciliana, leads into the Coranto, "Spring, the sweet spring". The marking – *Allegro pesante* – suggests the nature of this dance: for all its rhythmic dislocations it is deliberately heavy-footed and earthy. At the end there is a great choral shout of "Spring, the sweet spring" to a heartrendingly nostalgic harmonic sequence, and the music moves into the Brawles (the French *Bransle*). This *Allegro giocoso* is basically an orchestral movement with two choral trios. It is full of Lambertian syncopations, with a recurrent triadic figure first heard on the horns.

The second "Madrigal con Ritornelli" begins with the words "Autumn hath all the summer's fruitful treasure"; each verse of the poem ends with the ominous words "From Winter, Plague and Pestilence good Lord deliver us". The Rondo Burlesca *King Pest*, which comes next, was suggested by Edgar Allan Poe's grotesque story of Plague-ridden London in the reign of Edward III, though the Plague scenes in *The Unfortunate Traveller* will also have been in Lambert's mind. At times the triplet rhythms suggest Holst's *Uranus* and the *Apprenti-Sorcier* of Dukas. As has been mentioned, Lambert used a theme from his music for Salome's Dance in this movement. There is another musical quotation, two bars before 145 in the printed score, where it is marked *fff, pesante e ritenuto*. This is a reference to the phrase "Carry him to the burying ground" in the halliards shanty "Walk him along, Johnny". The association is with Heseltine. The clue is provided by a passage from Cecil Gray's biography of his friend:

> One evening in particular I remember vividly . . . when Peter gave an impromptu performance of a little-known sea shanty in the collection of Sir Richard Terry, entitled "Walk him along, Johnny", which he said he wished to be performed at his funeral. . . . Caparisoned in his African witch-doctor's robe and a huge soft black hat, he intoned the choral lines in a hoarse whisper, hopping and capering grotesquely like a vulture, in a kind of *danse macabre*, imbuing the artless little ditty with a nameless sense of dread and horror, and seeming almost to gloat over the thought of his own imminent decease. On a certain dark and gloomy December day only a few years later, in the old cemetery at Godalming, I was to recall involuntarily this strange performance, and in my mind's eye seemed to see him leaping around his own coffin, croaking sardonically "Walk him along, Johnny, carry him along; carry him to the burying ground".

The influence exerted on Lambert by Heseltine has been stressed in earlier pages, and the atmosphere Gray evokes in his anecdote is precisely that which Lambert wanted to convey in *King Pest*. The cumulative excitement of this Rondo makes an effective contrast with the final movement, the Saraband "Adieu, farewell earth's bliss", ushered in by bleak chords on the harps like the tolling of a funeral bell. It is in this movement that the solo baritone makes his appearance. The slow swaying of the music is punctuated by the refrain "Lord, have mercy on us". The mood is black: even when the chorus sings of the consolations of religion the soloist breaks in with a cry of "I am sick, I must die". The music ends very quietly on a high A, returning to the same single note with which the whole work began.

The first performance took place at Queen's Hall on 29th January 1936. The artists were Roy Henderson, the Philharmonic Choir and the BBC Symphony Orchestra under the composer. The rest of the programme, a curious one, was made up of Matthew Locke's *Music for His Majesty's Sackbuts and Cornetts* and Mendelssohn's *Die erste Walpurgisnacht*, both works conducted by Boult. From the viewpoint of the average concertgoer it was not an enticing programme. To be fair to those who planned it, it may be that their choice of the Mendelssohn work was made on the principle enunciated by Professor Grumbelius in Lord Berners' novel *Count Omega*.[1] Lambert was most unfortunate in the date of his first performance: George V had died on 20th January, and the concert took place between the death of the King and his funeral. People were in no mood for concert-going, and the papers were devoting little space to artistic matters. Most of the audience who assembled in Queen's Hall connected Lambert with two things: a vivacious and exuberant choral work (*The Rio Grande*) and a witty and entertaining book (*Music Ho!*); for it must be remembered that the new piece was Lambert's first on a large scale to come before the public for six years. The audience was confronted with a work which, despite the rhythmic impetus of some of its movements, was fundamentally "serious" and pessimistic. Had they been familiar with Lambert's *Piano Concerto*, they might have been less surprised, but most of them were not. Disconcerted, they gave *Summer's Last Will and Testament* a lukewarm reception, and the critics were more respectful than enthusiastic. Lady Wimborne, Walton's patroness, gave a party for Lambert after the first performance, but there was no disguising the fact that there was no triumph to celebrate.

---

[1] The Professor is commissioned by the millionaire Count Omega to arrange the first performance of young Emanuel Smith's Symphony. He tells the composer: "I have already drawn up the programme of the rest of the concert. It will be composed of the works of the great composers but I have purposely selected the most trivial and tedious so that they may serve as a foil to your own composition." His choice falls on Beethoven's *Weihe des Hauses* and Brahms' *Serenade*, Op. 16 ("a tedious work").

1. Constant and Florence Lambert arriving at Covent Garden for the first night of *Schwanda the Bagpiper* (1934).

2. (*Above*) Constant Lambert (1933).

(*Below*) Florence Lambert (1933).

3. *The Rio Grande* at Sadler's Wells, with Margot Fonteyn, Walter Gore and Beatrice Appleyard. (Victoria and Albert Museum, Crown Copyright.)

4. Angus Morrison by Maurice Lambert, R.A. (*c.* 1925).

5. (*Above*) "The Five Year Plan": an evocation of life in Soviet Russia by Florence and Constant Lambert and Anthony Powell (at the wheel).

(*Below*) Lambert in the character of a jealous husband interrupts a flirtation between his wife and Anthony Powell.

6. Part of Salome's Dance from the incidental music for Wilde's play which Lambert composed in 1931. The first three bars show the phrase which Lambert later used in the *King Pest* movement of *Summer's Last Will and Testament* (original ms.).

7. Lambert and Michael Ayrton working on *The Fairy Queen* 1946.

8. Humphrey Searle by Michael Ayrton (1965).

9. *Tiresias*, Scene I, with Michael Somes and Margaret Dale.

10. Studies for a portrait of Lambert, by Michael Ayrton (1946).

Summer's Last Will and Testament is Lambert's most ambitious work, an "urban pastoral" whose theme seems perfectly suited to his talents. But despite its many beautiful pages it lacks the urgency of the *Piano Concerto*. The first four movements form a satisfactory sequence and the final Saraband is moving, but in the central part of the work, the second Madrigal and the Rondo, the quality of the inspiration declines. Effective as *King Pest* is as a *genre* exercise in theatrical horror, it lacks the "charnel" quality its creator sought to convey. Lambert wrote the names James Joyce and Hogarth on his score for this movement, but it suggests far more the writings of Mrs Radcliffe or, at best, Poe. The staginess and theatricality of *King Pest* gravely detract from the impact of the work as a whole, so that what might have been a creation of blazing conviction and power becomes yet another exercise in that elegiac vein so abundantly represented in English choral music.

A fortnight after the first performance of *Summer's Last Will*, Lambert conducted his new Liszt ballet, *Apparitions*, at the Wells (11th February 1936). With its Ashton choreography and Cecil Beaton sets it scored a triumph ("the biggest success we have ever had at the Wells", wrote Lambert). He had selected the music, though it was orchestrated by Gordon Jacob. Some of the pieces chosen, like *Unstern* and *R. W.-Venezia*, were almost unknown at that time, and represent Liszt at his most daring and experimental. Lambert's sense of theatrical effectiveness was a major factor in the success of the ballet.

A passion for Liszt brought Lambert and the young Louis Kentner together about this time, and they became friends. Kentner had recently settled in England, and Lambert wrote a glowing notice of a Liszt recital he gave in London. This appeared in the *Sunday Referee* for 11th October 1936. Shortly afterwards Lambert and his wife entertained Kentner to dinner, and the two men found that they had in common not only their devotion to the Hungarian master and a highly emotional reaction to music in general but many other things, including a love of cats. Kentner went down with Lambert to a Liszt concert in Oxford the following month.

The story of this concert shows the trouble to which Lambert was prepared to go for a cause that he thought worth while: he possessed a generosity which is rarer among musicians than one would think, or wish. At that time Humphrey Searle was an undergraduate at New College. Much later he was the driving force behind the Liszt Society, which was formed in 1950 with Lambert as a founder member. The young Searle's feelings about the music of Lambert and Walton were akin to those of Denis ApIvor, which have been quoted on an earlier page. Searle had sung in a performance of *The Rio Grande* by the Oxford Opera Club (the conductor was Trevor Harvey, the pianist Joseph Cooper, and Robert Irving played percussion). Searle had recently become interested in Liszt, partly through reading Sacheverell Sitwell's book on him, partly through seeing *Apparitions*. He decided to organise in Oxford a concert of little-known and experimental music by Liszt to commemorate the 125th anniversary of his birth. He therefore wrote to Lambert, whom he had not met, to ask him if he would come to Oxford and conduct the *Malediction* for piano and strings. The concert was also to include a number of piano pieces, including the *Csárdás Macabre*, which Searle had reconstructed, using Liszt's incomplete autograph manuscript in the British Museum and a four-handed version Searle had found in the Liszt Museum at Weimar. Lambert wrote back agreeing to conduct and making some suggestions about the rest of the programme. Shortly afterwards the two men met and on 5th October Lambert wrote again:

> About the Liszt programme. It is a mistake to begin with *Nuages gris*, one of the most experimental and quietest of the pieces. If I were you I should start off with the *Wehnachtsbaum*. As regards this I imagine you are only doing a few of the best. Some of the Christmas ones are very bad and I suggest you confine yourself to *Polnisch, Hongroise, Abendglocken, Carillon* and *Jadis*. . . . I see you are doing the *Chromatic Galop*. . . . I suggest getting hold of the version for 2 pianos 8 hands which is a riot. The programme as a whole is most interesting and I very much hope to be able to help you. The only thing that would prevent me would be fuss concerning the new ballet at Sadler's Wells which comes on the next Tuesday.

The five pieces from the *Wehnachtsbaum* Lambert mentions were all used in *Apparitions*. The première of *Nocturne* (10th November) did not stop Lambert from going to Oxford, and the concert took place at the Carfax Rooms on Sunday, 8th November. Irving[1] played the

---

[1] Irving had gone down by this time and was helping with the British Music Drama Season presented by Albert Coates at Covent Garden in November–December 1936. Irving later became a ballet conductor at Covent Garden and a colleague of Lambert's before going to America as conductor of the New York City Ballet.

Malediction and the *Csárdás*, rather nervous, he says, because Kentner was in the front row. Lord Berners came over from his house at Faringdon, and Sacheverell Sitwell and Cecil Gray were also there. Despite the musical conservatism of Oxford, the concert was a great success and sold out.

Up to this point in his career Lambert had never conducted opera at Covent Garden: his only appearance there had been to conduct an interlude at the ballet in 1929. Beecham, who was in control of the 1936-7 winter season, invited Lambert to conduct Puccini's *Manon Lescaut* for three performances (4th, 7th and 12th January). Lambert agreed. He read the small print of his contract and came up with the following rhyme:

> Though at last I've been honoured by Beecham,
> I still may fall short of the prize
> Through war, epidemic, a fire in the theatre,
> Riot or Royal Demise.

Royal Demise had played hell with *Summer's Last Will*, and as luck would have it an influenza epidemic occurred in London during the opera season and houses were small. But *Manon Lescaut* was performed as planned, and Lambert, though "battling with a somewhat under-rehearsed ensemble" (Richard Capell) and with competent rather than brilliant leading singers (Augusta Oltrabella and Piero Menescaldi) acquitted himself well. "His interpretation had the great merit of bringing out all the life of the score" wrote Francis Toye in the *Morning Post*; "he played the music as if he loved (as I am sure he does) every bar of it; and that is the only way to do proper justice to Italian music in particular." Lambert loved Puccini at a time when it was fashionable in British musical circles to look down on him as a vulgarian. Unhappily Lambert had the opportunity to conduct only two more operas in the theatre during his lifetime.

Meanwhile he was preparing a new ballet for Sadler's Wells. This was *Les Patineurs*, first given on 16th February 1937, with music by Meyerbeer, chosen by Lambert from two little-known operas, *L'Etoile du Nord* and *Le Prophète*. The music from the latter had originally served as an accompaniment to a skating spectacle on a frozen lake, and was therefore completely appropriate. The ballet was an immediate and lasting success, thanks to Ashton's choreography and the cheerful melodiousness of the pieces Lambert had selected. *A Wedding Bouquet*, with words by Gertrude Stein, choreography by Ashton and sets and costumes as well as music by Lord Berners, followed on 27th April. Lambert was again in the pit. At these early performances the words were sung by a small chorus, but later, during the War, when the work was given with two pianos and there were no singers available, Lambert recited the text. He did this with such style that even when the Company regained an orchestra he continued to recite. It was perhaps as well that Miss Stein was never present at the wartime performances, for Lambert did not regard her text as sacrosanct and was apt to interject comments of his own. On one occasion the dancer playing the maid was taken aback to hear the words "Webster, your shoes are creaking!" issuing from Lambert's stage box. In June the Sadler's Wells Company were in Paris for the International Exhibition, and Lambert directed the première of Bliss's *Checkmate*, a ballet which, despite the cuts in the score which Bliss had made at Lambert's suggestion, was very far from being to the French taste.

That summer Lambert and his wife went with Ashton to stay at Raimund and Alice von Hofmannsthal's house in Austria. Mr von Hofmannsthal is the second and only surviving son of the poet and dramatist Hugo von Hofmannsthal, the collaborator of Richard Strauss, and his wife, who had been Alice Astor before her marriage, was a friend and patroness of Ashton. It was not a large house party: the idea was that Lambert and Ashton should work on a projected ballet, and neither their host nor hostess was expected to be there. In fact Mr von Hofmannsthal unexpectedly joined the party, which consisted therefore of himself, Ashton, Lambert, Lambert's wife and the baby Kit. For various reasons the situation was electric, and no one was in good spirits. So far as the Lamberts were concerned, he had begun to fall in love with a dancer and was weary of his marriage. His wife, aware of this, responded by making scenes. Things eventually reached such a pitch that Mr von Hofmannsthal picked Mrs Lambert up bodily and deposited her outside the house, where she was soon joined by her luggage. She returned to England with her child, while Lambert remained behind in Austria and continued to work on his ballet. When he returned to London he moved into a flat in Hanover Lodge (which he liked to refer to as his "shooting-box" or as "Hangover Lodge"), a large house in Regents Park belonging to Alice von Hofmannsthal where Ashton already had a flat. Lambert provided grounds for divorce by spending a night in a hotel with a woman hired for the purpose (they played cards all night) and the marriage came to an end. There appears to have been no lasting rancour between Lambert and his former wife, though there was a good deal of amusement later on when she married a Mr Hole (her nickname had been "Mouse"); and during the War, when the former Mrs Lambert was in uniform, headlines such as "German army advancing on Florence" were greeted by Lambert with gusts of laughter.

Neither Lambert nor his former wife showed a great deal of consistent enthusiasm or talent for parenthood, and the boy Kit came to regard 42 Peel Street (where his grandfather, aunt and uncle lived) as home. So far as Lambert's feelings for his son went, it should be recorded that on one occasion he went to a performance of *Boris Godunov* and was in tears during the scene of Boris and his young son, but without wishing to appear uncharitable one must say that when a man drinks as Lambert did and reacts emotionally to music as he reacted tears are often not far away. Momentary outbursts of this kind relieve the feelings but are no substitute for sustained care and attention. On the other hand Marie Nielson has written that "he used to take great care in choosing the books he took when he went to see Kit at school. I have never known an adult who could discuss the subtleties of Père Castor and Beatrix Potter as Constant could."

The next eight or nine years of Lambert's life were dominated emotionally by a deep and passionate affair with the dancer already mentioned, which disintegrated finally only shortly before Lambert's second marriage in 1947.

The collapse of Lambert's first marriage provided peace of a kind but left him far from happy. It was about this time that Denis ApIvor first met him, having been introduced into Lambert's circle by Cecil Gray. ApIvor describes himself as "an 'observing eye' who saw suffering and threatening disaster", never far distant from someone he held dear. At the time he first met Lambert he was a medical student, and subsequently a qualified doctor. Dr ApIvor specialised in anaesthetics, and Lambert used to say of him that he put people to sleep by day, unlike certain other composers who put them to sleep in the evening. ApIvor continues:

As a doctor I observed him and his way of life, and dreaded the worst. When I first met him we had been having dinner at Pagani's with Cecil Gray and went subsequently to Gray's home in Porchester Gate. On the way back in the taxi, Constant asked for my opinion about a certain drug for insomnia, a condition with which he was apparently all too familiar at the time. That was the first time I heard about the troubles, both mental and physical, which ailed him throughout his life. When one considers the matter dispassionately, he was really ill equipped to have to contend with the appalling life of drudgery of the workaday ballet conductor, and in that sense he was as much and more the victim of fate as any of us who have to grub a living and find the time to compose. He was extraordinarily sensitive and nervous. If dipsomania is a real illness, either of psychoneurotic or metabolic origin, as is believed in many quarters today, Constant was never fit to contend with life the way he had to. He used to say that he enjoyed drinking, and so to all appearances he did – yet he always seemed to me to be of all people the one who really needed to drink to dull a sort of over-awareness and over-sensitivity. He had fits of terrific depression, and when he was not depressed his most frequent bane was "boring" circumstances or "boring" people. The volatile and uproarious side of his character, of which I have never seen the like, was probably at least fifty per cent of himself, but on the above analysis at least a part of it was due to the urgent necessity of avoiding the ever-present abyss of ennui, leading to a vortex of depression.

Pagani's, in Great Portland Street, was a favourite resort of music cians and artists (Busoni used it a good deal). During the wartim- bombings it was destroyed, but an offshoot, also, though unofficially, called Pagani's, was still used by such people as Lambert, Edward Clark and Dylan Thomas. It profited from its proximity to Broadcast- ing House. Another restaurant patronised by Lambert was the Casa Prada, in the Euston Road, near Warren Street tube station. The pro- prietors had hit on the engaging idea of taking the signatures of the many famous artists who ate there and embroidering them into table- cloths which were then hung as décor on the walls. Humphrey Searle often saw Lambert lunching there on Sundays. They invariably ate separately, but frequently joined each other for coffee. They had very long conversations: on one occasion Lambert recited limericks, his own, Heseltine's and others, for two hours without stopping. On another occasion he insisted on their visiting Madame Tussaud's, where he sang (in a discreet *mezza voce*) the music-hall ditty about the man who went to the Chamber of Horrors every Saturday to see "the statute of dear old Ma". Sometimes Searle and Lambert went back to Hanover Lodge and played through absurd pieces on a mini-piano of which Lambert was very fond.

The ballet on which Lambert and Ashton had been working in Austria received its first performance at Sadler's Wells on 27th January 1938. This was *Horoscope*. The printed synopsis reads as follows:

> When people are born they have the sun in one sign of the zodiac, the moon in another. This ballet takes for its theme a man who has the sun in Leo and the moon in Gemini, and a woman who also has the moon in Gemini but whose sun is in Virgo.
>
> The two opposed signs of Leo and Virgo, the one energetic and full-blooded, the other timid and sensitive, struggle to keep the man and woman apart. It is by their mutual sign, The Gemini, that they are brought together and by the moon that they are finally united.

Lambert was interested in the occult and in astrology; they appealed to the romantic in him. There is an interesting if somewhat overwritten passage about him in the autobiography of Cecil Gray; though justly stigmatised by Angus Morrison as "a far-fetched and inaccurate character study" of Lambert the man, it has some relevance to *Horoscope*:

> He exhibits . . . a disconcerting blend of the most opposite extremes imaginable – a *fin de siècle* Frenchman with morbid *faisandés* tastes, and a bluff and hearty roast-beef-and-Yorkshire Englishman; Baudelaire and Henry Fielding combined, Purcell and Eric Satie, Ronald Firbank and Winston Churchill (to whom he bears an uncanny physical resemblance) . . . This schizophrenic, Manichean, ambivalent dichotomy is attributed by its somewhat (and no wonder!) harassed possessor to the fact that the date of his birth coincides, horoscopically, with the moment of the change from the zodiac sign of Leo to that of Virgo.

Whatever gave Lambert the idea for *Horoscope*, its subject is admirably suited for balletic purposes: there is enough plot, but not too much, and the action provides opportunities for sharp musical and choreographic contrasts.

The music begins with a short, eerie Prelude, a palindrome. Lambert told Searle that it had been dictated to him by Bernard van Dieren after that composer's death (April 1936). The piece is certainly quite unlike anything else Lambert ever wrote. There follows a Dance for the Followers of Leo, a brilliant, energetic movement, with a short solo for the Young Man to a march-like theme. The next movement, the Saraband for the Followers of Virgo, is a delicate, melancholy dance. The next pair of dances is a Variation for the Man, aggressively masculine in style, and one for the Woman, marked *Andante molto espressivo*. Then comes a Bacchanale, the first cousin of the Dance for the Followers of Leo. The repeated figure with which it opens sounds curiously like a much-accelerated version of the stealthy, sinister introduction to Stravinsky's *Oiseau de Feu*. The reminiscence was probably unconscious. In the Valse for the Gemini, Castor and Pollux dance to a melody whose use of tied notes over bar lines suggests a French *valse à deux temps*. After a *pas de deux* for the lovers, not a high point of the score and omitted from the concert suite, the ballet closes with an Invocation to the Moon and Finale, which begin mysteriously and build up to a great climax before dying away into silence.

The ballet was a great critical and popular success. Margot Fonteyn, to whom the score is dedicated, danced the Young Woman, Michael Somes the Young Man; the Gemini were Richard Ellis and Alan Carter, the Moon Pamela May. The sets and costumes were by Sophie Fedorovitch. *Horoscope* is the most finished of Lambert's ballets. It is admirably designed for the theatre, rhythmic, colourful and melodious. Until all his music faded into what one trusts is only a temporary oblivion the Concert Suite of five movements was the most often played of his works, apart from *The Rio Grande*. Lambert conducted this Suite at the "Proms" on 8th August 1938, and it is excellent light music – of which the twentieth century has produced little. *Horoscope* was as much a product of the romantic side of the 1930s – the decade of Garbo, Cecil Beaton and Rex Whistler – as was *Pomona* of the more astringent 1920s. Yet when one listens to the score analytically one grows aware that the music relies excessively on certain harmonic and rhythmic devices, notably the division, in fast movements, of common time bars into two threes and a two, and the use of triadic movement in the harmony (a mannerism one finds elsewhere in Lambert). *Horoscope* cannot compare for interest with the *Piano Concerto*, *The Rio Grande*, the *Li Po Poems* and parts of *Summer's Last Will* and *Tiresias*, but it is most effective as a ballet score. Unhappily the full score of the com-

plete work was lost, with the sets, in Holland in 1940, and does not
appear to have been reconstructed, though the Concert Suite is still
occasionally played. The ballet has never been revived: Ashton considered doing so for the twenty-fifth anniversary gala of the Sadler's
Wells Ballet in 1956, but rejected the idea. Lambert wrote one other
work in 1938, a short *Elegy* for piano, but *Horoscope* was his last large-
scale composition apart from the controversial *Tiresias*.

By now Lambert's friends Marie Nielson and Cecil Gray had married. During the summer of 1938 Mrs Gray's doctor ordered her to
stay in bed for a week, and as Gray needed a holiday she suggested that
he and Lambert should go over to France. Gray took Lambert to see
an island in the river at Chinon in Touraine which he and his wife
loved. Whether because of the gentleness of the French countryside,
the melancholy in himself, or the unaccustomed experience of being,
at least for a little while, unharried by money worries, Lambert almost
ceased to talk. He simply wanted to lie on the grass and dream. Disconcerted by the altogether unexpected phenomenon of Lambert without conversation, Gray returned to Paris, and wrote to his wife saying
that for all he knew Lambert was still lying on the grass in Touraine.
He had not said when he would be coming back to England. But in the
end he had to drag himself back and resume his London life, one in
which he was perpetually pressed for time and money and barely alone.
Gray's enjoyment of France in 1938 had been clouded by thoughts of
approaching disaster; it was the time of the Munich crisis. Lambert too,
with his francophile tendencies, hated what was happening in Germany.

Lambert was asked to conduct *The Rio Grande* at a festival at Frankfurt in June 1939, but refused, and tried, without success, to stop his
music being performed there at all. "I have the very strongest objection
to a note of mine being played in Germany under the present régime",
he wrote to Alan Frank of the Oxford University Press.

In 1939 Sadler's Wells mounted the full-length *Sleeping Princess* of
Tchaikovsky, the first non-Russian company to do so. There was a
royal gala at the Wells for Queen Mary on 2nd February, and on 22nd
March the Company moved to Covent Garden for another gala, this
time for the President of France. The entire work was considered too
long for the occasion, and so only Acts I and III were given, though
time was found for Beecham to conduct Debussy's *Ibéria* between the
Acts. Lambert was in charge of the London Philharmonic Orchestra
for the ballet. He had wanted the sets to be entrusted to Edmund Dulac,

and had this been done the results might well have been very attractive. Unhappily he was overruled (presumably by de Valois, always stronger on administration than on taste) and the décors by Nadia Benois were drab and dreary to a degree. This talented artist, who had done excellent work for Rambert, was quite unsuited to the Tchaikovsky ballet. Once again it was possible to gauge, if only negatively, the excellence of Lambert's visual instinct.

He returned to Covent Garden on 3rd and 11th May to conduct his second Puccini opera, *Turandot*. The cast was a good one: Eva Turner in the title role, José Luccioni as Calaf and Mafalda Favero as Liù. He restored certain passages that were usually cut and received good notices. The *Daily Mail*, for example, spoke of his "masterly command and great insight" and called it a "memorable performance".

Soon afterwards the ballet company embarked on a provincial tour, and Lambert was in Liverpool when war broke out between Great Britain and Germany.

VIII WARTIME AND AFTER

On the outbreak of war the Sadler's Wells Ballet re-formed at Cardiff and embarked on another provincial tour – six evening performances and three matinées in each town. In the absence of an orchestra the accompaniment was provided by two pianos, played by Lambert and the rehearsal pianist, Hilda Gaunt. Tours of this kind were to be a feature of the Company's existence during the war. A number of other pianists helped out – Angus Morrison, Mary and Geraldine Peppin, Harold Rutland and Marjorie Reed – but the main burden was carried by Miss Gaunt and Lambert. The latter complained in letters to friends that while he could conduct quite adequately after heavy drinking (as indeed he could), temporary abstinence was necessary if he was to acquit himself properly at the keyboard. No one who experienced the train journeys of the war years is likely to forget them. Everything took longer than it had in peacetime and the carriages were often in semi-darkness or even totally blacked-out. The dancers were often cold and hungry. Ashton and Lambert passed the time on this particular tour by reading the Bible, not always in a devout spirit; but from their reading came an idea for a new ballet, the music for which Lambert asked Walton to arrange from the works of Bach.

Travelling by train with Lambert in wartime was an eventful business. The painter Michael Ayrton tells the story of a journey they undertook together:

> One dull morning early in the year 1944, the Sadler's Wells Ballet Company reached Stoke-on-Trent in the course of its winter provincial tour. At that time I was myself working on the designs for the ballet *Le Festin de l'Araignée* for the company and had been asked, for reasons connected with the production, to travel up to discuss matters. Constant was going to rejoin the company as one of the two pianists who, during those bleak years, substituted for an orchestra. We decided to travel together and after a start which was delayed by Constant having inadvertently set light to a chair in his studio, and a late lunch at Pagani's restaurant in Great Port-

land Street, we arrived at the railway terminus exactly one hour and twenty-five minutes before the train was due to leave. Constant insisted on being in time for trains. We settled ourselves in an empty carriage and became deeply involved in a discussion of the relative merits of cats and fish and their representation in Oriental art. To my surprise, Constant pleaded the cause of fish as ideal pictorial material; the reason, it became gradually apparent, being that he had spent many profitable hours while on tour with the ballet, in learning to draw fish. Jealously, I proposed that my mastery of cat draughtsmanship was bound to exceed his amateur efforts, even though he had the advantage of that relatively easy vehicle for virtuosity, the stylised fish.

As the train began to move, Constant produced paper and pencil and executed in outline a small but lively carp. Between us, alternately, we drew cats and fish for some time until the available paper was exhausted. The argument was not exhausted. As dusk fell, Constant inscribed in pencil above the carriage door, a small goldfish, seen head on. Gradually, fish of many varieties and cats posed in numerous ways, came to decorate the available wall space. Night came on and we worked like Cro-Magnon man in total darkness. Occasionally, by the light of matches we inspected our work. Small cats appeared, riding large fish. Small fish were revealed inside large cats. Fish bit cats. Cats sat on fish.

In due time, only the ceiling remained virgin and it was not without difficulty, for we were both heavily built, that we climbed each into a separate luggage rack to continue, like twin Michelangelos, to draw upon the vault. At some time during this period of creative frenzy, the train drew up at a station and an elderly lady entered. Seeing no seat occupied, she relaxed comfortably and took out her knitting. Poor lady, she assumed the carriage was empty. She was wrong. The luggage racks were filled with reclining draughtsmen, but it was not until Constant observed that the ceiling was over-crowded, that she became aware of this. She disembarked and one can only be thankful that the train was still standing in the station.

Lambert's friends Alan Rawsthorne and Hyam Greenbaum and their wives had taken a house in Bristol. Both Jessie Hinchliffe (the first Mrs Rawsthorne) and Sidonie Goossens (Mrs Greenbaum) were players in the BBC Symphony Orchestra, then based at Bristol. Until they were bombed out Lambert stayed with them when he was within striking distance of the town. He spent the Christmas of 1939 in the country with another friend, Tom Driberg, the journalist and politician, but returned to London on Boxing Day for a short season, with orchestra, at the Wells. The outstanding event of this month of performances was the première of Lambert's second Liszt ballet, *Dante Sonata*, on 23rd January 1940. The music was an orchestration by Lambert of the elaborate *Après une lecture de Dante, Fantasia quasi Sonata*, which Liszt published as the last piece in the second volume of his *Années de Pélerinage* for solo piano. The ballet, with its theme of the conflict between the Children of Light and the Children of Darkness, and its Flaxman-inspired designs by Sophie Fedorovitch, caught the mood of the time perfectly. The emotional atmosphere it generated helped to keep the Company's morale high during the exhausting and often dispiriting tour that followed. This lasted until April, when the dancers came back to Sadler's Wells once more, and gave (on the 24th) the first performance of Walton's Bach ballet, *The Wise Virgins*.

In May there occurred the most dramatic incident in the history of the Wells company. They went to dance in Holland, at that point a neutral country, and were there when the Germans invaded. The dancers had to return hastily to England, abandoning, among other things, the décor and full score of *Horoscope* and that of *Dante Sonata*. Fortunately Louis Kentner (the soloist at the première) and Lambert had already recorded the Liszt work, and it was danced to records until there had been time to reconstruct the score: the set and costumes which were simple were re-made.

Lambert recorded a talk about the Company's adventures for the BBC. In it he described the morning of the invasion. There was a feeling of unnatural calm; they had all left Arnhem at midnight and travelled to the Hague. At about 3.30 A.M. the Germans attacked. Lambert and his colleagues watched from the roof of their hotel, some still in evening dress, others in dressing-gowns, as the parachutes, incendiary bombs and leaflets began to fall from the sky in the early dawn. The dancers did not know what chance they had of escaping to England – were they aliens or allies? After two days of waiting in a Hague full of spies and fifth columnists, they drove in dangerous circumstances to a cargo boat which brought them safely home. Lambert himself seems to have been the only "casualty": his war wound took the form of a speck of cigar ash in an eye, and he came down the gang-plank bandaged, somewhat to his embarrassment. His experience in Holland bore fruit in the form of an orchestral piece two years later, the *Aubade Héroïque*.

The male dancers were fast disappearing into the Forces, and Lambert and de Valois therefore decided to devise a comedy ballet with few demanding male parts, emphasis on the women dancers and an excellent role for Helpmann. This was *The Prospect Before Us* (first given, at the Wells, on 4th July), a comedy of eighteenth-century theatrical life using music arranged by Lambert from the works of his old enthusiasm, William Boyce. Its success was a tribute to the inventiveness and practicality of its creators, working in very difficult circumstances.

It is not surprising that in these conditions Lambert found time to compose very little music. In April, just before the visit to Holland, he made a setting of the Dirge from *Cymbeline*, "Fear no more the heat of the sun", for tenor and baritone soli, male chorus and strings. It was dedicated to Patrick Hadley, and first sung that year at Hadley's Cambridge college, Caius. In its very limited span this is one of Lambert's most moving works, personal in its utterance but imbued with the influence of Heseltine.

A less fruitful and perhaps surprising influence appeared in the score for a film which Lambert also wrote in 1940, though he made alterations to it subsequently before it achieved its final form: *Merchant Seamen*, originally called *Able Seamen*. In view of Lambert's well-known dislike for the English folksong school one would hardly have expected the shadow of his old teacher, Vaughan Williams, to make an appearance in his music at this late stage, but appear it did. Perhaps the subject-matter of the film, a semi-documentary about the Merchant Navy, did not appeal to Lambert; perhaps he felt that it called for a self-consciously "English" manner and therefore wrote a deliberate pastiche, just as he later composed pastiche-Russian music for *Anna Karenina*; perhaps he regarded it as hack work. At all events he produced a score which, while perfectly adequate as film music, completely lacks the distinction of Walton's work for the cinema. Lambert extracted a Concert Suite of five movements from it. After the *Fanfare*, a "salute to the heroism and gaiety of the Merchant Navy", there followed *Convoy in Fog*, a sombre piece with clarinets in their lowest register over a pedal note on piano and drums. *The Attack* was based on a scene in the film during which a ship is torpedoed. After *Safe*

Convoy, a seascape, the suite ended with a *March*, a straightforward movement with a "Celtic" tune as its trio section. The Fanfare betrays its authorship by its occasional reminiscences of *Horoscope*, but the rest of the Suite might be by any one of a number of English composers working dutifully but without inspiration.

In 1941 the ballet company found a fresh home at the New Theatre, and for the rest of the War they alternated seasons there with provincial, and, later, foreign tours. In 1943–4, for instance, they danced for forty-eight out of fifty-two weeks. During the second half of the War Lambert acquired assistants to help with the conducting (Julian Clifford in 1942–3, Alec Sherman in 1943–4 and Geoffrey Corbett from 1944 onwards) but it was an exhausting life for a man who was never physically strong. At the same time he was taking charge of concerts with the BBC Symphony and London Philharmonic Orchestras at Bristol, Cambridge, Bedford and other provincial towns. Nor were the programmes necessarily routine: the emphasis, partly because of the wartime mood and partly because of Lambert's own taste, was on French, Russian and English music, and there were a number of unusual and interesting concerts. In Cambridge, on 11th February 1942, for example, Lambert conducted Britten's *Sinfonietta*, his own *Piano Concerto* (with Kentner as soloist), *La Création du Monde* of Darius Milhaud and the first performance of Roberto Gerhard's suite *Don Quixote*.

About this time Lambert moved back to Peel Street to live for a time with his mother, who was now seventy, but his ballet and concert engagements often took him away from London. Marie Gray wrote of an unexpected visit Lambert paid to her house in the country about this time:

In the early days of the war we were sitting late one night in the Windmill talking with Walter Legge, who was our weekend guest. He suddenly asked if Constant was coming that weekend and we said no. Shortly after, the door handle banged and although I don't know how he got there at that time of night I wasn't surprised to hear Constant's voice. He had been to a wedding reception, then taken a negress to a swimming bath and felt a proper conclusion would be to sleep in a windmill – so there he was. Could he have a toothbrush? His case contained a score he was working on and six ties. One never knew what kind of day the next one would be or what mood one would be in and it was necessary to have the appropriate tie.

The score may have been that of the *Aubade Héroïque*, which Lambert wrote in 1942 and dedicated to Vaughan Williams on his seventieth birthday ("a fact which, to be quite frank, is relished by neither of us" wrote Lambert in a letter to Felix Aprahamian). The title was suggested by Debussy's *Berceuse héroïque* in honour of King Albert I of the Belgians and his soldiers (written in 1914). The choice of a French title, Lambert said, was not an affectation: "any English translation would become something like Auden or MacNeice and God defend us from that!" A note in the score says that "this short piece was inspired by a daybreak during the invasion of Holland, the calm of the surrounding park contrasting with the distant mutterings of war". The ballet company, writes Angus Morrison,

> were marooned for a few hours in a beautiful mansion standing in a park, with trees and lawns and wild deer grazing by a lake at daybreak. The contrast of this idyllic scene and the momentous events that were already shaking the world made a profound impression on him (Lambert) and out of it he fashioned a flawless little masterpiece. It has the dream-like quality of some exquisite Chinese painting, for although the distant mutterings of war are heard from time to time the urn-like stillness of the surrounding scene is never broken.

The work recalls its dedicatee in its pastoral character, and, as Richard McGrady has pointed out, the distant and ominous fanfares foreshadow similar effects in the slow movement of Vaughan Williams' *Sixth Symphony*.

Ashton joined the RAF, and to fill the gap Helpmann, the ballet company's *premier danseur*, began to turn to choreography, assisted with musical and theatrical advice by Lambert. He produced three ballets in 1942, all danced for the first time with orchestra in London. The first was *Comus*, first seen on 14th January. Helpmann wanted a subject that would permit the introduction of speech – he had already been successful as an actor and now wanted eventually to move in that direction – and his friend the producer Michael Benthall proposed Comus as a subject. Milton's original *Masque of Comus*, first performed at Ludlow Castle, had music by Lawes, but Lambert felt that music by

Purcell would be more suitable for a ballet. He therefore chose pieces from seven of Purcell's theatrical works and orchestrated them for the present purpose. The ballet had handsome designs by Oliver Messel, and was a success. *Hamlet* followed on 19th May. Leslie Hurry designed striking neoromantic sets and costumes, and the ballet, which showed the crucial events in Hamlet's life as a phantasmagoria passing before his eyes at the point of death, was a triumph. Tchaikovsky's overture, proposed by Lambert as music for the ballet, contributed greatly to its effect. On 24th November *The Birds*, with music by Respighi, was produced, a slighter affair altogether but again well received.

Lambert himself had little time to write ballet scores, and he asked Walton to write an original ballet for the Company to dance. This was *The Quest* (first performance 6th April 1943). Ashton, on leave, took charge of the choreography, John Piper of the sets. But the ballet could hardly be described as a collaborative effort. Walton was staying at Ashby St Ledgers, Lady Wimborne's house near Rugby, and his score arrived in bits and pieces by train. When the music for the final scene was slow in appearing, Walton helpfully sent a message that it would be composed of about two hundred bars of slow music in the manner of Vaughan Williams. The whole score was well below Walton's best standard, and this, combined with the somewhat improbable casting of Helpmann as the patron saint of England and the complications of the plot (based on *The Faerie Queene* of Spenser) ensured a rather short life for the work. It disappeared soon after the War. On the other hand the revival of *A Wedding Bouquet* was most successful.

Lambert had occasional opportunities to relax a little. Loving animals, he often visited the London Zoo, where he especially admired an orang-outang named Spike. In July 1943 he was in Manchester where he met Mr Gerald Iles, Superintendent of the Belle Vue Zoological Gardens, who wrote in 1954:

> Margot Fonteyn and Robert Helpmann had been to the Zoo to name two zebras, but after Helpmann had seen a llama he insisted that he must name that animal, which bore such a striking resemblance to himself, rather than a zebra! Miss Fonteyn named the other zebra after herself. . . . The following day Mr Lambert 'phoned me from his hotel to say that the two ballet stars had told him that they had had a delightful day in the Zoo and that there

was still a zebra spare without a name, and he wondered, as he adored animals, whether he might come along to the Zoo and name the remaining animal. I was delighted with his suggestion and so it was arranged. . . . After this initial visit Mr Lambert never failed to come to the Zoo as often as possible. . . . His passion and love for animals was almost matched by his delight in riding on our amusement devices. One particularly devilish device we have here called the "Octopus" captured his eye, and he insisted on having a ride. I had previously sampled the machine and decided never to go on again, but my duty as host compelled me to accompany Lambert on this occasion, and the ride attendant gave us a particularly long session, so that Lambert was soon calling for me to stop the thing as he was suffering from vertigo. I was pleased, however, that he was not very much upset by his experience, for he conducted at the ballet that night as well as ever.

Mr Lambert was particularly interested in small mammals and he was very much attached to a ring-tailed lemur called Lena which we had here at the time. I photographed him holding this animal and, on the same occasion, took one of him holding a python. . . . During one of his visits to the Zoo he saw our sea-lions go through one of their performances which concludes with a sea-lion playing *God Save the King* on a "Hornchestra", a specially made instrument consisting of trumpets which sea-lions can play by pushing the valves with their noses. Lambert was enchanted and promised to go straight back and write a special fanfare which the sea-lions could play at the forthcoming Circus. Unhappily he never lived to do this.

Lambert was also very fond of cats. He was President of the Kensington Cats' Club, and owned a number of cats at various times in his life. One of the last, which survived its master, was called Captain Spalding; the allusion is to a scene in a Marx Brothers film, when Groucho, arriving at a party in a litter carried by four dusky bearers, is greeted with cries of "Hurrah for Captain Spalding, the African explorer!" Three other Lambert cats were named Aimée, Semple and McPherson, after the well-known American evangelist. In a radio talk on "Cats in Music" Lambert inveighed against the "I love little pussy, her coat is so warm" school of cat-lovers, and extolled the masculinity of the cats of Russian folklore, notably the beast called Mr Samson Cat who formed an impromptu but happy partnership with the Widow Wolf and appeared as a character in Lambert's early ballet *Mr Bear Squash-You-All-Flat*.

In the first two months of 1944 Lambert composed incidental music for a production of *Hamlet* by the Old Vic Company at the New Theatre. Having scored a great success in the ballet of that name, Robert Helpmann wished to act the part, and did so in this production by Tyrone Guthrie and Michael Benthall. The other leading parts were taken by Pamela Brown (Ophelia), Margot Grahame (Gertrude) and Basil Sydney (Claudius). Lambert was offered a grotesquely low fee, and after a financial haggle produced a score that was the most conventional kind of Shakespearian incidental music, consisting of little more than fanfares, short songs and brief march-movements. It has no life outside the theatre.

Lambert's private life was not proving easy. He found living at Peel Street somewhat constricting, and was anxious to move. A favourite family story concerns an incident which occurred at about this time: Lambert's small son came downstairs for breakfast one morning and greeted his father with the words "Hello, pompous". This guileless remark completely disconcerted Lambert, who for days afterwards kept buttonholing friends and asking them if there was any truth in the suggestion. More seriously, it was not easy to carry on his affair with the dancer from the ballet company under his mother's roof. This also was not without difficulties, and at the risk of being accused of vulgar speculation one cannot help wondering whether Lambert's drinking must not have had an adverse effect on his virility. It is worth noting that though he had several affairs in his life he fathered only one child, or two at the most.

During the early years of the War Lambert had become friendly with the young artist Michael Ayrton. It was thanks to Lambert that Ayrton was commissioned to design the sets for Andrée Howard's ballet *The Spider's Banquet*, to Roussel's score, which was first given at the New Theatre on 20th June 1944. Lambert's colleagues had scarcely heard of Roussel, and were dubious about the choice of a young and at that time little-known painter as designer, but Lambert pushed the decision through. He and Ayrton found each other very sympathetic, and on his provincial and foreign tours Lambert sent Ayrton a series of postcards and letters. From Glasgow in November 1943 he wrote:

Extract from letter from my mother – "Kit has been indulging in black magic on Allhallow E'en which he seems to have enjoyed." What a family.

From Leeds a few days later Ayrton received one of those postcards (now seldom seen) which look as though they are made of some form of grained plastic:

This, I like to think, effectively disposes of our theory that the English landscape does not lend itself to plastic treatment. Do you know the work of F. H. Sikes? (You will soon).

On 13th January 1944 Lambert wrote from Peel Street:

What *mouvementée* lives lorry drivers seem to lead. On top of the man who stole (and in my opinion very reasonably) budgerigar seed in order to grow deadly nightshade, there is the lorry driver in tonight's *Standard* (actual cutting lost, alas) who after being married for three weeks got into his lorry and drove it at his wife. He was only given 4 months which must have been a disappointment. Did you notice, by the way, that the march in Barnby's *Rebekah* is called "The *Bride's* March"? Not Bridal March or Wedding March as you might hastily be led to suppose. It shows more insight into "feminine psychology" than I had previously credited the old boy with. I gather the old girls have got into a cabal . . . Joan rang up . . . at teatime. I gave imitations of FISH through the glass of the stage door and took down the conversation in shorthand on my shirt-cuff.

In spite of all the turmoil and strife we hope to make that Feb. weekend if physically possible. It all depends, alas, on Ensa.

If I don't see you before we will meet at the Gluepot on Friday.[1]

Very shortly after writing this letter Lambert moved in to share Ayrton's house at 4, All Souls Place, which no longer stands but had been used by Weber when completing *Oberon* on his fatal visit to London in 1826. Lambert, who remained there for over two years,

---

[1] Lambert referred to his female friend as "the old girl" or "my old girl" ("O.G." for short). The "Gluepot" was, and is, the nickname for the "George", a public house close to the site of Queen's Hall and to Broadcasting House and much used in former times by musicians. It owes its second name to Sir Henry Wood, whose players tended to "get stuck" there.

confirmed the arrangement in a letter written in London on his return
from a visit to Cambridge (27th February 1944):

Formal agreement enclosed as requested. I also agree to the comparatively reasonable clauses in the codicil which, however, has
certain *lacunae* you may have cause to regret when you are woken
up by the sound of *The Entry of the Gladiators* or *Boy Scouts of
Wisconsin, Forward Forever* on the Marimbaphone (not to mention
the dozen Singing Mice I purchased yesterday).

I am here (en route to Derby) to do a bit of eleventh-hour
recording with the man Legge. My address next week will be the
Midland Hotel, Derby, but the New Theatre is always a safe
business address.

Do get this week's *Picture Post* – it has some photographs of
that R.C.M. rehearsal including 3 of V.W. which make Breughel
look like Olive Snell and one of myself, cutting my throat while
conducting Humphrey Searle.

I envy you your fires – I am in an absolute fury at missing them.
I was sorry to hear the R.C.M. missed it but was consoled by the
fact that all the windows have been blasted so that the professors
have to teach in overcoats and catch influenza. The Fish with an
Ear for Music gave me a slight jolt the other morning, first of all
being introduced by one of the monoglot cretins at the University
Arms as "Mr Grossvoor" and then entering my bedroom in battle
dress and a hangover carrying under his arm a framed Medici print
which he presented to me with the conversational gambit "Is this
a Tintoretto?"

Without being a Borenius I was able to assure him that it ante-
dated Tintoretto by about 150 years, being one of those typical
Italian things with a parched landscape in the background, a rather
ineffective miracle in the middle distance, the foreground occupied
by a lot of pansies having a cocktail party, playing nap and getting
off with the waiter etc. Apparently K. Clark or CEMA or whoever
is responsible send the paintings down with a list of the titles but
fail to attach one to the other so a good time is had by all with
highbrow ATS labelling Rubens as Paul Nash and vice versa.

I'm glad to hear that the costumes . . . are finished – you must
show them to me the next time we play *Billiards Russe*. As regards
the drop curtain I propose not shooting until I see the off-whites of

their eyes. Please put your trust in a hardened old campaigner. The orchestration of the missing insects is being entrusted to Gordon Jacob who will do it well and carefully. I frankly can't manage it myself.

. . .

War on Two Fronts. This has now reached the stage of that famous welter-weight contest at Elsinore, viz. rapiers *and* daggers. To make things worse the two old girls in question are quite obviously going to GET TOGETHER with, I presume, pretty dire results for me. There are times when I seriously think of going back to my negress in the Fire Service.

Yours ever
Constant.

P.S. The semi-bombed-out cloakroom at St. Pancras has, pasted over it, the statement "No one is more profoundly sad than he who laughs too much". Without for one moment doubting the apothegm I can't really think the attendant has been burdened with undue hilarity on the part of his clients – he certainly wasn't this morning.

"The man Legge" refers to Walter Legge, who produced many of Lambert's records for Columbia and HMV. The "fish with an ear for music" is the late Alan Rawsthorne, then a sergeant in the Army and stationed near Cambridge, who had seized the opportunity to escape from his military colleagues for a day and go to see Lambert, ostensibly to ask him to identify a picture (which Rawsthorne knew perfectly well was not a Tintoretto).

Apart from his second marriage, which was also a comradeship, though not without its disagreements, Lambert's strongly emotional relationships, which were almost always with women, were not among his most successful. He established far more satisfactory *rapports* with colleagues and drinking companions like Ayrton and Rawsthorne, and with others less close to him but sympathetic in attitude, like some of the actors who played the clowns in his version of *The Fairy Queen*. Where sexual relationships were concerned he was apt to enter into them in a mood of high romanticism and then to discover painfully that everyday reality could not be made to fit with his original concepts: the result was distress for him and for the women he loved.

After *The Spider's Banquet* the next important balletic event in which Lambert was concerned was *Miracle in the Gorbals*, the dance drama by Helpmann, Arthur Bliss and Edward Burra which received its triumphant first performance in October 1944. It is doubtful whether the work would revive well after thirty years, but the three components coalesced to a remarkable degree, producing a *Gesamtkunstwerk* worthy of Diaghilev though far removed from his aesthetic. It was very well received in Eastern Europe after the War was over, though the French, predictably, disliked it.

It was about this time that Lambert began to broadcast for *Music Magazine*, then, as now, edited by Anna Instone.[1] He took the chance to speak out for his own enthusiasms, and during the period from 1944 to 1950 he talked on the air about Sousa, Suppé, Chabrier, Elgar, Walton, Berners and Puccini's *Manon Lescaut*.

Towards the end of 1944 Lambert flew to Southern Italy to conduct orchestras at Naples, Bari and other centres. The journey began at Lyneham in Wiltshire. John Pudney, the poet, was one of a party of prospective passengers who assembled in a requisitioned country house near the airfield. When a heavily-built figure smoking a cigar appeared the party at first thought it was Randolph Churchill, but it proved to be Lambert in khaki. He took his uniform seriously enough to practise saluting, and was chagrined to discover that the officer to whom he had to report on arriving in Italy was the reverse of military in manner. One day Lambert entered the "Gluepot" in uniform and was far from delighted to be greeted with cries of "Hello, Randolph!" But whether Lambert liked it or not there were similarities in appearance and manner, while both he and Churchill had been strikingly good-looking as youths and in later years showed the effects of frequent and heavy ingestions of alcohol.

Lambert and Pudney spent a long, wet weekend in Wiltshire. They had to sleep in a dormitory and were not permitted to walk more than a mile away from the house in any direction. Even then they could not speak to anyone they met. The melancholy deepened when Lambert discovered a piano in what had been a nursery and proceeded to play *Sheep may safely graze* over and over again, with ever-increasing sadness. As Lambert descended the gangway at Naples most of the music he was carrying was caught by the wind and ended up in the mud, but he and Pudney managed to reassemble it, and the Bari concert, which Pudney attended, would have been a great success had the lights not failed four times during the performance. In one of these blackouts

---

[1] The final edition of *Music Magazine* was broadcast on Sunday, 25 March, 1973.

Lambert could be heard at the piano playing *Sheep may safely graze* yet again, as an interlude between the Purcell, Handel and Vaughan Williams.

He wrote to Ayrton from Naples:

> You, my dear Michael, are naturally conversant with *Achilles in Sciro* by Pietro Metastasio and Domenico Sarro which, as every schoolboy knows, opened the San Carlo on Nov. 4th, 1737. But did you know that it was "a work subsequently hooted off the stages of almost every Opera House in Europe"? I like to think that the rare exceptions were due to *apathy* rather than admiration. Old Sarro seems to have had as much stamina as the brothers Ricci (or, for that matter, myself).
>
> The Aquarium here is a dream, and contains a museum of skeleton catfish, cuttle-fish, octopods, etc. (looked after by a man like Spoletta) which knocks the slats off Ernst, Miró, Dali and the boys. The guide book (your Christmas present) is second only to Goya Popular Painter. In the section labelled "Hermit Crabs" you get the following:— "the anemone, too, gets her share, for she walks around on the agile legs of her friend; and this is not only an unexpected pleasure for a beast condemned to sit still throughout life – these promenades bring a more material gain" . . . The entire work is up to this standard.
>
> If you see the man Gray, tell him I don't write because I don't wish to depress so typical a specimen of the *diavolo incarnato* as himself. He will understand. The strains of the American national anthem are floating through the window as I write. Naples occasionally reminds one of a London Telephone box and for the same reason . . .

Lambert's relish for the absurd shows very strongly in this letter. The brothers Ricci, Federico and Luigi, were Neapolitan composers; among Federico's operas was one called *La prigione d'Edimburgo*, based on *The Heart of Midlothian* and containing a once-famous barcarolle with the title "Sulla poppa del mio brick". Another interest, shared by Lambert and Cecil Gray, was Pietro Raimondi, a composer of vast output whose masterpiece was a trilogy of oratorios, *Potiphar, Joseph and Jacob*, designed to be performed either separately or simultaneously, according to taste. We are told that their reception was only moderate when they were given one after the other, but when they were combined (engaging the efforts of nearly four hundred musicians) the excitement of the audience knew no bounds and Raimondi fainted with emotion. Only death prevented Raimondi from putting the finishing touches to his "opera seria" *Adelasia* and his "opera buffa" *I quattro rustici*, also designed for simultaneous performance. "Goya Popular Painter" was a publication which had delighted Lambert with its unintentional humour. The message to Cecil Gray, who loved Italy, refers to the proverb "inglese italianato, diavolo incarnato" – "an Italianate Englishman is the devil incarnate".

There was another bulletin, from Bari, marked "3:00 A.M. 10/12/44":

Sunny Italy to you! The shindy made by the Adriatic plus complete lack of light, heat and water reminds one of a really ham version of *Wuthering Heights* by Cecil B. de Mille. Lights have just gone on hence late hour of script. Do you know this part of Italy? Superficially dull to begin with it ends up like a cross between the D. of M. and the more sinister parts of Wiltshire. Modern Bari is absolute hell – the old parts are terrific. Every conceivable influence from Moorish to Norman with neither of them knowing whether they were coming or going. Tomorrow I go to Brindisi and hope to see some odd sights on the way. Particularly the Trulli or conical houses.

All the slang in the dialects here is derived from English or Celtic. The old slang, I mean, not the OKAYS with which you are greeted by the brats in the slums. All the players in this orchestra (and for that matter the instruments) remind one of early paintings by you, so I feel quite at home.

Statues here of Piccinni and Mercadante are knock-outs. "YUGOSLAVIAN WINE SHOP" "Branded Liqors – Strong Drinks – Nobleman Assortment" is an encouraging sign.

Do you know the Palermo guide *Short History of the Catacombes?* The very curious sight HOW THEY DID THE MUMMI-FICATION. (Tried to get a copy but have copied out best bits.) Love to the old girl. Hope all goes well. Slightly harassed at the moment.[1]

---

[1] The "D. of M." is a reference to Webster's *Duchess of Malfi*, which Ayrton was illustrating at this time. The mixture of Moorish and Norman was something which Lambert was able to observe again on a visit to Palermo in 1949.

Rome proved as bizarre as the other places Lambert visited:

> I had idly thought that a journey of some 100s of miles by 'plane
> would have transported me to a grove of oranges, lemons, buxom
> peasant girls and chianti rather in the style of the paintings near
> King or is it Duke St.[1] Far from it. I am sitting in the freezing cold
> at an ebony wash-stand lit only by a dim ship's lantern, pestered
> by a charming but highly Baudelairian cat and surrounded by more
> books on Black Magic than I have ever seen before.
>
> My host, John Rayner, is in hospital at the moment following a
> mild car accident between Naples and Rome. . . .
>
> The electric light (1 hr. per day) has just been put on by the
> weeping Transylvanian maid so I hope my writing improves.
>
> To-morrow I am going to see a surrealist redhead . . . surrounded
> by cats and engaged in doing drawings for private editions of the
> old Marquis de S. It all goes to show.
>
> Rome is even stranger than Wiltshire (where I spent 3 days
> waiting for a 'plane. Goodness me!)
>
> Had fun in Naples at the opera. Ever seen *La Gioconda*? It is full
> of property boats. Final par. in libretto goes "As she falls to the
> ground the spy yells over her body 'Yesterday your mother
> offended me and I have drowned her!' but La Gioconda is already
> dead."
>
> Why is it that I can't lead a simple life?
>
> Love to the old girl.
>
> Yours
>
> CL.
>
> P.S. Cassino is remarkably like that painting you did of bad teeth
> inspired by Liszt's D. of D.[2]

Lambert was abroad again in 1945, with the ballet company to
France, Belgium and Germany, and on his own to Poland. The latter
trip was a success, though their distinguished visitor's drinking alarmed
the Polish players, not teetotal themselves. Cecil Gray, too, was
worried. He wrote to Ayrton:

---

[1] The pictures Lambert had in mind were genre paintings of the kind one
still sees in certain galleries in St James's, depicting merry rustic scenes,
gourmandizing cardinals and jovial monks. The artist engaged in
illustrating Sade was presumably Léonor Fini.

[2] Liszt's "D. of D." is his *Totentanz* for piano and orchestra, a work much
admired by Lambert, Ayrton and Gray.

I have seen Constant several times lately. He still goes up and down in his usual disconcerting fashion. The last time I saw him – two days ago – he was in great form; the time before very much under the weather. But taking the situation by and large I do not like the look of it at all. His emotional instability is becoming "chronic", as charwomen say. Of course we are all the same, but he takes it a stage further than the rest of us.

He was obviously in ebullient mood when he wrote to Ayrton, on 13th September 1945:

> Good news from home, I read with tears
> From friends I hadn't seen for years
> (Genuine ballad *circa* 1890)
> Telephone (tenant's) was installed 3 p.m. by a sexagenarian midget (ex-French-Horn player in the guards) who congratulated me on my playing of Prokofieff. The extension is on its way. No lights yet. Only liver.

Despite Lambert's ample experience he was still extremely nervous before going on to the platform to conduct. Taking part in the "Proms" was therefore an ordeal for him. The Henry Wood Promenade Concerts had been abandoned in 1944, but they resumed in 1945, and that year and the following one Lambert was an Associate Conductor. In 1945 he conducted ten concerts, completely or in part, with both participating orchestras, the BBC Symphony and the London Symphony. Much of the music he was allocated was to his own taste (like the *Sinfonia Concertante* of Walton and Borodin's *Second Symphony*) but he took his fair share of "standard classics" and, ironically, was asked to give the British première of Hindemith's overture *Cupid and Psyche*. The last night of the "Proms", 15th September, was shared by three conductors, Sir Adrian Boult, Basil Cameron and Lambert himself. Lambert's share included his friend Rawsthorne's *First Piano Concerto*. On the 17th, Lambert described the occasion to Ayrton:

> I am not sending on any letters as I fear that they might cross with your return. They look pretty dull anyhow and seem to lack financial and/or sexual appeal. I gave your address to C. B. Rees whose Baroque-cum-Cymric charm grows from day to day.
>
> The last night of the Proms was fantastic – rarely have spectators been so dithyrambic. You have possibly read of the wild orgy in which "the three conductors were pelted with flowers".

139

I have kept, as a souvenir, a large yellow chrysanthemum which caught **** **** a neat whang on the nose. May I point out (in hasty parenthesis) that autumn treasures thrown by enthusiasts at short distance can be more painful than the casual observer might be led to suppose. My own theory is that the whole thing was led by a gang of highbrows who objected to our *tempi*. I beat a retreat before they got on to the earthenware.

Old Fishface had a good call after his concerto (which in my humble opinion knocks the slats off **** ****, **** **** and the Girls). It was very well played by Phyllis Sellick and I was delighted to see that it had a bad notice from W. Glock...

MEA CULPA, I broke (though very slightly) into your bottle of Ronsonol. I think you will excuse me. I came back after the last night of the Proms *tout seul* and found I had damn all. Neurasthenia as usual had the better over my moral self. The *lacuna* will be restored ere your return. I have now got something of my own and in the immortal words of the late E. Lear

"He drinks a great deal of Marsala

But never gets tipsy at all."

NEWS FROM FAR AND NEAR

Philip Hendy (!) is apparently going to be the successor to Sir K. Clark. How much is the job worth? It might solve the problem of what to do with my child.

Your edition of the D. of M. was reviewed in the Observer under the heading "Black Magic".

The Emperor of Japan (bless his soul) is, we are told, renowned for his "excursions into marine biology".

Hoping this finds you as it leaves me viz. 47 sheets in the wind.[1]

An undated letter from the same period returned to the subject of Japan:

I hope that you (as a well-known follower of seismographical disturbances) will have had the prescience (to say the least) to observe that the sunsets this week have only been equalled by the ones following that rather grave earthquake in (only the other day), Japan.

---

[1] Philip (now Sir Philip) Hendy became Director of the National Gallery in 1946. "Old Fishface" is Rawsthorne.

It just shows what the atomic bombs can do. I am not being facetious (far from it). I thought you might appreciate this rare example of visuality on the part of a musician.

In October 1945 the Managing Director of the Australian Consolidated Press (publishers of the *Sydney Daily Telegraph* and the *Sydney Sunday Telegraph*) invited Lambert to spend six or seven weeks in April, May and June the following year conducting a symphony orchestra which was being formed in Sydney. Lambert declined, pleading pressure of work in Britain. It is tempting to speculate on what might have occurred if he had accepted, but in truth highly unlikely that he would have felt able to settle in Australia, even if he had been asked to do so. There was the family connection, it is true, but he would have been able to find few friends of his own temperament in Sydney or Melbourne.

He took on a series of concerts with the Hallé Orchestra in February 1946, but his major task was to train a largely inexperienced orchestra for the reopening of the Royal Opera House with a new production of *The Sleeping Princess* by the Sadler's Wells Ballet. There were to be spectacular new sets and costumes by Oliver Messel, and on 20th February the Company enjoyed one of the greatest triumphs in its history: one which reflected on de Valois, on Fonteyn, who danced Aurora, and on Lambert. From this point Covent Garden became the home of the ballet company. The intention was that when opera performances began Lambert should share conducting responsibilities with the Austrian, Karl Rankl, but, as will be seen, this arrangement got off to a bad start and Lambert conducted only two operatic productions.

During the 1946 "Prom" season Lambert took part in seventeen concerts; he was responsible for several first performances or British premières, including John Ireland's overture *Satyricon*, the suite from Bliss's ballet *Adam Zero* (which Lambert had conducted at Covent Garden) and more Hindemith – the *Symphonic Metamorphoses on Themes by Weber*.

On 29th September the BBC Third Programme came into being, and Lambert was an obvious choice to conduct concerts of little-known music for it. Humphrey Searle, who was working for the BBC at that time, obtained his services as often as he could. During the first fortnight of the Programme's existence Lambert conducted a concert of

Liszt rarities, and over the next five years he took part in many concerts as conductor or speaker. The composers represented ranged from Purcell to Berners, from Marschner to Benjamin Frankel. The programmes are so interesting that they have been listed in Appendix IV. Two particularly memorable performances were those of Warlock's *The Curlew* on 11th June 1947 and Liszt's *Faust Symphony* on 23rd December 1949. It was the first time Lambert had been able to conduct the latter work, with its personal associations for him. At one stage Lambert contemplated a Faust opera, and when Basil Ashmore suggested to him that he might consider the alternative idea of setting Heine's ballet text on the subject of Faust he received the proposal enthusiastically: but it came to nothing.

Often there would be two rehearsals in the same day, followed by a live broadcast in the evening. As the day progressed the atmosphere would change. At the morning rehearsal Lambert would slump in, slightly late and rather gloomy, and things would go wrong. After the mid-rehearsal break matters would start to improve, and by the afternoon they would be much better. But he always saved something up for the performance, which would be a great improvement on anything that had happened during rehearsal. Lambert also broadcast for the BBC Overseas Service, and introduced some of the programmes with the general title *Musical Curiosities* designed by Searle with the intention of bringing a little humour into the musical side of the Third Programme, which was inclined at times to be portentous. His most important broadcasts as a speaker were in *Façade*. By the 1940s Lambert's interpretation and his voice had deepened, and he had also acquired the habit of introducing at what he conceived to be appropriate points imitations of such persons as Winston Churchill, John Ireland and the late Professor Dent – "moving in classical metres" in "When Sir Beelzebub" was recited in Lambert's "Dent" voice. There was no malice in this, for Lambert was on the best of terms with both Dent and Ireland.

During the second half of 1946 Lambert's main preoccupation was one very dear to his heart: the first operatic production to be seen at Covent Garden after the War, a production of Purcell's *The Fairy Queen*. Lambert suggested it because it would employ three companies – dancers, singers and actors – and only at a theatre like Covent Garden could the mechanical side of the enterprise be properly handled. The work was full of magnificent music, and the resources of Covent Garden "gave one at last the opportunity to present the public with a whole evening of Purcell and to present him not as a museum piece but as a still vital theatrical figure". The preparation, culminating in the première on 12th December, occupied six months of Lambert's artistic life, during which he worked closely with the choreographer, Ashton, and the designer, Ayrton, whose house he was still sharing. This was the grandest result of Lambert's passion for Purcell, which had already produced two ballets and the 1931 *Dido*. He also gave some fine concert and broadcast performances of Purcell, including a full-length *King Arthur* on the air, with as much of the Dryden text as possible. Purcell, of course, is no longer neglected today, thanks to the admirable and sterling work of such enthusiasts as Britten, Pears, Imogen Holst and Philip Ledger. But Lambert was in the field long before them, and his greatest lesson – one that has been imperfectly learned – was to show that it was possible to play Purcell as full-bloodedly and uninhibitedly as Puccini without sacrificing stylistic rightness. By present-day standards he occasionally departed from the letter of the score in such matters as instrumentation, but his performances were invariably conceived and carried out in the right spirit, and they were never anaemic, mannered or effete; not did one feel that one was listening to Purcell filtered, as it were, through the gauze of another and a very different personality.

The Fairy Queen was presented in three acts and six scenes, and ran for three hours including two intervals. The libretto is a seventeenth-century hotchpotch, and had the work been presented in its original form it would have lasted at least twice as long. Purcell's music was naturally given priority. Lambert made a ruthless "acting edition" of the text, cutting the words to a minimum. He used Dent's libretto, which had restored as much of the original Shakespeare as possible, and collated it with Dennis Arundell's version, which, for scenic reasons, retained a certain amount of verse by the anonymous librettist. Theseus and the lovers were ignored; the action concentrated on Oberon and Titania, the immortals and the clowns.

Little of the music was sacrificed, but among the pieces that were dropped were the scene of the Drunken Poet and the duet for Coridon and Mopsa. One number from *Dioclesian* was introduced as a *pas de deux* for the Spirits of the Air (Fonteyn and Somes), another for a procession in Act Three. Dent collaborated on the instrumentation, and realised all the numbers where the harmony was indicated by figured bass alone. Lambert, assisted by Gordon Jacob, took charge of the rest. They introduced piccolos and tabor, but used them only for two "exotic" numbers, and a cor anglais, which, though anachronistic, was intended to represent its obsolete forerunner the tenor hautboy. Boris Ord played the harpsichord.

Act One contained a Masque of Night, Act Two a Masque of Love, Act Three a Masque of the Seasons. Ayrton decided to base his designs on those of Inigo Jones, because in his view it was fitting that the greatest English stage designer should, as it were, collaborate post-humously with the greatest of English composers. The anachronism worried few people and the designs were effective and often beautiful. The fifth living collaborator in the enterprise, with Lambert, Dent, Ayrton and Ashton, was the co-producer Malcolm Baker Smith, a qualified architect and a former art director for René Clair. The cast included Margaret Rawlings, Robert Helpmann, James Kenney, Michael Hordern, Edgar Evans, Constance Shacklock, David Franklin, Fonteyn, Michael Somes and Moira Shearer. The chorus were placed in two tiers on either side of the stage.

It will be clear that the entire project was Lambert's brainchild. Incredibly, it transpired not long before the opening date that David Webster, the General Administrator of the Opera House, planned to entrust the conducting of the work to the Austrian Karl Rankl, who had been appointed to take charge of the musical side of the Covent Garden Opera. Even in his native Austro-German repertory Rankl was hardly the most distinguished of conductors, and it would have been sheer musical folly as well as appalling tactlessness to hand over *The Fairy Queen* to him. Thanks in the first place to Michael Ayrton, this nonsense was prevented: the main performers (many of them by now friends and drinking companions of Lambert's) made it clear that they would not take part in the production unless its presiding genius was in the pit.

Lambert wrote:

> I can well see that some Purcell enthusiasts may accuse me of crimes of omission. All I can claim is that after a period of neglect lasting 250 years Purcell's major theatrical work was presented at our principal opera house not as a "period piece" enjoying its brief-lived *succès d'estime* but as a masterpiece of English theatrical art enjoying at last its rightly popular and spiritual due. The greatest

and most intelligent tribute I received was not from any academic source but from my local greengrocer, Mr O'Leary of Great Titchfield Street, who said, "What I liked about it was the balance of the thing. Not too much of anything. The right amount of singing, the right amount of speaking and the right amount of dancing."

Unhappily what pleased Mr O'Leary did not please everyone. Some of the solo singing did not meet Purcell's taxing demands. But the main trouble was that regular theatregoers, unlike Lambert's greengrocer, knew what they wanted to see before they even set foot in the theatre. Each of the three "publics" which attended wanted something different: the balletgoers were bored by the singing, the opera audience resented the dancing, and the Shakespeare-lovers from the Old Vic were appalled by the whole thing. Like all Purcell's stage works apart from *Dido*, *The Fairy Queen* presents immense problems to modern editors. The production was revived in Festival Year, 1951, with new choreography by John Cranko, and not seen thereafter.

During the winter of 1946–7 Lambert was at his lowest ebb, physically and mentally. Humphrey Searle remembers going with him from the BBC's Maida Vale studios to a pub for lunch, with snow on the ground. Lambert could scarcely walk, and as they trudged through the icy wilderness Lambert told Searle that he always called this part of London "Average Asia", having once seen a score of Borodin's orchestral piece with the title helpfully printed in three languages, thus:

IM MITTELASIEN   DANS L'ASIE MOYENNE
IN AVERAGE ASIA

One night after a concert Lambert had a long conversation with an orchestral player about edible fungi. The player promised to bring next day a book containing an illustration of a particular type of fungus they had been discussing. Next morning, at the rehearsal break – with Lambert not at his best – the player rushed up with the book open at a colour plate showing an enormous red toadstool with white spots. "There you are, Mr Lambert!" he cried. Lambert, with no recollection of the previous night's conversation, looked at the picture with horror and shuddered into a corner, saying: "What do you mean: there I am?"

Lambert was not only neglecting his physical appearance; as Professor Hutchings has made plain in his introduction to *Music Ho!* he was not necessarily an amiable figure at this time in his life. To some degree disappointment had soured him, and the reference to Mr

O'Leary's spontaneous enjoyment and instinctive understanding of *The Fairy Queen*, containing as it does an implied contrast with the reactions of professional musicians, is indicative of the way Lambert felt about much of the musical world. This state of mind resulted in apparent arrogance and sheer bad manners on occasion. At the end of the 1939–45 War Basil Ashmore was arranging some poetry readings with music, and wanted to perform *Façade*. Edith Sitwell suggested that he should get in touch with Lambert, who grudgingly agreed to see him; but when Ashmore visited Lambert the composer was both discouraging and offensive. *Façade*, he said, could not possibly be revived, and he sent Ashmore away without even offering him a cup of coffee. A year or two later, when Ashmore was drinking with Searle in a pub, and Lambert was also there, drinking alone, Searle introduced his companion to Lambert, not realising that they had met before. Lambert grunted and turned his back. But when Ashmore started to talk about Satie, who was almost unknown at that time, Lambert swung round and offered him a drink. The conversation continued for three hours, and thereafter Lambert was always courteous and friendly to Ashmore. This kind of behaviour seems to have been one of Lambert's ways of masking an intense sensitivity (the conductor Leslie Heward behaved in the same way at times). It is consistent with the sympathetic and understanding account of Lambert as a boy by his Housemaster quoted on page 33. The schoolboy, set apart by his lameness, used his sharp tongue "to amuse, to amaze and often to hurt"; the man, faced by the neglect of much he held dear and the success of much he despised, withdrew into a brooding hauteur, discarded instantly if a newcomer proved sympathetic.

Having taken charge of a production by the Sadler's Wells Ballet of Falla's *The Three-Cornered Hat*, with its choreographer, Massine, as the Miller (February 1947), Lambert escaped to Ischia for a holiday. Michael Ayrton went with him. There they renewed their acquaintance with Norman Douglas, then living on Capri. Lambert admired Douglas as a writer, and when the author of *South Wind* had been in London during the War, with very little money, Lambert, Ayrton and Cecil Gray formed a Norman Douglas Dining Club whose main function was to see that once a month Douglas had an enjoyable evening with an adequate amount of drink. Douglas seems to have been under the impression that his hosts were well off, which was far from being the case where Lambert and Ayrton were concerned, and since his capacity for drink was formidable the members of the Club found that they had to save money carefully against the monthly meetings. Ayrton painted while in Ischia, Lambert relaxed in the company of a Japanese soprano.

In May, after his return, there was a new production of *Turandot* at Covent Garden, which he conducted. Eva Turner sang the lead, as she had in 1939, Walter Midgley made a successful début as Calaf and Vera Terry sang Liù. Michael Benthall's production and Leslie Hurry's barbaric designs (so unlike the vapidly pretty sets with which the Webster régime later replaced them) added to the impact of the music. There were eight performances, the first on 29th May, the last on 1st July. Ralph Hill wrote in the *Daily Mail* that "both the Covent Garden Orchestra and the Opera Chorus played and sang with a vitality and a musical feeling which showed what can be accomplished under the right director" (not a remark calculated to appeal to Rankl). Indeed it was perhaps fortunate for the audience that Rankl had little interest in the Italian repertoire.

But all was not well. In the first place Lambert was drinking heavily. Curiously, the singers, orchestral players and dancers who worked under him at this time are agreed in saying that he was always in complete control in the orchestra pit (though his drinking cannot have been good for morale). Margaret Dale, a member of the ballet company at this period, concedes that if Lambert had been drinking before a performance the *tempi* might be a little slower than usual; but, she says, he was always consistent about such matters as the length of pauses and the relative timing between the sections of a ballet. One was aware from the first phrases from the pit how Lambert's general interpretation was going to go, and once that was established there was nothing to worry about on the musical side. Pamela May remembers how sensitive Lambert was to the needs of individual dancers: he always remembered that there was one section of Act II of *Le Lac des Cygnes* where she liked a slightly different *tempo* from the one favoured by Fonteyn. Dame Eva Turner confirms that Lambert was always "in command" of a performance, even when immediately afterwards he might be near collapse.

Alcohol was not the whole story. One night, conducting at Maida Vale, he had very little to drink, but when he went to his car he fell flat on his face in the snow. During the first American tour by Sadler's Wells, in 1949, he was in charge of a very taxing programme consisting of the whole of *Le Lac des Cygnes* and *Hamlet* as well; during the latter

147

he "blacked out" and had to be taken back to his hotel. On that occasion he maintained with pathetic earnestness that he had had nothing to drink. A member of the Company once found him lying outside a stage door in Liverpool. It seems likely that undiagnosed diabetes caused these comatose conditions. Lambert had suffered a great deal at the hands of well-meaning doctors as a boy, and he avoided them as far as possible. His diabetes, which was given as a cause of his death, was not established till then: there was no question of his forgetting to take his insulin, as was put about by some after he died – none had been prescribed.

There was a crisis in the summer of 1947. Accounts differ as to what actually happened. One of Lambert's senior colleagues is insistent that he was not asked to resign as Musical Director; it was merely felt that he should rest a little. On the other hand Lambert's future wife, the present Mrs Isabel Rawsthorne, states that he was given "the conventional way out"; either he could resign or he would be dismissed. She goes on to say that had she been one of those responsible for the running of the Opera House she would have acted as Lambert's colleagues did: "his physical and mental state at this time was such that he could not be relied upon to give *consistently* good performances". At all events Lambert wrote as follows to the late Sir David Webster on 2nd July:

As I explained to you this afternoon, I have with the utmost regret decided to leave the Sadler's Wells Ballet Company with which, as you know, I have been associated intimately for the last fifteen years and whom, if I may say so, I helped to carry through the very difficult war years at the expense of giving up my composing and conducting career. I feel now that the work is running on its own wheels and no longer needs the help of my experience. Among the many reasons which have induced me to take this decision have been the productions of *The Fairy Queen* and Puccini's *Turandot* in which, in sharp contradistinction to the balletic approach, I have received intimate collaboration and personal gratitude.

As I told you the other day I have taken on an important film which will involve my being free from the beginning of September to the end of November, so, apart from the preliminary work which I propose to start immediately after going abroad I will obviously be unable to give the hundred per cent support to the ballet which I have been able to give in the past. Since the situation has inevitably arisen I think it better that, howsoever regretfully, I should retire from my position as Musical Director and Conductor of the Sadler's Wells Ballet – though ,as someone who has been connected with it intimately for so many years, I shall always be pleased to give them my musical advice.

I am very sorry to have made this heavy decision. Please convey my regrets to the Trustees who I am sure will appreciate the sincerity of my inevitable action.

With very best wishes for the future of the ballet.

Both Sir John Anderson, who accepted the resignation on behalf of the Trustees on 21st July, and Webster, who wrote Lambert a personal letter, ignored – as one would have expected them to do – the sour note of this communication. Webster told Lambert that

the Sadler's Wells Ballet owes you an enormous amount of credit for the work they have done. Certainly no ballet company since Diaghilev has had such an outstanding list of musical works in their repertoire, and as far as English composers are concerned I am quite sure that never have they had such an innings with any other musical institution. It does you enormous credit. I remember hearing you many times in the early part of the war thumping on those pianos and I cannot imagine any greater work and labour, nor can I think of anybody else in the country of your standing who would have been willing to have given time to it. I personally am extremely happy that it is likely you are going to do more composing and I am sure the whole musical world will be glad also.

Since both men are dead there is no point in trying to conceal the fact that they disliked each other. The incident of *The Fairy Queen* had not helped, and Lambert's sense of humour grated on Webster, who did not like being referred to as "the Margravine of Ansbach". Nor, on the whole, did Lambert care for what might be described as the "musical businessman" as a type (Hubert Foss of the Oxford University Press was an exception, but then Foss was unusually gentlemanly for his trade). The kind of musical businessman who, as one of them put it, "liked tying up young English composers", filled Lambert with distaste. On one occasion he was passing the shop of a music publisher when he spotted the words "Cleaner required" in the window; it was with great difficulty that his companion restrained him from adding, in his unmistakable hand, the words "Experience Augean Stables Desirable". During his last sickness he did indeed, as was reported, ramble about *The Fairy Queen,* but not about the beauty of the music: rather about Webster's conduct in the matter. Lambert had made an immense contribution to the ballet company, damaging not only his musical career but his health thereby. It is difficult not to feel that his colleagues treated him shabbily at this point, and that they could have prevented his resignation if they had chosen to come to his support. They did not do so. Fortunately for them, if not for him, the bond was not to be completely broken for another four years.

Perhaps the greatest of his many achievements in this connection was to hold the balance between the two basic attitudes towards ballet, either of which, pushed too far, can debase the art form. During the years when Lambert was Musical Director, the Sadler's Wells Ballet never moved too far towards decorative abstraction, with music and scenery playing inferior roles. Nor did the Company's repertoire become overloaded with mere "dramas in movement" in which the choreography lacked distinction. The ideal was the Diaghilevian concept of a unity of three arts: choreography, music and décor. In this respect, as well as in the matter of musical standards, the Sadler's Wells Ballet would have been a very different and an inferior company without Lambert.

In October 1947 Lambert remarried. His wife was Isabel Delmer, whose marriage to the war correspondent Sefton Delmer had been dissolved the year before. Mrs Delmer, an artist, had been born Isabel Nicholas, and had been the friend and model of Epstein and subsequently of Giacometti. She had first met Lambert when she was about twenty, soon after the first performances of *The Rio Grande*. However she had gone to live in France in 1934, and returned to Britain only in 1940. While working in London during the War she had met Lambert again, but returned to France towards the end of the hostilities. Thus she and Lambert had not been close friends for long before their marriage. They had a good deal in common: an orientation towards France, stronger in her case than in his; the fact that they were both artists; and many friends. The second Mrs Lambert was of the left, while Lambert had no fixed political position, but many of his established friends were also left-wing. In his second marriage Lambert found an easy-going cama-raderie which suited him well, and at this time he made some physical recovery, even giving up alcohol entirely for some months; but this did not last. His mother and brother were less than enthusiastic about the marriage but Lambert was not inclined to pay too much attention to their views: he was after all over forty by now. Not long after the wedding the couple moved from Thurloe Square, whither Lambert had gone from All Souls Place, to 197 Albany Street, N.W.1. Albany Street is a long and pleasant road running alongside Regents Park, and the new house was a handsome one; it was therefore a shade misleading of Lambert to say, as he did, that he lived in Camden Town.

Denis ApIvor writes:

> When Constant married Isabel he came and lived a hundred yards or so from us, in Albany Street, and as a result I saw a good deal more of him. His favourite pub was the *York and Albany*. When he died, and I came into the bar and told the proprietress, she was very sad. "What a nice man he was!" she said, and then, in the same breath, "Must have spent five pounds here the other night."

He also used to like the *Edinburgh Castle*, a few paces from the *York and Albany*, because of an extraordinary Garden of Gethsemane which it possessed. At the end of this dreadful place ran the main line, and whenever a train passed Constant would totter across the few square yards of blackened paths, past the withered flower beds, and gaining the edge of the abyss he would peer down at the 7:45 or the 8:10 or what have you, on its way to Edinburgh or Glasgow. This attraction for trains must be almost unique among composers. But on fine evenings the *Edinburgh Castle* provided a beautiful view of the sunset, and it may be that he liked it for that reason also, as I remember him pointing out the colour of the sky on one occasion with an almost proprietary gesture.[1]

The film of which Lambert had spoken to Webster was a prestigious affair: *Anna Karenina*, directed by Duvivier, with a screenplay by Anouilh among others, costumes by Cecil Beaton, and Vivien Leigh and Ralph Richardson in the cast. The music used in the film fell into two categories: genuine Russian music for ball and theatre scenes (Glinka's *Valse-fantaisie*, the Overture to *Ruslan and Ludmilla*, parts of *A Life for the Tsar*, and the Prelude to *Eugene Onegin*) and Lambert's original music. The latter recalls Auric rather than Prokofiev in the sense that it is self-effacing rather than dominant film music; a great deal of it is modal in character, and there is a fair amount of appropriate and convincingly executed pastiche-Russian writing. Lambert's identity is sometimes betrayed, as so often in his work, by the cadences. The opening of the Venetian episode is accompanied by a Siciliana figure which Lambert later used for another brief love-idyll, that of the female Tiresias. Here it is called a *Forlane* – the Venetian gondoliers' dance of which the most famous instance in music is Ravel's, in *Le Tombeau de Couperin*.

Lambert's connection with the ballet was hardly broken: he was back at Covent Garden on 26th November to conduct the English première of Massine's "Mam'zelle Angot". At Christmas he and his wife began what was almost a tradition over the next four years: dinner on Christmas Eve at the Casa Prada, followed by a drive to Thaxted in Essex for midnight mass, at which Lambert wept copiously, and

---

[1] Intending pilgrims should be warned that the "York and Albany" has been modernized beyond recognition and it is no longer possible to see the main line from the garden of the "Edinburgh Castle".

then on to Tom Driberg's house at Bradwell for the holiday. The Bradwell visitors' book is full of typical entries by Lambert.

In May 1948 Lambert went north to conduct the Hallé Orchestra before going to Paris at the end of the month for his first holiday with his wife. He wrote from Manchester to his mother:

> The tour so far has been most successful and the general ambience far from unpleasant. The orchestra are not only first rate (particularly the strings) but an extremely pleasant crowd to be with. I stay in Manchester and go round with them by motor coach. Once out of Manchester it is lovely. Here to Sheffield over the moors and here to Morecambe through N.W. Lancashire are both very good trips, though Morecambe on a Sunday afternoon is not the ideal ambience for *Scheherazade*.
>
> No concert today so went to the Art Gallery.
>
> *Knock out* collection of Holman Hunts, and a very strange collection of medallion portraits in grisaille of poets by Blake. The portraits obviously copied from engravings, the fantastic decorations on each side obviously original. The gallery is more or less back to its old shape – *Birds in Flight* is on view again but not too well placed. – Side view against a wall, most irritating, but what can you expect from a gallery that states on a painting of Derain's that he died in 1916? What will London think tomorrow? Dashed off an interim present to Kit (2 Puffin books – all I could get).
>
> It's pleasant to be busy again.[1]

He wrote again twelve days later:

> So sorry not to have written before but this tour though extremely enjoyable and worth while in every way has been a little tiring and frequently after a long day's travelling and playing I have to sit up writing business letters including ones in French to Paris where I am conducting on June 3rd with an interesting modern English programme. Writing the programme notes in French was difficult but Isabel has corrected the grammar and they have been sent off in time.
>
> We go to Paris the day after my concert in London (Sunday week). It will be a great treat for both of us as we have had no holiday since we married and hope to stay for a few days after my hectic rehearsing. I have my last and most important Hallé concert

---

[1] *Birds in Flight* is a sculpture by Lambert's brother Maurice.

at the Opera House to-morrow. I gather it is practically sold out which is not bad for Whit-week in Manchester when they close down on everything except religious processions. Have been asked to do several concerts here next season including a large scale choral, orchestral and brass band concert in the circus ring at Bellevue. Hope to write a piece for the sea-lions at the same time (I have now got the entrée to their training quarters).

The working days have been hard but interesting. Days off in Manchester have been very dull apart from the Zoo but I have managed to get through business letters and read some Shakespeares which I knew only slightly or had forgotten. *Troilus and Cressida* is as marvellous as *All's Well That Ends Well* is boring. Now re-reading *Measure for Measure*.

Sent off a bird-book for Kit (serious illustrations and scientific notes) to atone for my rather perfunctory gesture.

Clifford (of London Films) wants to see me urgently re future prospects. So things seem to be looking up at last after a period which not unnaturally led to bitterness. Not that all is clear by any means but the combined invitations of the Hallé and the Orchestre National have consoled me for neglect in my home town.

As regards finance (which I loathe discussing as you know) your suggested present will be more than welcome and I hope it won't embarrass you in any way. It was unfortunate that I should have to pay double rent at a time when jobs were fading away. But with your help I shall be able to start on clear ground once again and with my life settled we shall both be able to concentrate on our work without worry and interference. I can't tell you how grateful I am. . . .

I was very sorry to see about Dick Wyndham and slightly irritated that all the papers referred to him as a reporter and never mentioned his painting which though not of great importance was very charming and highly competent. But after all even Andrew Marvell has a statue to him in which (I mean *on* which) he is described merely as M.P.

Must now brush up my Shostakovich and swallow what passes for food in this town.

In fact Lambert was to write no more film music. Kit Lambert was eventually sent to Lancing, on Tom Driberg's recommendation, but his father seldom saw him and he never stayed with Lambert and his second wife.

Lambert and Mrs Lambert enjoyed themselves in Paris, where both had many friends. He was able to renew contact with Darius Milhaud, and the concert (which included *Music for Orchestra*) was a success. On 18th June he accepted an Artistic Directorship of the Sadler's Wells Ballet at a fee of £500 a year, and there were to be guest appearances as a conductor as well. In the autumn he returned to Paris with Sadler's Wells to conduct at an ill-timed season at the Théâtre des Champs-Elysées (the Parisian theatre season had hardly begun) and stayed with his wife at a simple but sympathetic hotel in an unfashionable area. Lambert no longer felt completely happy with the ballet company. On 25th November he wrote to his mother:

> Just off for the opening of the ballet at Covent Garden, a place where I feel still slightly ill at ease, being received with the mingled welcome and suspicion that greets a cat that has been lost for a week.

After Christmas with Driberg he returned to the North for his series of Hallé concerts, which included works by Lambert himself, Russians he liked such as Balakirev, Glazunov and Liadov, and a *Belshazzar's Feast* at Belle Vue. When he appeared at Covent Garden on 24th March to conduct a revival of *Apparitions* he received a great ovation which can have left him in no doubt about the feelings of many of the ballet-going public, whatever reservations some of his colleagues within the Company may have had about him.

That year, 1949, the Festival of the International Society for Contemporary Music was to be held at Palermo, the capital of Sicily. Lambert was to conduct works by Lennox Berkeley, Mátyás Seiber and Searle. He went first to Paris, where he suffered severe stomach trouble, and when he arrived in Rome to rehearse the radio orchestra he was far from well. But he insisted on walking all over the Pincian Gardens to find the statue of the one-legged Italian motorcyclist (complete with cycle) heroically hurling his crutch at the Austrian enemy in the First World War. At Palermo the Festival authorities had put him and his wife into the Villa Igiea, a magnificent old-fashioned hotel on the western side of the city, approached via an insalubrious slum quaintly called Acquasanta. The hotel is set in large grounds overlooking the sea, under the rock mass of Monte Pellegrino. But the

Lamberts preferred the animation of Acquasanta to their hotel. It was in Palermo that Lambert finished his *Trois Pièces Nègres pour les Touches Blanches*, pieces for piano duet commissioned by the London Contemporary Music Centre and dedicated to Edward Clark, then President of the ISCM. Only the white notes of the piano are used, as the Satiesque title states, but Lambert managed to avoid monotony and the work is one of the finest of his small-scale pieces. There are an *Aubade*, a movement called simply *Siesta* and a *Nocturne*. The last deserves special mention, being most unlike Chopin and composed in a captivating quintuple rhythm of great verve and joyousness. Lambert stayed on in Sicily for a while after the Festival and came back to London in rather better health.

The new pieces were played by Mary and Geraldine Peppin at a concert sponsored jointly by the LCMC and the BBC in the Concert Hall of Broadcasting House on 17th May. Another first performance on that occasion was of the *Gold Coast Customs* of Humphrey Searle. Searle, who had dedicated the work to Lambert, wanted him to conduct it, but he chose to be joint speaker with the author of the poems, Edith Sitwell. He sat with her (she in a long gold cloak), reciting furiously against the music and conducting not only his distinguished co-speaker but the conductor of the orchestra (Leighton Lucas) as well. He was perhaps unwise to tax his strength in this way, but he enjoyed it, was as careless of his health as he was of his money, and liked to help other musicians in any way that he could.

It was about this time that he took up the cudgels on behalf of Satie once again. In recent years there has been a great revival of interest in this curious figure, and a good deal of his output is available on commercial records. In 1949 most English musicians knew little or nothing of his music and thought he was a joke (some, of course, still do). Lambert gave a talk on Satie for the BBC Third Programme and devised a group of three concerts, of which he himself conducted two. They included four first performances in Britain. Satie's most ambitious piece, *Socrate*, was one of these, and was broadcast on 17th June with Sophie Wyss, Megan Foster and a section of the London Symphony Orchestra under Lambert.

In the autumn the Sadler's Wells Ballet were to make their first visit to America, with Lambert in charge of the musical side. All the Company received visas without trouble, with two exceptions, of whom Lambert was one. At the American Embassy he was questioned about his visit to Poland after the War, but when the officials wanted to know what his father's initials stood for he was able to roar "George Washington". He got his visa.

The season was to open at the Metropolitan Opera House in New York on 9th October with a performance of *The Sleeping Princess*. Shortly after arriving Lambert wrote to his mother:

One's first two days in New York leave one with only two feelings:—

(A) A maniacal and continuous desire for iced water

(B) An even more maniacal and continuous desire to be translated immediately to some odoriferous slum in the south of Europe.

Everybody is most kind and nice. But I could not (as yet) feel more a stranger.

(Rends-moi le Pausilippe et la mer d'Italie.) (Gérard de Nerval.) Perhaps I am still suffering from the overlong flight which I only overcame by doping myself with Dr Child's pills.

Had my first rehearsal today at the Metropolitan.

Orchestra up to reasonable standard (about the equivalent to Covent Garden at its average) but most pleasant to deal with.

The town is extraordinarily beautiful by night, but during the day is rather drab. Not so modern or so chic as I had supposed. Rather suggesting a lot of buildings put up hastily for an International Exhibition and left there after the Exhibition had closed.

But as you know I am inclined to hasty prejudice.

He wrote again the day after the opening:

Opening night last night. Naturally great strain. First night nerves, no stage rehearsal, orchestra not too familiar with the music and a damp heat of over 80 degrees. But absolutely fantastic success from the start. Applause almost hysterical and record number of curtains. To one's great relief and surprise New York has been knocked sideways by the ballet as a whole and quite rightly by Margot in particular.

Notices exceptionally good particularly for this town where critics are notoriously "snooty".

(a) Seen on the first night. Gent wearing leopard-skin dinner jacket with white bow tie. (Presumably *not* one of those Englishmen who always dress for dinner even in the jungle.)

(b) The photograph of myself and cat in the programme bears

the rather ambiguous caption "Constant Lambert, guest conductor, and one of the artistic directors".

(c) "Even before the performance began, there was the reassuring figure of Constant Lambert at the conductor's desk" (The *New York Sun*).

At what stage of the performance, may I ask, do American conductors deign to put in an appearance?

There was a longer and more revealing letter to Mrs Isabel Lambert:

COLUMBUS DAY!!!

Darling Isabel,
Autobiography Chaps. III and IV (I don't think you've seen Chap. II yet).
III. Having spent 40 years before the mast I have no clear idea as to what it looks like, my behind having naturally been turned towards it. On the other hand I am an authority on the appearance of the bowsprit.
IV. There are certain things in life such as birth, fornication, and death which have their ups and downs. The only thing in life which can maintain a continuous level is *cafard*. Talk about *cafard*! Fortunately I am getting gradually acclimatized and can even distinguish between one street and another (which is more than most Americans do). I live rather symbolically between two avenues (both of which I have explored) – Park Avenue, which tries to be like Gloucester Gate without succeeding and Lexington Avenue which is vaguely like Camden High St. and quite frankly lets the whole fucking thing ride. I drink there rather gloomily after the show from time to time.

The only place in this curiously drab and *utterly dated* town (dated like an early UFA film or one of the more tedious works of Stravinsky) where I feel at home is the old Groucho Marx opera house, where fortunately I have to spend most of my time. . . . Wildly comic supper given us by the Irish anti-British Mayor of N.Y. in the garden of his super bungalow on East River. Telephone-pal Webster and Ralph Hawkes(!) literally crawling round me like lichen on an old church tower or slugs on a bunch of rhododendrons *(sic)*.

. . . Tonight after two *Sleeping Beautys* I can relax a little as I am only doing the middle part of the show including the *Aubade*

Héroïque which they play v. well. In *S.B.* the negro pages are done by actual negro children who are solemn, wide-eyed and enchanting.

Social life obviously going to be intolerable. Everybody I have met during the last 24 hours took part in *Romeo and Juliet* 1926. The only tolerable conversationalists are the taxi drivers. . . .

Gastronomic Notes

Food in general good and over copious but curiously tasteless and *sweet*. Much the best is the sea food which it is hard to spoil. They serve the blue-points with a tomato sauce to which has been added Lyles Golden Syrup in generous quantities but a really *Churchillian* scene will produce lemon and red pepper. *Pompano*, a flat fish like a small sole but with something of the texture of a tunny is well worth while. Deep sea scollops etc. all excellent. Californian Bergundy (sic!) disappointing. Chilian Riesling (no joking) excellent and is my staple beverage.

It has unfortunately been necessary to omit certain passages and names from this letter, but even in truncated form it conveys an excellent idea of Lambert's mood.

Lincoln Kirstein, who was at the opening night, wrote:

The hero of the occasion, according to Balanchine and myself, was Lambert; he had a fine band and the score never sounded so well; he is a genius for tempi; absolutely on the note in every variation; no boring bits; and he supports the dancers on the huge stage by giving them assurance with his authority. He whipped people up into applause, purely by sound; when nothing was really happening from a dancer he seduced everyone into imagining that she was divine. Anyway, he got an ovation; many people knew what he had done.

Lambert was indeed a conductor of great brilliance, and this despite the fact that he was almost completely deaf in his right ear. He was undoubtedly the finest British conductor for the ballet there has ever been, worthy to rank in this respect with Monteux, Ansermet and Desormière, who all conducted for Diaghilev. With his authority and enthusiasm, and the clarity, precision and strength of his beat, he played a much-abused repertory for all it was worth, and galvanised the dancers into giving their best. There seems little reason to suppose that he would not have distinguished himself equally in opera if he had been given the chance: what little he did was very good.

In the concert hall Lambert conducted so far as possible music with which he was in sympathy. His tastes were wide and eclectic: his fondness for the French and Russian repertory recalled Beecham, but he played far more contemporary music than Beecham did in later life and would frequently give highly professional and perceptive performances of music by friends and confrères whose aesthetic was far removed from his own. In temperament too he resembled Beecham in many ways, although Lambert, unlike the older man, was consistently kind and generous and incapable of spiteful public attacks on other musicians, such as those made by Beecham on Rankl and Kubelik. Lambert enjoyed conducting Haydn, Mozart, and the even-numbered Beethoven Symphonies, but the other Austro-German classics and romantics did not appeal to him, and he boasted that he had always managed to avoid having to conduct the Symphonies of Brahms. He particularly disliked portentousness, while he brought great dash and style to good light music – the waltzes of Waldteufel, the orchestral pieces of Chabrier, the ballets of Lord Berners. His gifts are well summarised in a letter which Edward J. Dent wrote to Angus Morrison on 20th May 1946. Dent had been to Covent Garden to see the ballet *Symphonic Variations*, to music by César Franck. Morrison had been the pianist, Lambert the conductor. Discussing Lambert's choice of tempi, Dent wrote:

> Constant is always right in these things: he is the best all-round musician we have in this country and it is really a great thing in our musical life that we have a man who is always unquestionably safe in scholarship, style, interpretation, sensitive understanding, and complete professional accomplishment, whatever he undertakes. I suppose many people would use that word "safe" in a disparaging sense, but that is not at all what I mean – perhaps I should have said "secure".

Lambert, then, made a great contribution to the triumph of the Sadler's Wells first American tour, but he wore himself out in the process, and his "black-out" in *Hamlet* was a bad omen. And once again after the initial excitements, *cafard* set in and he drank too much. It is therefore not surprising, perhaps, that his colleagues would not take him on the second American tour a year later; but he was deeply wounded by this decision and took it as yet another instance of the churlishness of the ballet world. He continued to conduct at Covent Garden. On 9th March 1950 he appeared at a Command Performance for the French President to direct a performance of his *Aubade*. On 5th May he took charge of the première of the Chabrier–Roland Petit–Antoni Clavé ballet *Ballabile*, for which he himself had chosen the music and carried out some of the orchestration. Robert Irving, now on the regular ballet conducting staff, did what else was necessary. Rehearsals were marred by a clash between Lambert and Petit in the presence of Lambert's son.

On 15th May there was a 21st Anniversary Performance at Sadler's Wells (in fact it was the 20th Anniversary of the Vic-Wells Ballet, but no one noticed until too late) and Lambert, seated on stage and fortified with champagne, recited *A Wedding Bouquet*. In June and July the Lamberts escaped to Valmondois, just north of Paris, to stay with friends. Lambert was working on a new ballet, to be called *Tiresias*. During June he wrote to his mother:

> Work is going slowly but not too badly. I always find it difficult at first to write in a new situation and this extremely lush landscape with its incredible shindy of bird song is at first a little overwhelming. We have three rooms, a really large studio for Isabel, a spacious bedroom and a smaller room with a piano, presumably Pleyel's experimental model but just good enough to compose on. No modern conveniences, no h. and c., *unusual* offices in the garden. Life could not be more simple. Brood about work and/or take a walk in the morning. Lunch outside. Then tentative composing in the afternoon. Evening walk down to the village which is not beautiful but very human. The only bistro is filled with a series of characters (much hand-shaking etc) for which any French film director would willingly sell his soul. Simple dinner and then non-professional music, ranging from Purcell to Chabrier . . . Tiresias is only just beginning to breed. Have sketched the prelude (which for final polishing I shall leave to the last), have finished the opening number (young girls in the nude somersaulting over bulls) and the last number in Scene I (pas de deux for copulating snakes leading to Tiresias' first change of sex). Am pleased with the latter. Still 3 more numbers to do even to finish Scene 1! . . .

I was very glad to have the letter from Kit who seems in good

F   161

and improving form. I am very much on the side of his idea of a French holiday . . . I know that he longs to go to Paris with us but the idea is, as you can see, out of the question. Our whole ambience there is far too sophisticated and he wouldn't pick up a word of French from our high-speed highbrow friends. (Though I am all for being thrown head first into sophisticated society at the age of twenty as happened in my case). . . . Flying to England on July 5th for a few days to conduct *Semele*. Will ring you but doubt if rehearsals will allow time for a visit. Isabel (trying to save a kitten's life with brandy) sends her love.

It does not appear to have occurred to Lambert that he might alter his Paris arrangements a little to permit his son to join him for some of the time.

Financial pressures and the offer of interesting programmes led Lambert to accept a number of conducting engagements in late 1950 and the first half of 1951. His friend Berners had died, and he arranged two commemorative concerts for the Third Programme: a selection of songs and piano pieces which he introduced on 16th February 1951 and an orchestral concert two days later which included the *Caprice péruvien* arranged by Lambert from Berners' only opera. There were also a memorable Purcell concert at the Victoria and Albert Museum; *Summer's Last Will* at the new Royal Festival Hall on 29th May, and for the BBC Home Service on 15th July (it had its first American performance at Ann Arbor in May); the *Fairy Queen* revival at Covent Garden; and two appearances at the Proms. But *Tiresias* was his main preoccupation.

Tiresias, the blind Theban seer, is probably most familiar as a character in *Oedipus Rex*. Walking as a youth on Mount Cithaeron he came on two snakes copulating. He struck the female snake and instantly became a woman. Seven years later he had a similar encounter and by striking the male snake regained his manhood. One day Hera was arguing with her husband Zeus about which of the sexes derived most pleasure from the act of love, and Tiresias, being uniquely qualified to give an opinion, was called upon for an answer. When he agreed with the god that woman enjoyed copulation more than man Hera struck him blind out of spite at being contradicted. Zeus gave him the gift of prophecy as compensation. When Tiresias died and went down to Hades he was the only person in the world of the dead whom Proserpine allowed to retain his intellect and memory unimpaired.

Lambert had proposed the subject of Tiresias to the Camargo Society when he was their conductor, but the copulation of snakes and the sex-changes of the protagonist were considered too "daring" for balletic use. According to Robert Irving the original idea when the project was accepted by Sadler's Wells was to produce a thirty-minute satirical piece (perhaps on the lines of those "send-ups" of classical mythology so beloved of French dramatists) but the theme so absorbed Lambert that what emerged was a "brooding tragedy" lasting over an hour. Lambert's sense of humour seldom deserted him for long, and he was undoubtedly alive to the comic aspects of the theme he had chosen. Indeed he and Randall Swingler delighted the bar of the "George" with a mime designed to demonstrate the differences in sexual behaviour between English and French snakes. Lambert took the role of a hearty British snake to whom sex was anathema, while Swingler played a highly-sexed French snake with a taste for erotic subtleties and refinements. But there was nothing in the ballet which finally emerged to suggest that there had ever been any satirical intention at all, and one wonders whether Mr Irving did not misconstrue Lambert's intentions in the matter.

In the ballet which Lambert was writing, Tiresias, first an athletic young man, became a woman and enjoyed a passionate love relationship with another man; having regained his manhood, he was asked the fatal question, blinded and endowed with prophetic gifts. The ballet was "about" bisexuality: in the lovemaking of the second scene one was made conscious that though Tiresias was now physically a woman he/she was still psychologically a man, and this ambivalence gave the episode a great piquancy. Why did Lambert find the subject absorbing enough to be resurrected after twenty years and pushed through against, if not the opposition, at least the indifference, of many of his colleagues?

One, and only one, of Lambert's friends has suggested that the root cause of his drinking was a deeply suppressed homosexuality. This cannot be proved nor disproved, but on the face of it it is unlikely, and many who knew him well regard the idea as ludicrous. There were many forces driving Lambert towards the bottle, and while gossip about him was rife there has never been any suggestion of the mildest homosexual escapade. The most one can point to is a hero-worship of Kit Wood and the fact that occasionally, at the many parties of the 1920s, Lambert was given to dancing, with more enthusiasm than elegance, with partners of either sex. For that matter he was once observed performing a

163

Coranto with Dylan Thomas, but the implications, if any, were alco-
holic rather than sexual. Unless one wishes to join the school of biography which sees homosexuality everywhere, one has to admit that
Lambert appears to have been completely heterosexual; and since he
was not given, so far as one can judge, to suppressing his emotions,
it would appear that if he had wished to sleep with a man or a boy he
would have done so. Moreover, for Lambert – inevitably with his sense
of humour – certain aspects of sexual inversion were a huge joke. A
great many of his limericks are concerned with sexual oddities, from
the straightforwardly "queer" to the completely bizarre. The rumoured
homosexuality of certain English composers for whose efforts Lambert
did not care was a convenient source of fun in private correspondence
with his friends, but he was the reverse of narrow-minded and he
numbered several homosexuals and bisexuals among his friends. In any
case, no one with a violent dislike of homosexuals could possibly have
worked as he did in the ballet world for 25 years. Yet if one is trying to
make a case for Lambert the robustly "normal" man one comes up
against his persistent though not invariable habit of choosing as love
objects the remote, the inaccessible, the exotic, the unsuitable. No conclusion appears possible, and it is unlikely that anyone will be able at
this stage to explain why Lambert was so determined to see staged a
story which, on the face of it, seemed not a particularly promising
subject for a ballet.

He was completely absorbed in writing *Tiresias*. Denis ApIvor has
written:

> During the last year of his life he was writing *Tiresias* and had to
> cancel most of his engagements to do so. For this work he got
> £250, which is not much for someone of his fame. I saw a lot of
> him during *Tiresias*, as I was working with him, doing some of the
> mechanical side of the scoring, as were Bob Irving and some others.
> He gave full directions, and we just wrote it out for him. There is
> no doubt that writing this work gave him tremendous happiness.
> He explored the humorous possibilities of the various situations in
> private. He felt that he was going to "épater" the bourgeois senti-
> ments of certain members of the ballet company and the public,
> which he certainly succeeded in doing. And also he took infinite
> delight in the domestic quarrel between Jupiter and Juno, which he
> said reminded him of his first marriage. But the effort of the work

was too much for him in his state of health; he became very irritable at the end, and was drinking too much again. Still he was in great form, and the night before the first night I was with him and Alan Rawsthorne at his house until the small hours, having a wonderful party, with Constant in an uproarious mood. They left for Alan's place, ostensibly to write the interludes until dawn. In fact the interludes were written in the "Nag" at lunchtime the next day. I went down in Constant's car to the dress rehearsal . . . and stood with him on the huge stage as the men were unrolling the scenery. He stood looking half up at the roof, and then, tapping his stick in a gesture of mock vehemence, he exclaimed with a grin "Whenever I come into the theatre I feel like a tiger that has smelled blood". I shall always remember that remark, as it was the clearest indication of how much the theatre really meant to him, expressed in a characteristic way before his own last dress rehearsal.

The ballet was first performed at a Gala in the presence of the Queen (now Queen Elizabeth the Queen Mother) on 9th July 1951. The rest of the programme was composed of *Les Patineurs* and the Balanchine *Ballet Imperial*. The choreography was by Ashton, the sets and costumes by Isabel Lambert (whom her husband had deliberately left alone in her work, though of course she knew better than anyone what he was trying to convey). The cast included Michael Somes and Margot Fonteyn, as the male and female Tiresias; Margaret Dale as the Neophyte; Pauline Clayden and Brian Shaw as the Snakes; John Field as the lover of Tiresias; and Alfred Rodrigues and Gerd Larsen as Zeus and Hera. The orchestra contained no upper strings at all, but a large percussion section and a concertante piano, played by the young Australian, Gordon Watson, whom Lambert had heard playing his *Piano Sonata* some time before and invited to participate. Watson had studied the *Sonata* with Egon Petri in California.[1]

The programme note by the composer had been written with some care, in view of the nature of the audience. It read as follows:

SCENE I.   IN CRETE, THERE LIES THE SCENE

Young girls in a gymnasium are attempting to somersault over the

---

[1] Petri, an admirer of Lambert's work, played Mozart's *Piano Concerto* in A, K 488, and Liszt's *Piano Concerto* No. 2, in A, under Lambert's baton at Manchester on 1st December 1938.

horns of a bull. The youthful Tiresias enters and displays his superior prowess. The young girls leave in mockery.

Tiresias executes a dance of athletic triumph. He is joined by his warrior friends, who pay him homage. Their dance is interrupted by a young Neophyte who tells him that priestesses wish to give him a wand of honour. He accepts it with reluctance and is left alone.

Two snakes enter. Tiresias strikes the female snake with his wand and is transformed into a woman.

SCENE II. IN THE MOUNTAINS

Tiresias, now a woman, is discovered alone. She is joined by a group of shepherds and shepherdesses but the shepherds do not appeal to her.

From behind a statue appears a stranger. They fall in love. The shepherds and shepherdesses celebrate the happiness of Tiresias and her lover. The Neophyte re-enters with the wand and the bacchanale is interrupted by the presence of the two snakes. Tiresias strikes the male snake and is changed back to a man.

SCENE III. A PALACE

Zeus, the God, and Hera, the Goddess, are disputing the relative happiness of the two sexes, each maintaining that the other is the happier of the two. Tiresias is called upon for a decision. He states firmly that he preferred his life as a woman. Hera, furious at being contradicted, strikes Tiresias blind. Zeus as recompense gives Tiresias the gift of prophecy.

Tiresias is a ballet about the mystery of sex rather than the mystery of love, and the use of phrases like "they fall in love", "the relative happiness of the two sexes" and "his life as a woman" was simply due to the fact that it was thought inadvisable to be too explicit in the presence of the Queen and a gala audience. What was meant was respectively "they are attracted to each other", "the relative enjoyment of the two sexes" and "his role as a woman".

As the slash of two whips introduced a solemn "motto" theme on three trombones the drop curtain appeared, showing a skeletal snake, its mouth open to strike, menacing another skeletal figure. The introduction presented the melodic material on which the whole work was to be based, and then the curtain rose on a set recalling the palace of

Minos at Knossos, dominated by the sinister symbols of the horned
bull and the snake-goddess. Its most striking feature was a massive bull
before which girl athletes danced to music marked by irregular, jagged
rhythms. To a trumpet solo, Tiresias sprang from behind the bull and
joined in the dance. After his short solo, percussive music, with
prominent cowbells, accompanied the entrance and dance of the warriors. In various states of the score this movement is called "Warriors",
"Dance guerrière" and "Sardana", the last a Catalonian dance of which
Lambert was fond. When the Neophyte appeared the music took on a
slow, solemn, sarabande-like quality. Two clarinets, moving in suitably
oily, reptilian contrary motion, denoted the appearance of the amorous
snakes, and when Tiresias struck the female the priestess and warriors
rushed back on stage to a thunderous restatement of the motto theme
as the hero vanished and reappeared high above the bull. He had been
transformed into a young woman.

After a short entr'acte the curtain rose again on a mountain scene
carried out for the most part in soft blues and greys, suggesting a
Chinese painting. The female Tiresias was alone with a white veil at
the front of the stage. She began to dance to a Siciliana introduced by a
solo oboe. When the Shepherds and Shepherdesses entered the music
changed, and an oriental-sounding theme, often moving in parallel
augmented fourths, started to alternate with a pentatonic motive,
harmonised with steadily increasing polytonality, that recalled the
opening of Ravel's *Piano Trio*. The *pas de deux* for Tiresias and her
lover had the languorous nostalgia of some parts of *The Rio Grande*,
and used thematic material from the second movement (*Siesta*) of the
Trois Pièces Nègres. Likewise the violent bacchanal, ushered in by a
stroke on the gong, drew on the *Aubade* from the same set of pieces.

The argument of the third scene was accompanied by reminiscences
and developments of the musical material already heard, and Tiresias'
unlucky decision was given point with a poignant reference to the love
music of Scene Two. After the catastrophe the motto theme was re-
stated and the music began to die away, with lonely soli for celli and
oboe over repeated notes on piano and celesta. The girls clustered
round the blind man, eager to have their fortunes told, and the curtain
fell slowly to the tapping of his stick.

So that the long work should be ready in time, a number of friends
and colleagues helped with the scoring. Robert Irving took the Warriors' Dance, the Cortège and Dance of the Priestesses, the first

Entr'acte and the Bacchanal; Christian Darnton the Dance of the Snakes; Humphrey Searle the Dance of the Shepherds and Shepherd-esses; Denis ApIvor the Dance of Tiresias-woman at the beginning of Scene Two and the quarrel in Scene Three; Gordon Jacob the *pas de deux*. The rest was shared between Lambert, Alan Rawsthorne and Elisabeth Lutyens. An enemy of Lambert's put it about that the entire orchestration had been taken over by these friends. This was hardly the case: Lambert pre-determined the sound quality and choice of instru-ments by excluding the upper strings and including a concertante piano part, and gave clear indications to his aides about what he wanted. The score as it stands may be regarded as his and not as a collaborative effort.

The music is unmistakably Lambert's: in particular his fondness for melodic motives moving in triads is noticeable. Despite its length, the work is far more tightly organised than any of his other ballets, and virtually all the melodic material derives from the group of motives heard at the outset. The bisexuality of the protagonist is symbolised by the tritone (first heard as an F sharp pedal against a C major chord) and this harmonic conflict dominates the climax of each scene and permeates the whole score. An occasional harshness, even brutality, in the sound arises from the polytonality and dissonance of some of the writing, the absence of upper strings and the abundance of percussion. This harks back beyond the blander works Lambert wrote in the 1930s to the asperities of the *Piano Concerto*. Yet there are moments of lyricism in his finest vein, such as the *pas de deux*.

Since the subject of the ballet was mythological rather than historical, the choice of a Cretan setting was legitimate, and in some ways it was a theatrical masterstroke. It enabled Isabel Lambert to base her designs (apart from the idyllic interlude of Scene Two) on the discoveries of Sir Arthur Evans at Knossos. Crete has always been a junction be-tween east and west, and suggestions of the orient (Scene Two again) were therefore in order; even the straw hats worn by the Shepherds, which at first suggested coolie headgear, may be seen in the Mediter-ranean. The Cretan locale also permitted the authors of the ballet to avoid hackneyed notions of a classical Hellas, all white robes, Doric columns and decorum, and provide a fitting background against which could be played out a story at once passionate, harsh, violent, hieratic and strange. More recently the poet and film director Pier Paolo Pasolini escaped from conventional notions of classical Greece by filming his *Edipo Re* in Morocco and using Rumanian and Japanese music in the sound track.

A lengthy, serious ballet like *Tiresias* was not the best choice for the kind of audience which appears at a Covent Garden gala, and the reception was polite but unenthusiastic. Few people saw the point of the Cretan setting. The monumentalism of the first and last scenes put people in mind of Lifar's mythological ballets; so did Ashton's choreography for these scenes, which was unusually "masculine" for him. The central scene was better liked, partly because Fonteyn danced in it. In the short-lived magazine *Foyer* (Autumn 1951 issue) James Monahan wrote:

> In these dances there are . . . lovely passages – none so pretty as when Fonteyn first begins to dance with her white veil or when, with John Field, she appears to imitate some charming Minoan pony, running in an elaborate, Disneyesque slow motion.

Sophie Fedorovitch liked the ballet; so did other hard judges like Marie Rambert and Lionel Bradley. But there were lukewarm reviews in every major paper.

The most hostile notices came from Richard Johnson in the *New Statesman* and Richard Buckle in the *Observer*. Johnson, speaking of the ballet as "a total loss", wrote: "Perhaps the music that Constant Lambert has composed is to blame. His arid score with its faint flavour of Borodin's *Danses Polovtsiennes* is not worthy of a musician who, besides being our most distinguished ballet conductor, is also an accomplished composer." Mrs Lambert's "garish sets", he said, "would do at a pinch for a provincial production of *Thaïs*." One wonders how many provincial productions of *Thaïs* Mr Johnson had seen: Massenet's tale of ascetics in the Thebaid and courtesans in Alexandria would scarcely have benefited from being acted out in settings dominated by the symbols of the Bull and the Snake. It was the kind of comment which raises an easy laugh amid the interval chatter in the Crush Bar at Covent Garden but which is revealed as not only spiteful but silly when committed to print.

Richard Buckle attacked on a broader front. Under the headline "Blind Mice" he wrote:

> Did you ever see such a thing in your life? Sadler's Wells has three artistic directors. See how they run. Ninette de Valois is too busy to supervise every detail of production; Frederick Ashton is too

easily reconciled to compromise; Constant Lambert, one imagines, looks in occasionally with a musical suggestion. Lambert cannot take all the blame for the idiotic and boring *Tiresias*, which was given its first production on Monday, although the scenario and music were his, and the designs by his wife. Ashton must have undertaken the choreography of such a work with reluctance and out of duty to his colleague, but de Valois should have forbidden it. Experimental risks must be taken even with the taxpayer's money – and this ballet must have cost £5,000 – but certain enterprises are clearly doomed to failure from the start. Such was *Tiresias*.

This naturally had the effect of closing the ranks at Covent Garden, and even those in the Company who had disapproved of *Tiresias* bitterly resented Buckle's attack. Lambert instructed his solicitor to demand an apology on the grounds – which seem reasonable – that Buckle had suggested that he did not earn his salary as an Artistic Director. Lambert's influence, taste, judgment and hard work had permeated the Company's entire output for twenty years, and to belittle them was foolish, if no more, in a man whose own contribution to ballet at that time had been, to say the least, marginal.

Osbert Sitwell wrote to the *New Statesman* defending and praising the work. Years later, when the ballet was performed in America, John Martin, the doyen of American ballet critics, writing in the *New York Times* (25th September 1955), called it "a ballet of subtlety and high distinction" and "a work of unquestionable greatness". "It is", he said:

> patently a work of deep devotion by all its collaborators. Constant Lambert conceived the highly experimental scenario and clothed it musically with an obviously passionate belief in it. Isabel Lambert's costumes and scenery are not only visually stunning, but, like the score, combine fine research, admirable style and the most carefully considered dramatic connotations. . . . The manner of the music, the décor, the movement, the action, is sharply archaic, with a kind of cruel finality about it, for all that it is never fierce or violent . . . you are likely to carry away with you a keenly aroused sense of psychological drama, as if you had had a revelatory glimpse of a curious and unknown philosophical territory. . . . The fact that it is lavishly produced tends to divert the unwary attention from the fact that it is not a spectacle but a delicate psychological fantasy with profoundly philosophical overtones.

Tiresias is unlikely to be revived as a stage spectacle, and the fact that the Oxford University Press did not see fit to publish it has hindered performance in the concert hall. Unlike Lambert's other ballets the music does not fall neatly into numbers. All three scenes contain fine music, but probably the second is the best. It could be played on its own, starting with the Siciliana and ending with the Bacchanal, for which a "concert ending" could easily be devised. This section of the ballet may well have been the finest music on an extended scale Lambert had written since the *Piano Concerto*.[1]

Lambert was a composer who found very early in his career the style which suited him, and he adhered to it throughout his creative life. This is not to imply that his music is monotonous, ranging as it does from the suavity of *Horoscope* to the astringent *Concerto*. His greatest period of musical creativity came early, from 1926 to 1931, and most of his best music was written then: the *Concerto, The Rio Grande*, the *Li Po Poems* and *Pomona*, for instance. In the 1930s his music grew smoother, and the principal works of that decade lack in the main the urgency of his earlier music. The few pieces that he wrote during the Second World War are not among his most important, but at the end of his life he found form again in two works, the tiny *Trois Pièces* and *Tiresias* itself.

As it happened Lambert was busy with conducting engagements after the première, and he attended a round of parties. After *The Rio Grande* and Ravel's *La Valse* at the Proms on 15th August he went to the Searles', where he seemed desperately ill. He suddenly collapsed on leaving and had to be helped to his car. But the following day, lunching with Edith Sitwell, he appeared better and cheerful. That same week he attended another party, given by Elisabeth Lutyens. Denis ApIvor tells the end of the story:

> On the Saturday night he called me up late, a few minutes before closing time, and asked me to meet Andrée Howard. He had been playing the score of *The Hollow Men*. We all went down the road for a last round before closing time. Constant bought this, which was indeed his last round.

---

[1] It was on the opening theme of *Tiresias* that Alan Rawsthorne based his *Improvisations on a Theme by Constant Lambert*, published by the O.U.P. in 1962, and dedicated to his wife. After Lambert's death his widow married Rawsthorne.

When we got back, there followed a little incident which was extremely pathetic in retrospect. He called for his little old gramophone and put on a record of his own performance of a waltz by Waldteufel called *Sur la plage*. He sat there listening to this with a smile on his face, and shortly after we left, as it was midnight.

This was undoubtedly the last music he heard, as he felt unwell on Sunday and did not get up. The next night, in the early hours of Monday morning, Isabel rang up, distraught, and we rushed over.

He was in a state of delirium tremens, seeing fiends and terrible visions, and threatening to jump out of the window. My wife did her best with him, and she and Isabel held him in bed while I summoned his own doctor. He was rushed to hospital by ambulance, and died.

The copy of *The Hollow Men*[1] stood open on the piano, his gramophone and records still lay where he had left them, and the room was full of muddled manuscripts and dusty notes. He was looking forward to a tour in Edinburgh, but never saw the mile of pubs, nor the French countryside which he promised himself after the Edinburgh Festival was over.

Lambert died in the London Clinic on 21st August, two days before his forty-sixth birthday. The official Death Certificate gives the causes of death as broncho-pneumonia and diabetes mellitus. No one had thought to tell his mother, brother nor son until it was too late, and after his death Alan Rawsthorne telephoned Maurice Lambert with the news. He in turn telephoned his wife Olga at Peel Street, suggesting she should leave him to break it to Lambert's mother when he arrived back from his studio. But the elder Mrs Lambert guessed what had happened before being told. The funeral was at St Bartholomew the Great, Smithfield, the Memorial Service in St Martin-in-the-Fields. Lambert's ashes were placed in Brompton Cemetery, where his grandfather was, and where his mother and brother later joined him.

---

[1] *The Hollow Men* was a work by Dr ApIvor which Lambert had conducted and whose sinister atmosphere led him to suggest the composer to Miss Howard as composer for her forthcoming ballet *A Mirror for Witches*. It was the last instance of Lambert's Diaghilevian flair for bringing balletic collaborators together.

In his obituary for the *New Statesman* Osbert Sitwell wrote:

> I must record my opinion that he would be alive today had it not been for the savage onslaughts of the critics on . . . *Tiresias.* Such is the rage of the uncreative against the creative that nearly the whole body of critics, ignoring all Lambert had done, both for music and for British ballet, jumped on him as if he were a criminal. And they felled him just at the moment when he was unwell and seriously overworked. By this act solely will the critics responsible be remembered in future.

This provoked a letter from the critic Scott Goddard, a riposte from Edith Sitwell, and an extended return to the attack by the irrepressible Buckle.

What is the truth of the matter? One cannot but agree with the late Sir Osbert about the inherent unmemorability of ballet critics, apart perhaps from Gautier, who had, after all, other claims to fame. On the other hand the idea of Lambert being "felled" by Buckle and the rest of them seems on the face of it quite ludicrous. Lambert himself had been a critic, and a cutting one. If an artist exposes his work to critical appraisal he must bear what is written about it, however fatuous it may be.

It seems probable, nonetheless, that Lambert's death at this particular time was due to two things: the tension and exhaustion of getting *Tiresias* on to the stage, and the disappointment and anticlimax of its critical reception. It must be remembered that the ballet was his first major work for fourteen years, and his first for Covent Garden. He probably intended it to complete the process of restoring his position in the Company (which had hit its lowest point in 1947 and was gradually being re-established) and, more importantly, to stake his claim to a position in English music of a kind he had once held but was in danger of losing. Fatigue and the blow of the critical reception drove him back to the bottle. Given his health and his way of life, death would probably have come soon in any case; but one cannot be sure. It was not given him to live long enough to enjoy the acclaim and respect that surround those other two builders of the ballet, Dame Ninette de Valois and Sir Frederick Ashton, in their declining years.

Soon after Lambert's death his widow authorised Elisabeth Lutyens to make considerable cuts in the ballet. In truncated form it remained in the repertory for about four years. After Lambert had died, Fonteyn,

Somes, Dale and the other principals seemed to be dancing it with a peculiar intensity, as if in tribute. Then Fonteyn relinquished her role to Elvin, and in time *Tiresias* was dropped.

The BBC broadcast two memorial concerts in January 1952. That same month the Society for Twentieth Century Music gave its inaugural concert at Hampstead Town Hall, and the *Eight Poems of Li Po* and the *Piano Concerto* were played as an unofficial tribute to Lambert's memory. At the beginning of the concert a large black cat appeared on the platform. Throughout the performance there it stayed; and at the end it stalked off and was never seen again.

APPENDIX I

THE COMPOSITIONS OF CONSTANT LAMBERT

A *Student Works*

1. **GREEN FIRE:** rhapsody for orchestra
   composed: 1923 (?)
   unpublished; score probably lost
   first performed: 28th June, 1923, at a Royal College of Music
                     Patrons' Fund Rehearsal, by the Royal
                     Albert Hall Orchestra under Gordon Jacob

2. **TWO SONGS** on poems by Sacheverell Sitwell
                     Serenade (words from "The People's
                         Palace")
                     The white nightingale (words from "The
                         Hundred and One Harlequins")
   composed: 1923
   instrumentation: soprano, flute and harp
   duration: 3′ 00″
   unpublished; ms in BBC Library
   first performed: 6th March, 1924, at the Royal College of
                     Music, London

3. **PRIZE-FIGHT:** Realistic Ballet in One Act
   composed: 1923–4; revised and rescored in 1925
   instrumentation: flute, piccolo, oboe, two clarinets, bassoon,
                     two horns, cornet, trombone, percussion
                     (two players), harmonium, and strings
   duration: 15′ 00″
   unpublished; ms (full score) in BBC Library
   unperformed (?)

4. **CONCERTO**
   composed: 1924
   instrumentation: piano, two trumpets, timpani and strings
   duration: 26′ 00″
   unpublished; ms (two-piano score only) in BBC Library
   unperformed (?)

5. Mr BEAR SQUASH-YOU-ALL-FLAT: Ballet in One
Act based on a Russian children's tale
composed: 1923–4 (completed June 1924)
instrumentation: flute (doubling piccolo), clarinet, bassoon,
trumpet, trombone, percussion (two players),
piano
duration: 15′ 00″
unpublished; ms (full score) in BBC Library
unperformed (?)

6. OVERTURE: for piano duet
composed: 1925
duration: 4′ 00″
unpublished; ms in BBC Library
see THE BIRD-ACTORS (B15)

7. ADAM AND EVE: suite dansée
composed: 1924–5
duration: (?)
unpublished in this form; partial ms in BBC Library
see ROMEO AND JULIET (B12), POMONA (B13) and
THE BIRD-ACTORS (B15)

8. SUITE in three movements: for piano
composed: 1925
duration: 8′ 00″
unpublished; ms in BBC Library
first performed: 19th March, 1925, at the Royal College of
Music, London, by the composer

9. TEMA: for piano
composed: (?)
duration: 1′ 00″
unpublished; ms in BBC Library

10. ALLA MARCIA: for piano
composed: (?)
duration: 2′ 00″
unpublished; ms in BBC Library
see ROMEO AND JULIET (B12)

11. PASTORALE: for piano
composed: 1926
duration: 3′ 00″   This is identical with:

176

CHAMPÊTRE: for chamber orchestra
unpublished in this form; ms (full score) in BBC Library
first performed: 27th October, 1926, at the Aeolian Hall,
London, conducted by Guy Warrack

B *Published and Mature Works*

12. ROMEO AND JULIET: ballet in two tableaux
composed: 1924–5, London; 1926, Monte Carlo
instrumentation: flute, piccolo, oboe, two clarinets, bassoon,
two horns, two trumpets, trombone, tim-
pani, percussion, strings
based on ADAM AND EVE (A7), with omissions and addi-
tions; includes ALLA MARCIA (A10); later used, with
further changes, as ADAM AND EVE, by the Camargo
Society, 1932
duration: 30' 00"
published: Oxford University Press, 1926
dedication: La Nijinska
first performed: 4th May, 1926, by the Diaghilev Ballet at
Monte Carlo, conducted by Marc-César
Scotto

13. POMONA: ballet in one act
composed: 1926, Chelsea and Renishaw
instrumentation: flute, piccolo, oboe, two clarinets, bassoon,
two horns, two trumpets, trombone, tim-
pani, triangle, strings
written as a Divertimento in seven movements; when it became a ballet a Passacaglia from ADAM AND EVE (A7)
was included in it; the first movement of the ballet (Intrata)
is the piano Pastorale/orchestral Champêtre (A11)
duration: 24' 00"
published: Oxford University Press, 1928
dedication: A.B. (Angela Baddeley)
first performed: as a Divertimento, 16th November, 1926, at
the Chelsea Music Club, London, by the
London Chamber Orchestra, conducted by
Anthony Bernard; as a ballet, 9th September,
1927, by the Company of the Colón Theatre,
Buenos Aires

14. EIGHT POEMS OF LI PO

composed: 1926–9

instrumentation: voice and piano or voice, flute, oboe, clarinet, string quartet, double-bass

duration: 13′ 00″

published: four songs with piano (*A Summer Day*; *Nocturne*; *With a Man of Leisure*; *Lines Written in Autumn*), Oxford University Press, 1927

three songs with piano (*The Ruin of the Ku-Su Palace*; *The Intruder*; *On the City Street*), J & W Chester, 1928

one song with piano (*The Long-Departed Lover*), Oxford University Press, 1930

The instrumental version is available from Chester

dedication: Miss Anna May Wong

first performed: instrumental version (seven poems only) 30th October, 1929, at the Aeolian Hall, London, by Odette de Foras (soprano) and an ensemble conducted by the composer

15. THE BIRD-ACTORS: overture

composed: 1925

instrumentation: flute, piccolo, oboe, two clarinets, bassoon, two horns, two trumpets, trombone, percussion (two players), strings

originally written for piano duet (A6); used as the Finale of ADAM AND EVE (A7); dropped when that work became ROMEO AND JULIET (B12); rescored 1927 as THE BIRD-ACTORS

duration: 4′ 00″

ms score at Oxford University Press

first performed: 5th July, 1931, at the Camargo Society, as an interlude, conducted by the composer

16. MUSIC FOR ORCHESTRA

composed: 1927, London

instrumentation: two flutes, piccolo, two oboes, cor anglais, three clarinets, two bassoons, double bassoon, four horns, three trumpets, three trombones, tuba, timpani, percussion, strings

duration: 12′ 00″

published: Oxford University Press, 1930
dedication: Lord Berners
first performed: 14th June, 1929, by the Wireless Orchestra,
  conducted by Leslie Heward

17. ELEGIAC BLUES

composed: November 1927
instrumentation: solo piano; or two flutes, oboe, two clarinets,
  bassoon, two horns, two trumpets, trom-
  bone, percussion (one player), strings
duration: 2' 00"
published: J and W Chester, 1928
dedication: Florence Mills

18. THE RIO GRANDE

composed: 1927
instrumentation: solo piano, two trumpets, two cornets, three
  trombones, tuba, timpani, percussion (five
  players), strings, chorus
  The percussion comprises bass drum; tenor
  drum; side drum; Chinese tom-tom; tam-tam;
  tambourine; castanets; triangle; cymbals;
  Turkish crash (large suspended cymbal);
  xylophone; jeu de timbres (keyed glocken-
  spiel); small cow-bell; Chinese Block
duration: 15' 00"
published: Oxford University Press, 1930
dedication: Angus Morrison
first performed: 27th February, 1928, by the BBC, with
  Angus Morrison (piano), and the Wireless
  Chorus and Orchestra, conducted by the composer; first performance in the concert hall
  12th December, 1929, at Manchester, with
  Sir Hamilton Harty (piano), and the Hallé
  Orchestra, conducted by the composer

19. SONATA: for piano

composed: 1928–9, Toulon and London
duration: 20' 00"
published: Oxford University Press, 1930
dedication: Thomas W. Earp

first performed: 30th October, 1929, at the Aeolian Hall, London, by Gordon Bryan

20. **JEW SÜSS**: incidental music to the play by Ashley Dukes after Feuchtwanger

composed: 1929 (?)

unpublished; score possibly lost; included a "Mars and Venus" ballet using music by Domenico Scarlatti, arranged by Lambert

first performed: 19th September, 1929, Duke of York's Theatre, London, conducted by the composer

21. **CONCERTO**

composed: 1930–1

instrumentation: solo piano, flute (doubling piccolo), three clarinets (one doubling E flat, and one bass, clarinet), trumpet, trombone, percussion (including temple blocks, maraca and tom-tom), cello, double-bass

duration: 25′ 00″

published: Oxford University Press, 1933

dedication: to the memory of Philip Heseltine

first performed: 18th December, 1931, at the Aeolian Hall, London, by Arthur Benjamin (piano) and an ensemble conducted by the composer

22. **SALOME**: incidental music (nine movements) to the play by Oscar Wilde

completed: 3rd May, 1931

instrumentation: clarinet, trumpet, percussion, cello

unpublished; ms in BBC Library

first performed: 27th May, 1931, at the Gate Theatre, London, conducted by the composer

23. **SUMMER'S LAST WILL AND TESTAMENT**

composed: Summer 1932–Winter 1935, London

instrumentation: triple woodwind (including piccolo, cor anglais, bass clarinet, double bassoon), four horns, three trumpets, two cornets, three trombones, tuba, timpani, percussion (three players), two harps, strings, chorus, baritone solo

duration: 52' 00"
published: Oxford University Press, 1937
dedication: Florence (Lambert)
first performed: 29th January, 1936, at the Queen's Hall,
London, by the BBC Symphony Orchestra,
the Philharmonic Choir and Roy Henderson (baritone), conducted by the composer

24. HOROSCOPE: ballet in one act

composed: 1937, London and Austria
instrumentation: three flutes, piccolo, two oboes (doubling
cor anglais), two clarinets, two bassoons,
four horns, three trumpets, three trombones,
tuba, timpani, percussion, (two players),
harp, strings
duration: 35' 00"
published: Oxford University Press, 1938
dedication: Margot Fonteyn
first performed: 27th January, 1938, at Sadler's Wells Theatre,
London, conducted by the composer

25. ELEGY: for piano

composed: 1938
duration: 3' 00"
published: Oxford University Press, 1940
dedication: Harriet Cohen

26. DIRGE from Cymbeline

composed: 1940
instrumentation: tenor and baritone soli, male chorus, strings
duration: 7' 00""
published: Oxford University Press, 1942
dedication: Patrick Hadley
first performed: November 1940, at Caius College, Cambridge, with piano accompaniment (Angus
Morrison); first performance of full version
23rd March, 1947, BBC broadcast, with
Martin Boddey (tenor), Hervey Alan (baritone), the BBC Men's Chorus and the
Boyd Neel Orchestra, conducted by the
composer

27. AUBADE HÉROÏQUE
composed: 1942
instrumentation: two flutes (doubling piccolo), oboe, cor
anglais, two clarinets, two bassoons, two
trumpets, percussion, harp, strings
duration: 7' 00"
published: Oxford University Press, 1944
dedication: Ralph Vaughan Williams on his seventieth birthday
first performed: 21st February, 1943, at Golders Green,
London, by the London Symphony Orches-
tra, conducted by the composer

28. MERCHANT SEAMEN: film music
composed: 1940; concert suite of three or five movements
arranged 1943
instrumentation (short suite): two flutes (doubling piccolo),
two oboes, two clarinets, two bassoons, four
horns, three trumpets, three trombones, tuba,
timpani, percussion (two or three players),
harp, piano, strings. For the full suite a
third flute (doubling piccolo), cor anglais,
bass clarinet and xylophone are added
duration (short suite): 12' 30"
published (suite only): Boosey and Hawkes, 1944
dedication: The Orchestras of the Royal Marines
first performed (suite): 15th May, 1943, at the Theatre Royal,
Norwich, by the London Philharmonic
Orchestra, conducted by the composer

29. HAMLET: incidental music to the play by Shakespeare
composed: 1944
instrumentation: flute (doubling piccolo), two trumpets, percussion
unpublished; ms in BBC Library
first performed: 11th February, 1944, at the New Theatre,
London

30. ANNA KARENINA: film music
composed: 1947
unpublished; photocopies of ms in BBC Library
no concert suite exists

31. TROIS PIÈCES NÈGRES POUR LES TOUCHES BLANCHES: for piano duet

composed: 1949, London and Palermo
duration: 8' 00"
published: Oxford University Press, 1950
dedication: Edward Clark
first performed: 17th May, 1949, at a BBC/London Contemporary Music Centre Concert in the Concert Hall, Broadcasting House, London, by Mary and Geraldine Peppin

32. TIRESIAS: ballet in three scenes

composed: 1950–1, Valmondois (Seine-et-Oise) and London
instrumentation: triple woodwind, full brass, percussion, solo piano, celli, double-basses
duration (original version): 68' 00"
unpublished
first performed: 9th July, 1951, at the Royal Opera House, Covent Garden, London, by the Sadler's Wells Ballet, the Covent Garden Orchestra and Gordon Watson (piano), conducted by the composer

C *Arrangement of Music by Other Composers*

33. LES RENDEZVOUS: ballet based on music from the opera "L'Enfant prodigue" by AUBER

unpublished

34. CAPRICE PÉRUVIEN: orchestral work based on the opera "Le Carrosse du Saint-Sacrement" by BERNERS

published: J & W Chester

35. Eight SYMPHONIES by BOYCE

edited, arranged and scored for strings and optional wind
published: Oxford University Press

36. Three OVERTURES by BOYCE:

The Power of Music; The Cambridge Ode; Pan and Syrinx

edited, arranged and scored for strings and optional woodwind
published: Oxford University Press

37. **THE PROSPECT BEFORE US:** ballet based on music
by BOYCE
unpublished

38. **BALLABILE:** ballet based on pieces by CHABRIER,
chosen by Lambert and orchestrated as
follows:
Ballabile: Lambert
Introduction: Lambert
Valse romantique No. 1: Mottl
Sous Bois (Dix pièces pittoresques): Chabrier
Bourrée fantasque: Mottl
Mélancolie (Dix pièces pittoresques): Lambert
Tourbillon (Dix pièces pittoresques): Robert Irving
Joyeuse Marche: Chabrier
España: Chabrier
unpublished in this arrangement

39. **HARLEQUIN IN THE STREET:** ballet based on pieces
by COUPERIN, chosen by Lambert and
orchestrated by Gordon Jacob
unpublished in this arrangement

40. **CONCERTO** for piano and small orchestra, arranged
from Organ Concerti by HANDEL
published: Oxford University Press

41. **APPARITIONS:** ballet based on pieces by LISZT,
chosen by Lambert and orchestrated by
Gordon Jacob
Consolation No. 3, in D flat
Valse oubliée No. 1
Schlaflos
Ungarisch (*The Christmas Tree*)
Polnisch (*The Christmas Tree*)
Jadis (*The Christmas Tree*)
Galop in A minor
Elegy No. 2
Evening Bells (*The Christmas Tree*)
Scherzoso (*The Christmas Tree*)
Carillon (*The Christmas Tree*)

Unstern
Mephisto Waltz No. 3
R.W.—Venezia
unpublished in this arrangement

42. DANTE SONATA: ballet using an arrangement for
piano and orchestra by Lambert of
D'après une lecture de Dante for piano
solo by LISZT
unpublished in this arrangement

43. LES PATINEURS: ballet based on music from the operas
Le Prophète and *L'Etoile du Nord* by
MEYERBEER
published (suite): Boosey and Hawkes

44. THE BIRTHDAY OF OBERON: choral ballet based
on *The Fairy Queen* by PURCELL
unpublished in this form

45. COMUS: ballet (eighteen numbers) based on music by
PURCELL from:
The Indian Queen
The Fairy Queen
The Masque in *Dioclesian*
The Tempest, or *The Enchanted Island*
The Virtuous Wife
The Gordian Knot Unti'd
The Married Beau, or *The Curious Impertinent*
published (overture and eleven numbers): Boosey and
Hawkes

46. THE FAIRY QUEEN: by PURCELL
edited by Lambert in association with Edward J. Dent
instrumentation: two flutes (doubling piccolos), four oboes
(the third and fourth doubling cor anglais),
two bassoons, four trumpets, timpani, tabor,
strings, harpsichord continuo
unpublished in this edition

47. MARS AND VENUS: ballet arranged from the music of
Domenico SCARLATTI
unpublished in this arrangement

48. HOMMAGES AUX BELLES VIENNOISES: ballet
arranged from the music of SCHUBERT

published: Oxford University Press

APPENDIX II

RECORDINGS

A *Records made by Lambert*

Unless otherwise indicated, all these records are 78 rpm and Lambert appears as conductor

Hallé	Hallé Orchestra
Liverpool	Liverpool Philharmonic Orchestra
LPO	London Philharmonic Orchestra
PO	Philharmonia Orchestra
SWO	Sadler's Wells Orchestra

Composer	Work	Other artists	Record Label	Number
Auber	Fra Diavolo – Overture	LPO	HMV	C 3084
	Le Chevalier de Bronze – Overture	LPO	HMV	C 3061
	Les Diamants de la Couronne – Overture	LPO	HMV	C 3071
Bartók	Portrait, Op. 5 No. 1	Szigeti/PO	Columbia	LX 1531
	Seven Rumanian Folk Dances	PO	Columbia	DX 1221
Berlioz	Rêverie and Caprice	Szigeti/PO	Columbia	LX 946
			reissued on HMV	HQM 1224 (33 rpm)
Bizet	Roma – Carnaval	Liverpool	Columbia	C 3518
Borodin	In the Steppes of Central Asia	PO	Columbia	DX 1449
	Symphony No. 2, in B minor	Hallé	Columbia	DX 1125–8

187

Composer	Work	Other artists	Record Label	Number
Boyce arr. Lambert	The Prospect Before Us – Suite	SWO	HMV	C 3181–3
Chabrier orch. Lambert	Ballabile	PO	Columbia	DX 1736
Chabrier	Joyeuse Marche	LPO	HMV	C 3112
	Le roi malgré lui – Danse slave	An orchestra	HMV	C 3218
Délibes	Le roi l'a dit – Overture	LPO	HMV	C 3080
Delius	Hassan – Intermezzo and Serenade	Hallé	HMV; reissued on HMV	C 3273; 7P 264 (45 rpm)
	Koanga – La Calinda	Hallé	HMV; reissued on HMV	C 3273; 7P 264 (45 rpm)
	On hearing the first cuckoo in spring	LPO	HMV	B 8819
	Piano Concerto	Moiseiwitsch/PO	HMV	C 3533–5
Glazunov	Stenka Razine	Liverpool	Columbia	DX 1107–8
Grieg	Sigurd Jorsalfar – Homage March	Hallé	Columbia	DX 1037
Lambert	Elegiac Blues		private	(Lambert: piano)
Lambert	Horoscope: Dance for the Followers of Leo; Valse for the Gemini; Invocation to the Moon and Finale	Liverpool	Columbia	DX 1196–7
Lambert	Horoscope: Saraband for the Followers of Virgo; Bacchanale	PO	Columbia; reissued on Columbia and HMV	DX 1567–8; 33SX 1003 (33 rpm); HQM 1078 (33 rpm)
	Pomona: Siciliana only		private	(Lambert: piano)

Composer	Work	Other artists	Record Label	Number
Lambert	The Rio Grande	Harty/St Michael's Singers/Hallé	Columbia	L 2373–4
	The Rio Grande	Greenbaum/Chorus		
		PO	Columbia	DX 1591–2
			reissued on Columbia	33SX 1003 (33 rpm)
			and HMV	HQM 1078 (33 rpm)
Liszt	Apparitions: Galop	PO	Columbia	DX 1568
orch. Jacob	Apparitions: Cave Scene and Finale (Mephisto Waltz No. 3)	PO	Columbia	DX 1560
Liszt *orch.* Lambert	Dante Sonata	Kentner/SWO	Columbia	DX 967–8
Meyerbeer	Les Patineurs: Suite	SWO	HMV	C 3105
orch. Lambert			*reissued on* HMV	7P 102 (45 rpm)
Meyerbeer	Le Prophète: Coronation March	LPO	HMV	C 3112
Offenbach	Orphée aux Enfers: Overture	LPO	HMV	C 3110
Purcell	Chaconne in G minor	PO	Columbia	DX 1230
	Dido and Aeneas	Hammond/Baillie/ Coates/Noble	HMV	C 3471–7
Purcell	Comus – Suite	Hallé	Columbia	DX 1076–7
arr. Lambert				
Rawsthorne	Street Corner – Overture	PO	HMV	C 3502
	Symphonic Studies	PO	HMV	C 3542–4
			reissued on HMV	CLP 1056 (33 rpm)
			and Music for Pleasure	MFP 2069 (33 rpm)
Rimsky-Korsakov	Ivan the Terrible: Overture	Liverpool	Columbia	DX 1140
	Skazka	PO	Columbia	DX 1485–6

Composer	Work	Other artists	Record Label	Number
Rossini	William Tell: ballet music	SWO	HMV	B 8900-1
Suppé	Morning, Noon and Night in Vienna	PO	Columbia *reissued on* Columbia	DX 1665 SED 5504 (45 rpm)
	Pique Dame: Overture	PO	Columbia *reissued on* Columbia	DX 1746 SED 5506 (45 rpm)
Tchaikovsky	Hamlet	Hallé	Columbia	DX 1101-2
	Romeo and Juliet	An orchestra	HMV	C 3216-8
	Symphony No. 4, in F minor	Hallé	Columbia	DX 1096-1100
	Symphony No. 5, in E minor	LPO	HMV	C 3088-92
	The Sleeping Princess: Suite	SWO	HMV	C 3081-3
Waldteufel	Estudiantina: Waltz	PO	Columbia *reissued on* Columbia *and* Columbia	DX 1693 33S 1006 (33 rpm) SED 5506 (45 rpm)
	Pomona: Waltz	PO	Columbia *reissued on* Columbia	DX 1713 33S 1006 (33 rpm)
	Sur la plage: Waltz	PO	Columbia *reissued on* Columbia *and* Columbia	DX 1755 33S 1006 (33 rpm) SED 5504 (45 rpm)
	The Skaters: Waltz	PO	Columbia *reissued on* Columbia *and* Columbia	DX 1674 33S 1006 (33 rpm) SCD 2097 (45 rpm)
Walton	Façade: Suites Nos. 1 and 2	PO	Columbia *reissued on* Columbia	DX 1734-6 33SX 1003 (33 rpm)

Composer	Work	Other artists	Record Label	Number
Walton	Façade: eleven numbers	Edith Sitwell/Walton	Decca	T 124–5 (K 991–2) (Lambert: speaker)
	Note: ten of these were reissued on Decca OUP 110 (45 rpm), a limited edition sold with a special edition of the "Façade" score published by the Oxford University Press			
Warlock	Capriol Suite	A string orchestra	HMV	C 2904
	Serenade for Strings	A string orchestra	HMV	C 2908
Weinberger	Under the spreading chestnut tree: Variations	LPO	HMV	C 3148–9

B *Records of Lambert's Music Under Other Conductors*

Composer	Work	Other artists	Record Label	Number
	Eight Poems of Li Po	Young/Argo Chamber Ensemble/Groves	Argo	RG 50 (33 rpm)
	Horoscope: Suite	London Symphony/Irving	Decca *reissued on* Decca Eclipse	LXT 2791 (33 rpm) ECS 657 (33 rpm)
	Horoscope: Valse for the Gemini	Royal Opera House Orchestra/Irving	HMV	HQM 1078 (33 rpm)
	Piano Concerto	Watson/Argo Chamber Ensemble/Groves	Argo	RG 50 (33 rpm)
	Piano Concerto	Pressler/Chamber Ensemble/Bloomfield	MGM	E 3081 (33 rpm)

191

C *BBC Recordings*

The BBC has recorded a certain amount of music by Lambert for use by foreign broadcasting stations. While these recordings are not generally available to the public, the British Institute of Recorded Sound has copies of most of them and they are therefore accessible to the student. The works concerned are as follows:

Horoscope – suite
> British Ballet Company/Lambert
> London Symphony Orchestra/Lloyd-Jones

Merchant Seamen – suite
> BBC Symphony Orchestra/Lambert

Music for Orchestra
> Philharmonia Orchestra/Lambert

Pomona
> British Ballet Orchestra/Lambert
> London Symphony Orchestra/del Mar

Summer's Last Will and Testament
> Herincx/BBC Chorus and Choral Society/BBC Symphony Orchestra/Sargent

Trois Pièces Nègres pour les Touches Blanches
> Rodney Bennett/Williamson

In addition, the British Institute of Recorded Sound possesses tapes of BBC performances of the *Elegy* (Peter Wallfisch), the *Merchant Seamen* suite, the *Li Po Poems*, the *Piano Sonata* (Louis Kentner) and *Romeo and Juliet*.

APPENDIX III

BIBLIOGRAPHY

A *Sources*

CLARKE, Mary: The Sadler's Wells Ballet. A. & C. Black, 1955.

COHEN, Harriet: A Bundle of Time – the Memoirs of Harriet Cohen. Faber, 1969.

de VALOIS, Ninette: Come Dance With Me. Hamish Hamilton, 1957

DREW, David: Modern French Music. *In* European Music of the Twentieth Century, edited by Howard Hartog. Penguin, 1961, pp. 252–310.

GRAY, Cecil: Peter Warlock: a memoir of Philip Heseltine. Cape, 1934.

GRAY, Cecil: A Survey of Contemporary Music. OUP, 1924.

GRIGORIEV, S. L.: The Diaghilev Ballet 1909–1929. Constable, 1953.

HUGHES, Robert: The Art of Australia. Penguin, 1966, rev. 1970.

"HUGHES, Spike" *pseud.* (*i.e.* Patrick Cairns): Opening Bars. Pilot Press, 1946.

"HUGHES, Spike": Second Movement. Museum Press, 1951.

KOCHNO, Boris: Diaghilev and the Ballets Russes. Penguin Press, 1971.

LAMBERT, Amy: Thirty Years of an Artist's Life – the Career of G. W. Lambert, ARA. Sydney, Society of Artists, 1938.

LEWIS, Cecil, *ed.*: Self-Portrait (taken from the letters and journals of Charles Ricketts, RA, collected and compiled by T. Sturge Moore). Peter Davies, 1939.

LIFAR, Serge: Ma Vie (*translated by* J. H. Mason). Hutchinson, 1970.

McCULLOCH, Alan: Encyclopedia of Australian Art. Hutchinson, 1968.

PUDNEY, John: Home and Away. Michael Joseph, 1960.

ROSENTHAL, Harold: Two Centuries of Opera at Covent Garden. Putnam, 1958.

SITWELL, Osbert: Laughter in the Next Room. Macmillan, 1949.

SITWELL, Osbert: Tales My Father Taught Me. Hutchinson, 1962.

SMITH, Bernard: Australian Painting 1788–1960. OUP, 1962

SOKOLOVA, Lydia: Dancing for Diaghilev, edited by Richard Buckle. John Murray, 1960.

van DIEREN, Bernard: Down Among the Dead Men. OUP, 1935.

The Art of George W. Lambert, ARA. Sydney, Art in Australia Ltd., 1924.

B *Chronological Bibliography of Lambert*

1. ZOETE, Beryl de: Constant Lambert. *Monthly Musical Record*, April 1929, pp. 97–9.
   (The Younger English Composers – III)

2. EVANS, Edwin: Walton and Lambert. *Modern Music*, April/May 1930, pp. 26–31.

3. RUBBRA, Edmund Duncan: Constant Lambert's Sonata. *Monthly Musical Record*. Dec. 1930, p. 356.

4. EVANS, Edwin: Constant Lambert. *Chesterian*, June 1931, pp. 181–7.

5. LAMBERT, Constant: Music Ho! Faber, 1934; 2nd ed 1937; Penguin, 1948; 3rd ed with an introduction by Arthur Hutchings, Faber, 1966.

6. FRANK, Alan: The Music of Constant Lambert. *Musical Times*, Nov. 1937, pp. 941–945.

7. BROOK, Donald: Constant Lambert. *In his* Conductor's Gallery. Rockliff, 1945, pp. 85–7.

8. FOSS, Hubert: Constant Lambert. *In* British Music of Our Time, edited by A. L. Bacharach. Penguin, 1946, 2nd ed 1952, pp. 168–174.

9. GRAY, Cecil: [Constant Lambert]. *In his* Musical Chairs. Home & van Thal, 1948, pp. 288–91.

10. FAIRY QUEEN: Purcell's "The Fairy Queen" as presented by The Sadler's Wells Ballet and The Covent Garden Opera. John Lehmann, 1948.

11. BEAUMONT, C. W.: *in his* Complete Book of Ballets. Putnam, 1949.
12. HERBAGE, Julian: Constant Lambert. *Canon*, April 1950, pp. 549–51.
13. FRANK, Alan: Constant Lambert. *Music Teacher*, Jan. 1951, pp. 19–20.
    (Contemporary Portraits No. 5) Reprinted *in his* Modern British Composers. Dobson, 1953, pp. 80–85.
14. BUCKLE, Richard: Constant Lambert. *Ballet*, April 1951, p. 46.
15. *NEW STATESMAN & NATION* [Constant Lambert]: 14/7/1951; 21/7/1951; 1/9/1951; 8/9/1951; 15/9/1951.
16. FOSS, Hubert: Constant Lambert. *The Times*, 22/8/1951.
17. RACE, Steve: Constant Lambert. *Melody Maker*, 1/9/1951, p. 11.
18. FOSS, Hubert: Constant Lambert. *Gramophone*, Sept. 1951, p. 73.
19. KOLODIN, I.: The Inconstant Lambert. *Saturday Review*, 8/9/1951, p. 39.
20. FOSS, Hubert: Constant Lambert. *Musical Times*, Oct. 1951, pp. 449–451.
21. FOSS, Hubert: Lambert – "Horoscope". *Halle [Magazine]*, Oct. 1951, pp. 18–20.
22. HUSSEY, Dyneley: Constant Lambert and the Ballet. *Dancing Times*, Oct. 1951, pp. 9–11.
23. MANN, William: Constant Lambert – the composer. *London Music*, Oct. 1951, pp. 26–28.
24. de VALOIS, Ninette: Constant Lambert – an appreciation of his work. *Dancing Times*, Oct. 1951, pp. 7–9.
25. BUCKLE, Richard: Constant Lambert. *Ballet*, Nov. 1951, pp. 12–15.
26. WEBSTER, David: Constant Lambert – an appreciation. *Opera*, Nov. 1951, p. 656.
27. MORRISON, Angus: Constant Lambert – obituary. *RCM Magazine*, Nov. 1951, pp. 107–110.
28. STEWART, Michael: Constant Lambert – obituary. *The Blue* (Christ's Hospital School Magazine), Dec. 1951, p. 61.
29. HOWES, Frank: Constant Lambert. *Ballet Annual 6*, 1952, pp. 50–53.
30. AYRTON, Michael: Sketches for a Portrait [of Lambert]. *Ballet Annual 6*, 1952, pp. 88–96.
    (Reprinted *in his* Golden Sections, Methuen, 1957, pp. 123–35.)

31. DENT, Edward J.: Constant Lambert 1905–51 – an appreciation. *Covent Garden Books* No. 6, Ballet 1950–52, Royal Opera House, 1952.
32. FOSS, Hubert: The Music of Constant Lambert. *Listener*, 24/1/1952, p. 158.
33. SEARLE, Humphrey: Constant Lambert. *Music Survey*, Feb. 1952, pp. 384–6.
34. BUCKLE, Richard: [Lambert] *in his* The Adventures of a Ballet Critic. Cressett, 1953, pp. 220–223.
35. RADLEY, T. B.: First and Last Things. *In* The Christ's Hospital Book, Hamish Hamilton, 1953, pp. 305–307.
36. HUROK, S.: Constant Lambert. *In his* S. Hurok Presents ... The World of Ballet. Hale, 1955, pp. 272–9.
37. HANSLER, George: The Choral Writing of Constant Lambert. *In his* Stylistic Characteristics and Trends in the Choral Music of Five Twentieth Century British Composers – a Study of the choral works of Benjamin Britten; Gerald Finzi; Constant Lambert; Michael Tippett; and William Walton. New York University, Ph.D. Thesis, 1957, pp. 88–142.
38. IRVING, Robert: Constant Lambert. *In* The Decca Book of Ballet, edited by David Drew, Muller, 1958, pp. 184–190.
39. COOKE, Deryck: Another Look at "Music Ho!". *Listener* 29/11/1962.
40. LINDSAY, Jack: [Lambert]. *In his* Fanfrolico and After, Bodley Head, 1962, pp. 94–5.
41. HOWES, Frank: [Lambert]. *In his* The English Musical Renaissance, Secker & Warburg, 1966, pp. 272–4.
42. McGRADY, Richard: The Music of Constant Lambert. *Music & Letters*, July 1970, pp. 242–58.
43. PALMER, Christopher: Constant Lambert – a postscript. *Music & Letters*, April 1971, pp. 173–176.
44. PIRIE, Peter J.: The Lost Generation of Composers. *Music & Musicians*, May 1972, pp. 36–40.

C *Major Encyclopedia Articles on Lambert*
COLLES, H. C.: *Grove* IV, supplementary vol. (5), 1940, pp. 340–41.
AVERY, Kenneth: *Grove* V, vol. 5, 1954, pp. 29–32.
WILLIAMSON, Winifred F.: *Die Musik in Geschichte und Gegewart*, vol. 8, 1960, cols. 121–2.

APPENDIX IV

LAMBERT'S CONCERTS FOR THE BBC THIRD PROGRAMME

Date		Works performed	
10th October 1946	Liszt	Two Episodes from Lenau's Faust	
		Galop in A minor	
	Schubert-Liszt	Les Morts, for orator, chorus and orchestra	First performance in England
		Cavalry March	
	Liszt	Hamlet – Symphonic Poem	
		Es muss ein Wunderbares sein – song with orchestra	
		Die Vätergruft – song with orchestra	
		Hungarian Coronation Mass – Graduale	
17th October 1946	Balakirev	King Lear – Overture	
	Lambert	Aubade Héroïque	
	Sibelius	Symphony No. 6, in D minor	
	Rameau-Gevaert	Castor et Pollux – Suite	
	Chabrier	Suite pastorale	
21st November 1946	Marschner	Hans Heiling – Overture	
	Tchaikovsky	Variations on a Rococo Theme	
	Glinka	Prince Kholmsky – incidental music	
	Dargomizhsky	Kazachok	
	Berlioz	The Trojans – Dance of the Slaves	

Date	Works performed	
21st November 1946	Berlioz	La Captive – song with orchestra
	Liszt	From the Cradle to the Grave – Symphonic Poem
		Mephisto Waltz No. 2
4th January 1947	Purcell	Dido and Aeneas
5th January 1947		Dido and Aeneas (repeat)
6th January 1947	Lambert	Piano Concerto (soloist: Kyla Greenbaum)
	Walton	Façade (Lambert, speaker; Leighton Lucas, conductor)
16th January 1947	Lambert	Summer's Last Will and Testament – King Pest
25th January 1947	Berlioz	Les Francs-Juges – Overture
	Field	Piano Concerto No. 2, in A flat
	Liszt	A Symphony to Dante's Divina Commedia
23rd March 1947	Purcell-Holst	The Gordian Knot Unti'd – Suite
	Lutyens	Concerto for bassoon and string orchestra
	Dowland-Warlock	Suite
	Lambert	Dirge from Cymbeline First performance of full version
	Jaubert	Trois Intermèdes
7th June 1947	Lambert	Summer's Last Will and Testament
11th June 1947	Warlock	The Curlew (Bernac, singer; Lambert, conductor)
18th June 1947	Walton	Façade (recording of performance on 6th January 1947)
13th August 1947	Lambert	Piano Concerto (recording of performance on 6th January 1947)
2nd October 1947	Lambert	Eight Poems of Li Po (Martin Boddey, tenor)
		(In this concert Louis Kentner played the Siciliana from Pomona, the Elegy, and the Saraband for the Followers of Virgo from Horoscope)

Date	Works performed	
14th November 1947	Balakirev	King Lear – Overture
	Roussel	Pour une fête de printemps
	Bax	The Tale the Pine Trees Knew – Symphonic Poem
	Lambert	Music for Orchestra
16th February 1948	Bartók	Two Portraits, Op. 5
		Suite No. 2, Op. 4
1st May 1948	Marschner	Hans Heiling – Overture
	Liszt	Two Episodes from Lenau's Faust
	Weber	Euryanthe – Wo berg' ich mich
	Dukas	Symphony in G
24th August 1948	Hadley	Ephemera
	Lambert	Eight Poems of Li Po (Martin Boddey, tenor)
7th October 1948	Marschner	The Goldsmith of Ulm – Overture
	Barber	Violin Concerto
	Glazunov	Symphony No. 2, in F sharp minor
12th October 1948	Rimsky-Korsakov	Ivan the Terrible – Overture
	Berkeley	Piano Concerto
	Sibelius	Luonnotar
		Symphony No. 6, in D minor
10th December 1948	Walton	Façade (Lambert, speaker; Leighton Lucas, conductor)
19th December 1948	Tchaikovsky	Mazeppa – Gopak
		Symphony No. 3, in D – Alla tedesca
	Liadov	Eight Russian Folk Songs

199

Date		Works performed
19th December 1948	Glinka	Valse-fantaisie
	Rimsky-Korsakov	Mlada – Procession of the Nobles
		The Snow Maiden – Suite
23rd December 1948	Berlioz	Les Francs-Juges – Overture
	Bartók	Violin Concerto
	Balakirev	Symphony No. 1, in C
1st January 1949	Handel	Alexander's Feast
23rd January 1949	Purcell	King Arthur
25th January 1949		King Arthur (repeat)
31st January 1949	Walton	Façade (recording of performance on 10th December 1948)
1st February 1949	de Machaut-Arnold	Double Hocquet
	Mozart	Divertimento No. 11, in D
	Stravinsky	Octet
6th March 1949	Handel	Semele
13th March 1949		Semele (repeat)
17th May 1949	Searle	Gold Coast Customs (Lambert and Edith Sitwell, speakers; Leighton Lucas, conductor) First performance (BBC/London Contemporary Music Centre Concert)
22nd May 1949	Purcell	Dido and Aeneas
24th May 1949		Dido and Aeneas (repeat)
30th May 1949	Auber	Masaniello – Overture
	Satie	Jack in the Box
	Ravel	Pavane pour une Infante défunte

Date		Works performed	
30th May 1949	Lambert	The Rio Grande (Kyla Greenbaum, soloist)	
	Chabrier	Le roi malgré lui – Danse slave; Entr'acte, Barcarolle; Fête polonaise	
14th June 1949	Satie orch. Roland-Manuel	Prélude de la porte héroïque du ciel	
	Satie orch. Poulenc	Gnossienne No. 3	
	Satie	Je te veux (song)	
		La belle excentrique	First performance in England
		En habit de Cheval	First performance in England
		Les Aventures de Mercure	
		Socrate	First performance in England
17th June 1949	Purcell	The Yorkshire Feast Song	
25th June 1949	Rameau	Hippolyte et Aricie – Suite	
	Purcell	The Masque in Dioclesian	
23rd July 1949	Searle	Fuga giocoso	
		(recording of a performance at the Festival of the International Society for Contemporary Music, Palermo, April 1949)	
29th July 1949	Berkeley	Symphony No. 1	
	d'Indy	Istar – Poème dansé	
	Borodin	Symphony No. 1, in E flat	
	Satie orch. Roland-Manuel	Prélude de la porte héroïque du ciel	
23rd September 1949	Satie orch. Debussy	Gymnopédie No. 2	
	Satie	Je te veux (song)	

Date		Works performed	
23rd September 1949	Satie	La belle excentrique	
		Socrate	
4th December 1949	Purcell	Ode for St Cecilia's Day, 1683: Welcome to all the pleasures	
		The Masque in Dioclesian	
9th December 1949	Searle	Gold Coast Customs (Lambert, speaker; Leighton Lucas, conductor)	
12th December 1949		Gold Coast Customs (repeat)	
21st December 1949	Purcell	Welcome Song for King James II: Ye tuneful muses	
		The Masque in Dioclesian	
23rd December 1949	Liszt	A Faust Symphony	
6th January 1950	Purcell	The Tempest, or The Enchanted Island	
8th January 1950		The Tempest (repeat)	
14th January 1950	Gluck	Alceste – Act I	
		Iphigénie en Tauride – Act III	
		Repeated Gluck programme of previous night.	
15th January 1950	Liszt	La Notte	First broadcast performance in England
10th February 1950		Grand Solo de Concert	First broadcast performance in England
		Héroïde Funèbre – Symphonic Poem	
		Totentanz	
		Hunnenschlacht – Symphonic Poem	
21st February 1950	ApIvor	The Hollow Men	First performance
	Frankel	The Aftermath	First broadcast performance
	Gerhard	Pandora – Suite	First performance of the Concert Suite
		(BBC/London Contemporary Music Centre Concert)	

202

Date	Works performed	
28th May 1950	Handel	Alexander's Feast
3rd June 1950	Lambert	Summer's Last Will and Testament
8th July 1950	Handel	Semele
9th July 1950		Semele (repeat)
12th August 1950	van Dieren	Serenata, Op. 16, for nine instruments
		Sonetto VII of Edmund Spenser's Amoretti, for tenor and eleven instruments
1st October 1950	Handel	L'Allegro ed Il Pensieroso
2nd October 1950		L'Allegro ed Il Pensieroso (repeat)
30th December 1950	Magnard	Symphony No. 3, in B flat minor
	Bliss	Adam Zero – ballet
5th February 1951	Purcell	The Fairy Queen (excerpts)
9th February 1951		The Fairy Queen (excerpts) (repeat)
16th February 1951		Introductory talk and presentation for first Lord Berners Memorial Concert
18th February 1951		Second Lord Berners Memorial Concert
	Berners *arr.* Lambert	Caprice péruvien
	Berners	Trois Morceaux pour orchestre
		The Triumph of Neptune – Suite
		Fantaisie espagnole

Two Memorial Concerts of Lambert's music were broadcast by the Third Programme

Date	Works performed
29th January 1952	London Philharmonic Orchestra, conducted by Robert Irving
	Pomona
	Music for Orchestra
	Horoscope – Suite
	Summer's Last Will and Testament – King Pest
20th January 1952	Martin Boddey (tenor)
	Henry Cummings (baritone)
	Kyla Greenbaum (piano)
	London Philharmonic Choir
	London Symphony Orchestra Chamber Ensemble, conducted by Norman del Mar
	Eight Poems of Li Po
	Piano Concerto
	Dirge from Cymbeline

INDEX

In this index Lambert's works, including arrangements, have been entered in the alphabetical sequence in *italic*. No other composer's music has been so entered, entry in these cases being as a subheading of the composer in question. No entries for specific ballets have been made under any name other than the composer.

The Introduction, appendices and illustrations have not been indexed. Page references in *italic* are to footnotes.

Abbreviations are entered where they would be in the sequence if spelled out, similarly with numbers. Definite and indefinite articles have been dropped for indexing purposes. All personal names have been indexed under their original form with a reference from later forms. Accents on foreign words and names have also been omitted.

INDEX

INDEX